D0758710

WITHDRAWN
UTSA LIBRARIES

Secured Transactions Reform and Access to Credit

European Bank
for Reconstruction and Development

ELGAR FINANCIAL LAW

Series Editor: Takis Tridimas, *Queen Mary, University of London, UK*

This important new series comprises of high quality monographs on a wide range of topics in the field of financial law, hosting work by established authors of international reputation, alongside younger and more emerging authors. The series is synonymous with original thinking and new, challenging research. The subjects under consideration range from financial services law, through securities regulation, to banking law and from financial fraud, through legal aspects of European Monetary Union and the single currency, to the legal workings of international financial institutions.

Titles in the series include:

Law and Corporate Finance
Frank B. Cross and Robert A. Prentice

Secured Transactions Reform and Access to Credit
Edited by Frederique Dahan and John Simpson

Secured Transactions Reform and Access to Credit

Edited by

Frederique Dahan

The European Bank for Reconstruction and Development

and

John Simpson

The European Bank for Reconstruction and Development

ELGAR FINANCIAL LAW

Edward Elgar

Cheltenham, UK • Northampton, MA, USA

© European Bank for Reconstruction and Development 2008

All rights reserved. No part of this publication may be reproduced, stored in a retrieval system or transmitted in any form or by any means, electronic, mechanical or photocopying, recording, or otherwise without the prior permission of the publisher.

Published by
Edward Elgar Publishing Limited
The Lypiatts
15 Lansdown Road
Cheltenham
Glos GL50 2JA
UK

Edward Elgar Publishing, Inc.
William Pratt House
9 Dewey Court
Northampton
Massachusetts 01060
USA

A catalogue record for this book
is available from the British Library

Library of Congress Control Number: 2008932877

Mixed Sources
Product group from well-managed
forests and other controlled sources
www.fsc.org Cert no. SA-COC-1565
© 1996 Forest Stewardship Council
FSC

ISBN 978 1 84720 598 8

Printed and bound in Great Britain by MPG Books Ltd, Bodmin, Cornwall

Library
University of Texas
at San Antonio

Contents

Contributors

Marie-Elodie Ancel, Professor in Law, University of Paris XII

Thorsten Beck, Chairman, European Banking Center, Department of Economics, Tilburg University, The Netherlands and formerly Senior Financial Sector Economist, Development Research Group, World Bank

Frederique Dahan, Senior Counsel, European Bank for Reconstruction and Development

Nuria de la Peña, Director of Legal Operations, Center for the Economic Analysis of Law

Thomas Engelhardt, LFS Financial Systems

Heywood Fleisig, Director of Research, Center for the Economic Analysis of Law

Martin Holtmann, Head, Microfinance Group, Global Financial Markets Department, International Finance Corporation and formerly Lead Financial Specialist, CGAP

Florencio Lopez-de-Silanes, Professor of Finance and Law, EDHEC Graduate School of Business and NBER

Diana Lupulescu, Director, Chamber of Commerce and Industry, Romania

Katarína Mathernová, Deputy Director, European Commission and formerly Adviser to the Deputy Prime Minister, Slovak Republic

Benjamin Regitz, LFS Financial Systems

Mehnaz S. Safavian, Senior Economist, Private and Financial Sector Development, South Asia, World Bank

John Simpson, Secured Transactions Project Leader, European Bank for Reconstruction and Development

Foreword

Access to credit and secured transactions may now be considered main stream components of law and finance reform, but it has not always been the case.

In 1991, when the European Bank for Reconstruction and Development (EBRD) started its operations in the transition economies of Central and Eastern Europe, it was obvious to all observers that private investment was required, and that this needed to be underpinned by sound financial laws and institutions. It was equally clear to the EBRD that these reforms required the offer of considerable and sustained technical assistance to these countries. This was the purpose of the Secured Transactions Reform Project set up by the EBRD's Office of the General Counsel in 1992.

Interestingly, what was initially seen as an arcane niche has now become a core component of international technical assistance. Financial institutions active in the field understand, of course, that sound banking principles require the use of collateral to maximise the certainty of repayment of debt, but the significance of legal reform in allowing for collateral has not always been appreciated. The choice of collateral is driven by the circumstances, such as the availability of assets, value, and market liquidity. At a minimum, the law should efficiently provide such a choice to lenders and borrowers. Yet, in 1992 this was not the case in any of the EBRD's countries of operations, and is still not the case in too many jurisdictions today. The Bank's first-hand experience of the business environment and enterprises operating in the region (as presented in the in-depth surveys that the Bank conducted in conjunction with the World Bank) also confirmed that access to finance was a major constraint to transition and growth. The considerable investment by the EBRD in financial banking and non-banking institutions in the region in the form of equity and debt reinforced the case for simultaneously fostering the development of sound laws and institutions that support the functioning of debt and equity markets. Over the years, the annual Transition Report published by the EBRD's Office of the Chief Economist has emphasised progress and gaps in this respect.

Much has happened in the last 15 years, but the task is not complete. We observe that secured transactions reform remains an area where better understanding and knowledge dissemination are required. This is the effort to which this volume seeks to contribute. Built on an international workshop that took place at the EBRD's headquarters in London in 2006, the work brings together some of the best experts in the field and allows them to share their personal experience and understanding of the subject matter with great generosity and passion. We are sincerely grateful to them for their time and commitment.

As, in our view, this volume brings a new and truly global vision of secured transactions reform, it is essential reading for those working in development who want a first initiation to the subject. But it also challenges the pre-conceived views of those who think they know the subject – for instance, the assumption that mortgages and pledges are two different instruments which should be analysed and regulated separately; or those who think that measuring the economic impact of secured transactions reform is impossible or pointless. The book also brings together detailed case studies of reform – or, as interestingly, failed reforms – and puts forward suggestions as to what are the ingredients for, and obstacles to, the success of the reform.

The view of the EBRD is that reform is best initiated and led by local stakeholders, but one key obstacle for those involved, especially the countries themselves, is the lack of information. For this reason the workshop offered them an opportunity to share their experience. A key role for the international financial institutions and other assistance providers is also to make readily available core information (economic and survey data, legal analysis . . .) and give technical advice to enable the best use to be made of that information. Over the years, the EBRD has published a number of documents, starting with the *Model Law on Secured Transactions*, the *Guiding Principles for the Development of a Charges Register*, the *Core Principles for Secured Transactions Law* and several surveys, precisely to enable the countries to deepen their understanding of the subject and make informed choices.

It is not by accident that the work gives much space to voices and experiences from civil law countries: the legal traditions of all of the EBRD's countries of operations have civil law origins. While open to considering modern instruments developed in other systems, the EBRD is eager to propose civil-law-compatible solutions. Civil law countries have sometimes been depicted as unable to adapt to modern financial markets, but the developments in Central and Eastern Europe in the past 15 years show that countries with a civilian tradition are also capable of rapid evolution. In fact, the region is widely recognised to have made more progress in secured transactions reform than any other part of the world.

Most importantly, the volume is evidence of the formidable synergy that can be developed between lawyers and economists when they are prepared to listen to and learn from one another. The EBRD is very proud of the fact

that the Office of General Counsel and the Office of the Chief Economist
have collaborated for many years, sharing data and analytical framework
in order to ensure that both legal solutions are designed to address economic needs and that economic analysis takes into account the complexity
and subtlety of legal and institutional systems.

Of course as some chapters explain, secured transactions is only one
component of a complex modern financial system. Just reforming secured
transactions is unlikely to bring about the economic benefits of deeper and
broader access to credit that a developing country seeks. If, however, as
some authors convincingly argue, secured transactions reform has been
neglected in the past, this work will hopefully ensure that it is now given the
prominence it deserves.

Emmanuel Maurice, General Counsel, EBRD
Erik Berglof, Chief Economist, EBRD

PART 1

Access to credit and secured transactions in a
global world

1. Turning the key to credit: credit access and credit institutions

Florencio Lopez-de-Silanes[*]

1.1 INTRODUCTION

Access to credit is essential for individuals and firms. It is the largest source of finance across countries. But there are marked differences in credit access around the world: while New Zealand, the Czech Republic and Hungary have large credit markets and easy access to loans, Russia, Albania or Argentina do not. The poor credit conditions in many countries make it imperative to understand what explains credit access in a world context and to draw attention to successful strategies. In this chapter we focus on understanding the institutional framework for credit that is required to support access, and present the empirical evidence on the link between those institutions and credit markets. Understanding and assessing the effects of the institutions that impact this market may be essential to unlock the key to credit.

As summarized in Djankov et al. (2007), there are two broad views about the institutions that impact private credit. The 'information' view argues that the prevalence of asymmetric information in financial markets, in the form of adverse selection or moral hazard, prevents an efficient allocation of lending (see for example Stiglitz and Weiss 1981, Pagano and Jappelli 1993 and Jappelli and Pagano 1999 and 2002). The implication is that better institutions that fill up the information gap between lender and borrower should lead to deeper credit markets and better financing terms for firms and individuals. An alternative, although not necessarily opposite view, focuses on the prevalence of agency problems in lending transactions. Under the 'control rights' view of credit access

---

[*] The author would like to thank the financial support of this research provided by EDHEC Business School, Paris School of Economics, the University of Amsterdam, the Inter-American Investment Corporation and the European Bank for Reconstruction and Development. The present chapter draws heavily on the ideas, data and work undertaken in the past few years with my co-authors Simeon Djankov, Oliver Hart, Rafael La Porta, Andrei Shleifer and Robert W. Vishny.

institutions, the fundamental problem is the potential expropriation of outside investors by those insiders in control of the firm (see Hart and Moore 1994, 1998, La Porta et al. 1997 and Hart et al. 1997). In this view, the law and its enforcement are key mechanisms of creditor protection and facilitators of credit access. The implication of this view is similar to that of the information argument: strong creditor protection should lead to deeper credit markets and better financing terms for firms and individuals.

Both of these views share in common the idea that, in some countries, there are certain market imperfections that are partly responsible for the current poor credit conditions. Under the first set of theories, it is adverse selection problems that are important, while the latter theories emphasize agency costs. An alternative theoretical view to these two strands of the literature would argue that credit institutions do not matter, as firms and individuals find mechanisms to provide borrowers with credit and to ensure lenders of their returns and thus successfully circumvent deficient laws and institutions (see Easterbrook and Fischel 1991 and La Porta et al. 1998 for a summary of such arguments). Ultimately, the effect of institutions on credit access is an empirical question. The main objective of this chapter is to review the existing evidence on these theories, to provide a comprehensive cross-country set of tests that could help empirically disentangle these two views, and to draw some lessons for developing countries.

There are many laws, rules and institutions that form the framework for private credit. Adopting a simple timeline structure of the credit process, one could group these institutions into four basic categories: (1) registering property; (2) information sharing arrangements or credit bureaus; (3) collateral rules and creditor rights; and (4) contract enforcement. The first two groups are more closely tied to the information view, while the latter two sets of institutions are mostly illustrative of the control rights view. The current chapter expands the existing evidence and comprehensively tests for the impact of these four groups of institutions in a sample of close to 130 countries. The analysis follows along the lines of La Porta et al. (1997 and 1998) and Djankov et al. (2007), expanding their coverage with the use of the largest data sets available from these sources and the World Bank *Doing Business Reports*. Our econometric results show that the establishment of credit bureaus, stronger creditor rights and simpler civil procedure rules have a large economic impact on credit access. The chapter also draws other more specific prescriptions for each area of institutions analyzed. Finally, when drawing an agenda for potential reform, particular attention is given to bankruptcy and judicial reform due to their large impact on the empirical results.

The chapter is divided in to six sections. After this introduction, section 1.2 sets up the conceptual framework, reviewing the two views of credit access institutions and their measurement. Section 1.3 is devoted to the presentation of the data for the cross-section of countries. The ultimate question is whether countries with poor frameworks for credit actually suffer, and section 1.4 is devoted to test if institutions matter and if so, which ones matter most. Section 1.5 takes on the task of analysing potential reforms of institutions supporting access to credit and their policy implications when taking into account the politics of reform. Finally, section 1.6 concludes with some final thoughts and a future agenda.

As previously mentioned, there are multiple sets of rules and institutions that play a key role in the credit process. The institutions surrounding the registration of property and the various information sharing arrangements such as credit bureaus, are more closely related to the information view outlined above. Meanwhile, collateral rules, creditor rights and contract enforcement are more closely linked to the control rights view.

1.2 CONCEPTUAL FRAMEWORK AND MEASURES

In this chapter we consider the effect of law and regulations on credit access. The first question is whether credit institutions matter at all for credit markets. An important tradition in law and economics, originating in the work of Coase (1960) and Stigler (1964), holds that some laws and regulations may be irrelevant, as firms and consumers who need credit and care about their reputation work to produce signals or changes in their arrangements, effectively circumventing a deficient institutional framework. The empirical prediction of this view would be to find no impact of information or control institutions on credit access across countries.

An alternative view argues that law and institutions matter (for example Johnson et al. 2000 and La Porta et al. 1999, 2000, 2008). This brings us to the next level of questions addressed in this chapter: if institutions matter for credit access, which institutions matter most? At this deeper level, there are two main views about the set of appropriate institutions that foster credit access. These views are not necessarily exclusive and could very well work as complementary aspects of a stable environment that promotes access to credit. What is clear is that their predictions sharply contrast with those from the null hypothesis that market participants will by themselves engage in activities to overturn deficient institutional frameworks and overcome the market imperfections that hamper credit access.

1.2.1 Two Views on Credit Institutions

The first view on the influence of institutions on credit access is also the oldest. Banks, and lenders in general, depend on the availability of information about borrowers that allows them to screen them and control their actions during the life of the loan. But reliable debtor information may be difficult or impossible to obtain. Informational asymmetries where creditors are at a disadvantage, either in the form of adverse selection or moral hazard problems, have been postulated as the cause of the wedge between lending and borrowing rates (Dotsey and King 1986), of inefficiencies in credit allocation, and of credit rationing (for example Stiglitz and Weiss 1981 and Jaffee and Russell 1976).

The core of these arguments is that the prevalence of asymmetric information in financial markets prevents an efficient allocation of credit (Pagano and Jappelli 1993, Jappelli and Pagano 1999 and 2002). Although collateral can alleviate the situation, lenders' unrestricted reliance on collateral may still have a pernicious impact on credit-market efficiency (Manove, Padilla and Pagano 2001). Therefore, the information view of credit access argues that information sharing increases competitiveness in credit markets and improves credit allocation and access. The implication is that institutions that fill up the information gap should lead to deeper credit markets and better financing terms for firms and individuals. The second institutional view of credit access emphasizes the prevalence of agency problems. In the framework used by Modigliani and Miller (1958), access to credit, and other forms of financial capital, is only determined by the cash flows that accrue to creditors and other investors. This implies that the size of credit, debt and stock markets should be proportional to the GNP of each country. But the data shows differently: there are marked differences in access to finance across countries with similar GNP (La Porta et al. 1997, La Porta et al. 1998). In order to explain these differences, we need to recognize that debt not only entitles lenders to receive payment of interest and principal, but also entitles them to exercise certain rights to recover the debt in case of default.

In the extreme, creditors would be unwilling to lend money at any interest rate if their control rights did not allow them to seek redress from debtors who have defaulted on their financial obligations. Creditors and management would benefit from the elimination of the agency conflict if they could write a complete contract that specified what the manager should do with the funds and how he would give them back to investors in all states of the world. Of course, a complete contract cannot be implemented in practice, making it necessary for management to have a level of discretion (Grossman and Hart 1986). Management discretion, although a cost-effective way of dealing with the separation of ownership and control, can unfortunately be used to expropriate creditors through outright expropriation, transfer pricing, asset stripping, large dividend payments, or investments that risk the creditors capital betting for high pay-offs with very small probabilities when firms are in financial distress.

The arguments of the control rights view are linked to a long tradition in regulatory economics (see for example Landis 1938) and more recently in the area of corporate and securities laws and the regulation of self-dealing (see La Porta et al. 2006 and Djankov et al. 2008). According to this view, the law and its enforcement are key mechanisms of creditor protection and act as facilitators of credit access. Lenders will be more willing to provide more finance at better terms if they receive legal rights in case of default and an ability to enforce them (see Hart and Moore 1994, 1998, Townsend 1979, Aghion and Bolton 1992, Hart et al. 1997). An institutional framework that provides for strong and enforceable creditors protection should map into deeper credit markets and better financing terms for firms and individuals.

1.2.2 Information Sharing Institutions

Arrangements for registering property as well as those that facilitate the flow of information provided by credit bureaus speak more closely of the information view of institutions. Property registries and credit bureaus mainly serve as ex ante mechanisms that allow creditors to screen and monitor borrowers.[1] As argued by the information view, the borrowers' characteristics and their payment performance may be crucial elements for lenders' survival. This kind of information is difficult and costly to obtain. In the classic asymmetric information model, the asymmetry is exogenous and either the borrower's actions are not transmitted to the lender, or the lender fails to see a relevant set of characteristics of the borrower.

Property registries are the first steps in the ladder of institutions for credit and constitute a basic step to ensure the rest of the process functions. Asserting the ownership of assets (via regulations of tracking property rights, registration of security interest, notifications of liens on assets, etc.) is an essential ingredient in the chain of credit access. Being able to efficiently register property is a cornerstone of securing transactions since assets provide the needed collateral to ensure creditors that if payment is

---

[1] Strictly speaking, some of these institutions can also be at work after the original loan has been given as some of the information helps monitor borrowers and take further decisions down the line, such as credit renewals, etc.

not received, there is an asset with a clear ownership title that can be easily taken over.[2] An expedient and cost-effective system for registering assets and giving notices of liens over the asset to the public are key elements in this area. In order to proxy for these institutions, we use the index of 'registering property' developed for the *Doing Business Report* of the World Bank for over 130 countries (available at www.doingbusiness.org). This index records the full sequence of procedures that need to be followed to register property on a transfer of a piece of land and a building from a seller to an acquiring corporation. Appendix Table A1.1 gives a more detailed definition of all variables used in this chapter and their sources. Appendix Table A1.2 in turn provides the basic statistics of the variables in this study. A full data set at the country level is available from the author upon request.

The second group of information institutions aims at accessing borrowers' information and makes it available. Banks may try to gain access to information through direct requests and visits to the clients. But these methods may be costly or unreliable. This is where the role of credit registries or bureaus comes in: lenders may be able to gain knowledge about potential new borrowers if there are mechanisms to exchange information between lenders. The function of the credit bureaus is to collect, file and make available the information that is provided by the members.

It is often more effective and cheaper to acquire potential borrowers' information by exchanging whatever information a particular lender has with that of other lenders. As borrowers solicit credit from various institutions across time, they leave a path of information that can be very useful down the line. Each lender may only have access to a certain part of the borrower's information at a point in time and obtaining the rest may be too expensive. If all lenders interact and pull their information together, a fuller picture of the borrower emerges. Credit bureaus tend to be more effective if they operate under reciprocity rules, where lack of information provision leads to no access to the others' information.

Sharing information may lead to improved outcomes if it increases the degree of competition amongst lenders (Vives 1980), overall higher lending volume, and improvements in the allocation efficiency of loans. It allows lenders to make more accurate predictions about the payment probabilities of borrowers. Borrowers may themselves behave better when information sharing facilities exist. As in the case for property registries, the existence of credit bureaus may reduce the incentives to over-borrow from several banks at the same time without any of them knowing.

---

[2] Registering title is only possible for assets that have uniquely defineable features such as land, buildings, motor vehicles, shares. This is not possible for goods such as stock in trade, small equipment, and intangibles like accounts receivable.

Although the increased coverage of credit bureaus can have a positive effect on credit allocation, we should not forget that membership in a credit bureau has costs and benefits. While there is a clear benefit of better information about potential borrowers, the members of the bureau give up their privileged information to competitors. Even under such circumstances, increased information sharing may still have a positive impact on the volume of credit if severe adverse selection forces safe borrowers out of the market, as in Pagano and Jappelli (1993).

Our proxies for information sharing institutions are also explained in detail in Appendix Table A1.1. They come from Djankov et al. (2007) and other World Bank indicators. The first set of proxies we use take into account the existence of credit information facilities and the differences between public registries and private credit. A second measure we use is the index of the depth of credit information, which is computed by looking at the rules that affect the scope, accessibility and quality of credit information available through either private or public bureaus. This index includes variables such as: the existence of positive and negative credit information and data on firms and individuals; a relatively long history of the data; the collection of information on loans of a certain size; and the legal right of borrowers to access their data. A final measure in this group of institutions is the coverage of public and private credit bureaus as a percentage of the adult population in each country. Overall we have six different measures that provide complementary aspects that may be at work in the information sharing view of credit institutions.

1.2.3   Control Rights Institutions

Collateral and creditor rights, emerging from law and regulations, and the quality of legal enforcement are institutions that are intimately tied to the control rights view of credit access.

The role of collateral is crucial in lending. When moral hazard and agency problems abound, borrowers have an incentive to use the financial resources from loans in an unproductive manner that could benefit themselves at the expense of creditors. Beyond reputation loss, which has a limit, adverse selection and agency problems could be partially mitigated by borrowers offering collateral which the creditor can seize and enforce if the terms of the loan are not met (see Fleisig, Chapter 3, this volume). Seizable collateral aligns the incentives of creditors and borrowers and adds a credible commitment to the relationship. The disciplinary role of collateral is a cornerstone to the theory of control rights and incomplete contracts developed by Hart (1995) and others.

There is empirical evidence that suggests that collateral is indeed very important for access to credit. Collateral requirements are very large in developed and developing countries. In the United States, almost 40 percent of the loans of small business and close to 60 percent of their value are secured. These requirements are even higher in emerging markets. Unfortunately, not all firms and individuals have access to seizable collateral. Small firms and lower-income consumers typically lack sufficient collateral (see Safavian, Chapter 4, this volume). For this reason, a set of institutions that expands the range of possible forms of collateral and facilitates its seizability in the case of default is likely to improve credit access, particularly for those at the bottom. The kinds of assets that can be registered and/or used for collateral, the priority of secured creditors outside of bankruptcy, and the possibility of seizing and selling collateral out of court increase secured creditors' rights and should foster the development of credit markets.

Collateral alone cannot be the solution to the problem of access to credit. The improvement of creditor rights and their enforcement may make banks less likely to require collateral, as they feel their rights stemming from the credit agreement alone can be respected. Efficient reorganization and liquidation procedures that protect the interests of creditors are also essential as they give power to creditors to enforce their claims in a timely and orderly fashion. In principle, we would like to measure the ability of creditors to use the law to force firms and individuals to meet their credit commitments. In practice though, creditor rights are difficult to assess for two main reasons. First, most countries have in place both reorganization and liquidation procedures, but these are used with varying frequency and so this may confer different levels of protections to creditors. For example, a country could be deemed very protective of creditors if it offers strong rights in liquidation and weak protection in reorganization, provided that the reorganization procedure is seldom used. Second, creditors, unlike shareholders, do not have homogeneous claims against the firm, that is, they differ in the priority of their claim. As a result, it is possible that measures that favor some creditors (for example unsecured creditors) may hurt others (for example secured creditors).

In order to undertake a cross-country analysis of rules of collateral and creditor rights, we use two sources of data, which are explained in Appendix Table A1.1 along with more detailed definitions. The data collected by La Porta et al. (1997 and 1998) to score creditor rights look at both reorganization and liquidation because almost all countries rely to some extent on both procedures. In assessing creditor rights, they also take the perspective of senior secured creditors, in part for concreteness, and in part because much of the debt in the world has that character. The creditor rights index we use aggregates the various rights that secured creditors might have in liquidation and reorganization. Restrictions on the debtor's ability to seek unilateral protection from creditors (for example by petitioning for bankruptcy with no right for creditors to block such petition), mandatory dismissal of management in reorganization, lack of automatic stay on assets (that would prevent secured creditors from enforcing their claims by seizing and realizing collateral), and absolute first priority for secured creditors in liquidation, all contribute to this index. As for the data that looks at collateral rules and rights, we use the World Bank data published in the *Doing Business Report*, which are based on the original La Porta et al. (1998) approach, but adds more specific variables dealing with the kinds of assets that can be used as collateral, the ability to grant or take security in the property, the priority of secured creditors outside of bankruptcy, and the ability of seizing and selling collateral out of court.

The final set of measures tied to the control view captures the quality of contract enforcement. Monetarizing a claim is highly dependent not only on the rights of secured creditors afforded by bankruptcy procedures, but also on the efficiency of court-led or out-of-court enforcement processes. Legal rules are only one element of creditor protection; the enforcement of these rules may be equally or even more important. If good laws are not enforced, they cannot be effective. Likewise, lenders may enjoy high levels of protection despite bad laws if an efficient judiciary system can redress expropriations by management. In this way, strong legal enforcement may serve as a substitute for weak rules.

The literature has used several proxies for the quality of enforcement of laws in different countries. Most of these measures are collected by private credit-risk agencies for the use of foreign investors interested in doing business in the respective countries. The drawback of these indices is that they are subjective and there may be some correlation with the current economic situation of the country, and not so much with the actual quality of enforcement. For this reason, in this chapter, we prefer to use the measures developed by Djankov et al. (2003b) which provide an objective view about the functioning of civil procedures used to resolve a dispute in courts. These measures form an index of restrictions or complexities (called 'formalism index') in the resolution of a bounced check through courts and are intimately related to the efficiency of the court system and the quality of enforcement, as the empirical tests in that paper show.[3] Finally, as a

---

[3]   The resolution of these cases involves lower level civil trial courts in all countries (unless Alternative Dispute Resolution is used). Because these are the courts whose functioning is relevant to most of a country's citizens, the focus on the regulation and efficiency of such courts is appropriate in a development context and is

robustness check, we also use another measure on the procedures to collect overdue debt through court which has been collected by the World Bank based on the methodology in Djankov et al. (2003b). This measures the number of procedures involved from the moment a plaintiff files the lawsuit in a payment dispute to the actual moment of the payment. This measure, developed by the World Bank in 2004, follows basically the same methodology as the sub-index of 'independent procedural actions' and has been expanded to cover 133 countries (as opposed to 109). Detailed definitions and summary statistics are provided in Appendix Tables A1.1 and A1.2.

1.3 CREDIT ACCESS INSTITUTIONS AND THEIR DETERMINANTS ACROSS COUNTRIES

In this section we present the cross-country evidence on the patterns of credit access institutions and explain some of their main determinants econometrically. The section follows on the 'legal origin' tradition started in La Porta et al. (1997 and 1998) assembling cross-country data. [4] Laws and regulations in different countries are typically not written from scratch, but rather based on or transplanted (voluntarily or involuntarily) from a few legal families or traditions. In general, laws come from two broad traditions: common law and civil law. Most English-speaking countries belong to the common law tradition. The common law family includes 36 countries (or 27 percent of the sample) who are former British colonies, and other nations like Thailand and Israel who modeled their initial corporate laws on the laws of England.

The rest of the world belongs to the civil law tradition, derivative of Roman law, which has four main families. The French legal family, which

---

essential for understanding the workings of the enforcement framework. The components are sub-indices of measures of various aspects of the legal structure or the extent of regulation of dispute resolution: (1) the use of professional judges and lawyers (as opposed to lay judges and self-representation); (2) the need to make written as opposed to oral arguments at various stages of the process; (3) the necessity of legal justification of various actions by either disputants or judges; (4) the regulations on evidence gathering; (5) the level of superior review of the decisions by higher courts; (6) the presence of various statutory interventions during dispute resolution (such as service of process by a judicial officer); and (7) the number of independent procedural actions required by law. Each category includes a number of measures of regulation of dispute resolution.

[4]   A full classification of countries by their legal origins can be found in La Porta et al. (2008) and Djankov et al. (2008).

is based on the Napoleonic Code of 1804, includes France, Spain, Portugal and their colonies, as well as developed countries like Italy and the Netherlands. It also includes nations such as Russia, Romania and Albania, which after the fall of the Berlin Wall have returned to their previous main source of legal tradition. It is the most extended legal family in the world, with almost half of the countries in our sample (64 nations). The German legal family, based on Bismarck's Code of 1896, has had less influence, and accounts for close to 14 percent of our total sample including Austria, Germany, Japan, South Korea, Switzerland and Taiwan. Like the French legal family, it has also been revived in many other Eastern European countries that have made a transformation after the fall of communism in the 1990s, such as Poland, Latvia and the Czech Republic. The third is the Scandinavian family, which legal scholars describe as also influenced by Roman law but 'distinct' from the other two civil families in many ways. It is very small and only includes the four Nordic countries of Denmark, Finland, Norway and Sweden. Finally, there are some countries, such as Cuba, that have basically kept their 'socialist' legal tradition, with a civil law origin, but heavily transformed and influenced during the era of communism. We classify them as a separate 'socialist' legal family for our purposes. The other reason to classify countries per legal origin (other than the similarity of their norms) is that research has shown that access to credit is a more pronounced problem in countries with a civil law origin. We thus want to explore whether this may be linked to their institutions and, if this is the case, which ones.

Tables 1.1 and 1.2 present the data on the institutions of information sharing and control rights as outlined in the previous section for all the countries in our sample.[5] The definitions and summary statistics of each variable can be found in Appendix Tables A1.1 and A1.2.

1.3.1 Information Sharing Institutions

Panel A of Table 1.1 shows the average index or value by legal origin for the seven measures that proxy for information sharing institutions. The first column shows the number of procedures that have to be undertaken to register property. For the average country in the world, there are six procedures that are required. Although there are some differences by legal origin, they are not statistically significant, with the exception of Scandinavian countries that have substantially simplified property registration procedures. The second, third and fourth columns of Table 1.1 present the data on

---

[5]   Due to space reasons, these tables only present the averages of the indices, but country level data is available from the author.

Table 1.1 Credit information sharing institutions by legal origin

	Procedures for registering a property	Public registry	Private registry	Information sharing	Credit information index	Public registry cov.	Private registry cov.
				Panel A: Means			
Common law legal origin	6.39	0.25	0.50	0.69	2.94	1.39	23.97
German legal origin	5.28	0.61	0.56	0.94	3.89	1.38	26.29
Scandinavian legal origin	2.75	0.00	1.00	1.00	4.50	0.00	55.60
Socialist legal origin	7.09	0.18	0.00	0.18	1.27	0.77	0.02
French legal origin	6.58	0.77	0.36	0.91	3.11	7.45	14.22
Sample average	**6.09**	**0.53**	**0.41**	**0.80**	**2.72**	**3.63**	**16.79**
			Panel B: Tests of means (t-statistics)				
Common vs German	1.16	2.72 ***	−0.38	−2.13 **	−1.54	0.00	−0.23
Common vs Scandinavian	1.86 *	1.13	−1.95 *	−1.29	−1.35	0.46	−1.55
Common vs Socialist	−0.58	0.46	3.25 ***	3.28 ***	2.28 **	0.32	2.12 **
Common vs French	−0.30	−5.74 ***	1.37	−2.78 ***	−0.38	−2.50 **	1.58

Notes:
* significant at 10%
** significant at 5%
*** significant at 1%

Table 1.2 Credit control rights institutions by legal origin

Panel A: Means

	Creditor rights and collateral						Enforcement measures	
	Restrictions for reorganization	No automatic stay on asset	Secured creditors first	Management does not stay	Creditor rights index	Creditor collateral index	Formalism index	Procedures for enforcing
Common law legal origin	0.42	0.50	0.72	0.64	2.28	6.25	2.81	26.83
German legal origin	0.22	0.50	0.89	0.72	2.33	5.78	3.59	26.28
Scandinavian legal origin	0.25	0.25	1.00	0.25	1.75	6.25	2.91	19.75
Socialist legal origin	0.36	0.27	0.73	0.82	2.18	5.64	3.73	31.18
French legal origin	0.27	0.30	0.45	0.30	1.31	3.59	4.41	35.84
Sample average	**0.31**	**0.38**	**0.62**	**0.49**	**1.80**	**4.86**	**3.53**	**31.54**
	Panel B: Tests of means (t-statistics)							
Common *vs* German	1.41	0.00	−1.39	−0.60	−0.19	0.83	−3.24***	0.19
Common *vs* Scandinavian	0.63	0.94	−1.21	1.51	0.93	0.00	−0.23	1.19
Common *vs* Socialist	0.31	1.32	−0.03	−1.11	0.29	0.91	−2.14**	−1.13
Common *vs* French	1.56	2.04**	2.66***	3.49***	4.04***	7.17***	−7.42***	−3.86***

Notes:
  *   significant at 10%
 **   significant at 5%
***   significant at 1%

credit bureaus. Columns two and three represent the average percentage of countries that have public registries and private credit bureaus respectively. The next column shows the percentage of countries that have at least one of the two types of credit bureaus, that is, public registries or private credit bureaus. As the data shows, almost 80 percent of the countries in our sample of 133 countries have at least one type of registry. Across legal origins, the socialist countries are markedly different from the rest of the world as only 18 percent of them have some kind of public registry or private credit bureau. Latin American countries, presenting a French legal origin, and Scandinavian countries are those with the highest scores: all of these countries have one or both. If we look further into what type of institutions exists in each country, we notice that three in four French and German legal origin countries operate public registries, as compared to one in four for common law countries. As Djankov et al. (2007) have recently pointed out, public registries seem to be a feature of civil law countries. German legal origin countries, however, also have a high percentage of private credit bureaus (higher than common law nations) whereas French legal origin nations do not.

The credit information index is in the fifth column of data in Table 1.1. This measure summarizes the rules affecting the scope, access and quality of the credit information of these bureaus. The data maps with previous results on the existence of information sharing facilities: Latin American countries, including French legal origin countries, and Scandinavian legal origin countries tend to receive the highest scores. The data on the coverage of the information by these bureaus (columns 6 and 7) reveal interesting patterns: although public registries are more common, their coverage tends to be more limited. In the average country in the world, the coverage of the adult population by private bureaus is 17 percent, while that of public registries is about 3 percent.

If one were to summarize the evidence for French legal origin countries, they do not seem to lack information sharing institutions or quality and accessibility of information. Some countries classified within this legal family, such as Latin American countries, actually score higher than most regions in the world, with the exception of very developed countries. At first sight, the data thus suggest that the lack of credit in French legal origin countries may not be due to an absence of information sharing institutions.

1.3.2 Control Rights Institutions

Table 1.2 presents data on institutions that, based on the control rights view, support creditor rights and contract enforcement. Table 1.2 is based on the index of creditor rights originally developed by La Porta et al. (1998)

as well as the expansion undertaken by the World Bank's *Doing Business Reports* to include more collateral specific variables. The results show a sharply different pattern for French legal origin countries compared to the other legal families, which is much more distinctive than what was found in relation to information sharing institutions (in Table 1.1).

Creditor rights and collateral rules are statistically significantly weaker in French and socialist legal origins than in common law nations and even in German legal origin countries. As shown in Table 1.2, creditors have no say in whether the firm's reorganization petition is accepted or declined in 73 percent of French legal origin countries, while this is the case in only 58 percent of common law nations. If the petition is successful, an 'automatic stay' is triggered in 70 percent of French legal countries, as opposed to only 50 percent of common law countries. Finally, in case of liquidation, secured creditors are not paid first in 55 percent of French legal nations, contrasting with 28 percent for common law countries. Rather, the state and the firm's employees take priority. The creditors' predicament is aggravated by the fact that the debtor not only will write the reorganization proposal, but will continue to run the firm pending the resolution of the bankruptcy procedure (which may take several years) in 70 percent of French legal origin countries, as opposed to only 36 percent of common law countries. The average aggregate creditor rights score for the French legal origin countries is 1.31, while the average common law country score is 2.28. The results of collateral index, as shown in Table 1.2, column 6, are very similar: French legal origin countries trail basically every other legal origin category. The contrast is sharpest in the results of the French legal origin countries compared with those of the common law origin countries (see Panel B of Table 1.2).

Table 1.2 also presents the data on enforcement institutions (see Djankov et al. 2003b). Column 7 of Table 1.2 presents the average score by legal origin of all the components of the 'formalism index'. A vast comparative law literature suggests that the extent of regulation of dispute resolution varies systematically across legal origins (see for example Damaska 1986). In particular, civil law countries are generally deemed to regulate dispute resolution more heavily than common law influenced countries. The data in Table 1.2 is a striking empirical confirmation of this proposition. Based on most sub-indices, as well as the overall index of formalism and the index of procedures for enforcing contracts, we find a more formal approach to enforcement and 'proceduralism' in the civil law (especially French civil law) countries, than in common law countries. On most individual components of the process, French legal origin countries show higher scores (which evidence a more formal approach to enforcement) than the world average, and certainly than common law countries. One could argue that formalism of dispute resolution is not in itself evidence of inefficiency. Such formal regulation may guarantee fairness of the process, or result from a lack of law and order. Nonetheless, when this data is mapped to several survey measures of judicial efficiency (that is, the expected duration of each type of disputes, perceived impartiality of courts, equal access to non-discriminatory judiciary, enforceability of contracts, etc.) the results show that formalism of civil procedure is a strong predictor of lower judicial efficiency, even controlling for the level of per capita income (Djankov et al. 2003b). These empirical results also do not support the hypothesis mentioned above that the quality of enforcement institutions can substitute or compensate for the inadequacy in creditor rights and collateral law.

Table 1.3 puts the information on all institutions together in a table of correlations. There are four main results. First, there may be a slight substitution between the case of registering property and other information sharing proxies. Second, countries opt for either public registries or private bureaus. Meanwhile, although a higher presence of any kind of information sharing institution is correlated with a higher coverage of the population, only the presence of private bureaus is positively significantly correlated with better quality of the information collected. Third, all control rights institutions are highly correlated with each other indicating that these indices tend to move together. Finally, and most interestingly, there is not a lot of evidence for the substitution hypothesis amongst the two groups of institutions. More precisely, it seems that countries that have a model based on public registries lack the rest of the institutions for credit access. This may be suggestive of different regulatory styles, as Djankov et al. (2003a) argue: the regulatory styles of different countries may involve more or less government intervention.

1.3.3 Determinants of Credit Access Institutions: Beyond Legal Families

To try to understand the determinants of credit institutions, we must also look at potentially exogenous sources of variation linked to legal, political, cultural or economic characteristics of nations (see La Porta et al. 1999). There are traditionally three sets of variables that the literature has used to proxy for these deeper country characteristics:

1. The first set of instruments proxies for economic theories of institutions. As economic wealth expands, better institutions become affordable. GDP per capita, which is highly correlated to the geographical latitude of the capital city of the country, is a good proxy for some of the exogenous reasons that allow countries to grow richer. In

Table 1.3 Correlations of credit access institutions

	Procedures for reg. a property	Public registry	Private registry	Information sharing	Credit information index	Public registry coverage	Private registry coverage	Creditor rights	Collateral index	Formalism index
Public registry	0.001 / 0.988									
Private registry	-0.187 / 0.031 **	-0.287 / 0.001 ***								
Information sharing	-0.179 / 0.040 **	0.540 / 0.000 ***	0.424 / 0.000 ***							
Credit information index	-0.139 / 0.087 *	0.123 / 0.160	0.754 / 0.000 ***	0.660 / 0.000 ***						
Public registry coverage	-0.006 / 0.943	0.373 / 0.000 ***	0.184 / 0.035 **	0.198 / 0.023 **	0.328 / 0.000 ***					
Private registry coverage	-0.226 / 0.005 ***	-0.217 / 0.013 **	0.034 / 0.708	0.090 / 0.311	0.040 / 0.652	0.018 / 0.825				
Creditor rights	0.047 / 0.592	-0.219 / 0.011 **	0.163 / 0.062 *	-0.106 / 0.224	0.248 / 0.004 ***	-0.048 / 0.587	0.183 / 0.036 **			
Creditors collateral index	-0.171 / 0.035 **	-0.420 / 0.000 ***	0.252 / 0.003 ***	-0.087 / 0.318	0.175 / 0.030 **	-0.088 / 0.277	0.320 / 0.000 ***	0.559 / 0.000 ***		
Formalism index (check)	0.135 / 0.203	0.420 / 0.000 ***	-0.093 / 0.385	0.166 / 0.120	0.116 / 0.272	0.281 / 0.007 ***	-0.266 / 0.011 **	-0.255 / 0.016 **	-0.517 / 0.000 ***	
Procedures for enforcement	0.138 / 0.091 *	0.213 / 0.014 **	-0.288 / 0.001 ***	-0.072 / 0.410	-0.236 / 0.003 ***	-0.038 / 0.646	-0.297 / 0.000 ***	-0.238 / 0.006 ***	-0.368 / 0.000 ***	0.544 / 0.000 ***

Notes:
  * significant at 10%
 ** significant at 5%
*** significant at 1%

locations closer to the equator, diseases are rampant, leading to lower productivity and efficiency which affects the rate of investment and growth over time.

2. The second set of instruments, already used in this chapter to partition the data in previous tables, was developed by La Porta et al., (1997 and 1998) and pertains to the different legal origin of countries. Under the legal origin theory, a country's approach to regulation is shaped by its legal tradition.

3. The third set of theories of institutions brings politics in play. The essence of these theories is that political divergence in societies, emerging from cultural, social, religious or ethnic interests, impacts the choice of regulation and institutions as, for example, those in power try to stay in power and transfer resources to themselves and away from other groups. Following this theory, one could use ethno-linguistic fractionalization in a country as a measure, as in La Porta et al. (1999), or religion composition, which also captures more explicitly the cultural aspects that could drive regulation and government policies.[6]

Tables 1.4 and 1.5 show the results of regressing each of our 11 measures of credit access institutions on various sets of variables that capture the essence of the theories of institutions. In each of the tables, we run Tobits and Probits regression specifications, but very similar results are obtained if we run simple OLS regressions as an alternative econometric specification. These tables also split the French legal family into those countries from Latin America and the rest, to ensure that the effect we find in French legal origin countries is not driven by the Latin American countries alone, which are perceived as among the least investor-friendly economies.

There are three main results to draw from these two tables:

1. Country wealth is an important determinant of credit access institutions: richer countries have lower levels of procedures to register property, a higher presence of private bureaus of credit, higher coverage and quality of information collected by information sharing

---

[6] According to cultural theories (Weber 1958, Banfield 1958, Putnam 1993 and Landis 1938), societies hold beliefs that can shape institutions. Societies' distrust and intolerance affect regulation and legislation. Following the approach of other papers, Table 1.5 uses as a set of variables the percentage of the population in 1980 that belonged to the five largest religions in the world: Catholic, Muslim, Orthodox and Buddhist with the omitted variable being Protestant. As an alternative we have also used the same variables for the 1900, but the results do not change.

Table 1.4 *Determinants of credit access institutions*

	Procedures for reg. a prop. (a)	Public registry (b)	Private registry (b)	Information sharing (b)	Credit Information Index (a)	Pub. reg. coverage (a)	Priv reg. coverage (a)	Creditor rights index (a)	Creditors collateral index (a)	Formalism index (check collection) (a)	Procedures for enforcing (a)
Log(GDP per capita)	-0.410 (0.162)**	-0.066 (0.034)*	0.231 (0.043)***	0.085 (0.026)***	0.843 (0.102)***	1.970 (1.042)*	21.220 (2.506)***	0.180 (0.071)**	0.427 (0.096)***	-0.165 (0.052)***	-2.277 (0.583)***
Scandinavian legal origin	-2.482 (1.495)*				-0.525 (0.912)	-81.417 (0.000)	-14.032 (17.361)	-1.022 (0.644)	-1.204 (0.890)	0.506 (0.382)	-0.664 (5.386)
German legal origin	-0.523 (0.815)	0.371 (0.103)***	-0.208 (0.139)	0.150 (0.092)	0.207 (0.501)	7.129 (5.274)	-19.789 (10.252)*	-0.111 (0.351)	-0.841 (0.485)*	1.062 (0.233)***	1.866 (2.936)
Socialist legal origin	0.336 (0.942)	-0.142 (0.198)		-0.449 (0.189)**	-1.214 (0.619)*	4.283 (6.883)	-33.349 (17.193)*	0.077 (0.406)	-0.233 (0.561)	0.781 (0.361)**	2.320 (3.393)
French (other) legal origin	-0.160 (0.611)	0.491 (0.091)***	-0.385 (0.119)***	0.181 (0.082)**	-0.122 (0.385)	15.875 (4.277)***	-36.042 (9.251)***	-1.279 (0.269)***	-2.531 (0.364)***	1.203 (0.192)***	7.757 (2.202)***
French (LAC) legal origin	0.706 (0.755)	0.451 (0.083)***	0.271 (0.165)		1.954 (0.467)***	23.035 (4.883)***	12.906 (9.200)	-0.787 (0.329)**	-2.701 (0.450)***	2.182 (0.206)***	10.370 (2.722)***
Constant	9.461 (1.293)***				-3.662 (0.830)***	-27.875 (8.817)***	-149.063 (21.054)***	0.918 (0.565)	3.051 (0.770)***	4.105 (0.428)***	43.886 (4.658)***
Observations	132	128	117	108	132	131	131	132	132	88	132

Notes: Standard errors in parentheses
* significant at 10%
** significant at 5%
*** significant at 1%
(a) Tobit regressions censored at zero
(b) Probit regressions, marginal coefficients shown

21

Table 1.5 Determinants of credit access institutions

	Procedures for reg. a prop. (a)	Public registry (b)	Private registry (b)	Information sharing (b)	Credit information index (a)	Pub. reg. coverage (a)	Priv. reg. coverage (a)	Creditor rights index (a)	Creditors collateral index (a)	Formalism index (check collection) (a)	Procedures for enforcing (a)
Log (GDP per capita)	−0.365 (0.160)**	−0.060 (0.036)*	0.233 (0.046)***	0.087 (0.027)***	0.838 (0.105)***	1.582 (1.091)	20.424 (2.560)***	0.201 (0.073)***	0.470 (0.098)***	−0.162 (0.055)***	−1.848 (0.583)***
Scandinavian legal origin	−1.771 (1.463)				−0.738 (0.927)	−77.064 (0.000)	−16.737 (17.560)	−1.186 (0.655)*	−1.699 (0.890)*	0.620 (0.389)	−0.742 (5.313)
German legal origin	−0.758 (0.829)	0.403 (0.099)***	−0.205 (0.164)	0.151 (0.082)*	0.319 (0.530)	6.267 (5.638)	−16.430 (10.955)	0.049 (0.372)	−0.482 (0.505)	1.013 (0.241)***	4.124 (3.011)
Socialist legal origin	−1.084 (1.079)	−0.175 (0.236)		−0.536 (0.199)***	−0.776 (0.717)	3.229 (7.447)	−19.403 (18.835)	0.260 (0.483)	0.264 (0.656)	0.560 (0.457)	3.161 (3.916)
French (other) legal origin	−0.745 (0.634)	0.496 (0.236)	−0.342 (0.128)***	0.191 (0.080)**	0.076 (0.415)	13.887 (4.444)***	−27.891 (10.548)***	−1.138 (0.291)***	−2.224 (0.386)***	1.007 (0.224)***	7.961 (2.301)***
French (LAC) legal origin	0.691 (0.955)	0.495 (0.087)***	0.274 (0.222)		2.092 (0.617)***	18.259 (6.244)***	15.950 (13.049)	−0.437 (0.432)	−2.088 (0.581)***	2.019 (0.282)***	14.894 (3.466)***
Buddhist	0.791 (0.999)	−0.142 (0.213)	0.304 (0.161)*	0.139 (0.123)	−0.032 (0.645)	−4.676 (7.561)	−0.052 (14.193)	−0.235 (0.453)	−1.475 (0.612)**	0.070 (0.311)	−0.823 (3.628)
Catholic	0.837 (0.802)	−0.044 (0.156)	−0.059 (0.180)	−0.076 (0.129)	−0.364 (0.519)	7.045 (5.126)	−7.554 (11.749)	−0.461 (0.364)	−1.002 (0.488)**	0.286 (0.251)	−3.543 (2.913)
Muslim	2.299 (0.680)***	0.155 (0.130)	−0.211 (0.157)	−0.052 (0.099)	−0.627 (0.440)	4.630 (4.453)	−16.238 (11.099)	−0.154 (0.311)	−0.549 (0.414)	0.398 (0.249)	4.896 (2.469)**
Orthodox	2.551 (1.098)**	0.119 (0.207)	−0.198 (0.184)	0.066 (0.130)	−0.813 (0.711)	4.263 (6.860)	−24.336 (17.647)	−0.352 (0.494)	−0.915 (0.668)	0.330 (0.399)	−1.892 (3.987)

22

Constant	8.285 (1.295)***				−3.395 (0.864)***	−27.064 (9.320)***	−138.154 (21.665)***	0.866 (0.586)	3.105 (0.788)***	3.953 (0.454)***	39.539 (4.701)***
Observations	132	128	117	108	132	131	131	132	132	88	132

Notes: Standard errors in parentheses
* significant at 10%
** significant at 5%
*** significant at 1%
(a) Tobit regressions censored at zero
(b) Probit regressions, marginal coefficients shown

institutions, higher creditor rights and collateral rights indices and better measures of contract enforcement. The only exception is that richer nations tend to have fewer public registries.

2.   French civil law countries have statistically significantly higher presence of public bureaus and higher credit coverage. They also show, consistent with previous tables, a much lower level of all types of control rights institutions. Among the two sub-groups of French origin nations, Latin America is mostly responsible for the results on information sharing institutions. If we compare the two sub-groups, Latin American countries have in fact a much higher presence of both public and private credit bureaus. The two sub-groups look remarkably similar in terms of control rights protection results (which are low). Strikingly, French legal origin countries have poor quality of enforcement, even after controlling for per capita income.

3.   If we compare the results in Tables 1.4 and 1.5 we observe that adding religious composition does not add much explanatory power. Legal origin seems to explain a much larger portion of the variation of credit access institutions.[7]

These results are useful for interpreting the findings in the next section, where we look at outcomes of institutions in the credit markets, since they speak about an important exogenous component of credit access institutions and lower the concern of potential endogeneity problems.

1.4   DO CREDIT ACCESS INSTITUTIONS MATTER?

The previous sections showed that credit access institutions vary a lot according to the legal family to which the country historically belongs and wealth levels. However the fundamental question is whether this matters for access to credit per se. Accordingly, in this section, we examine the evidence on the influence of credit access institutions on credit market outcomes.

Table 1.6 presents our measures of outcomes for access to credit for the sample of 133 countries across legal origins.[8] Columns 1 and 2 show the

---

[7]   The only cases where religion seems to enter marginally significantly is for the cases of creditor and collateral rights, where Catholic and Muslim countries show marginally lower protections.

[8]   Appendix Tables A1.1 and A1.2 provide detailed definitions, sources and basic statistics of these measures.

Table 1.6 Credit access measures by legal origin

Country	Time for reg. a prop.	Cost of reg. a prop.	Time for closing a business	Cost for closing a business	Recovery rate for closing a business	Time for enforcing	Cost for enforcing	Private credit to GDP
				Panel A: Means				
Scandinavian legal origin	14.75	2.53	1.78	5.75	79.53	151.50	5.48	0.84
Socialist legal origin	60.91	2.45	3.45	12.00	22.65	322.27	21.87	0.11
French legal origin (other)	92.75	10.03	3.88	17.90	24.12	433.09	37.08	0.35
French legal origin (LAC)	80.20	4.50	3.75	15.70	26.93	471.10	23.03	0.33
French legal origin	88.83	8.30	3.84	17.18	25.00	444.97	32.69	0.34
Sample average	**85.56**	**6.66**	**3.27**	**16.79**	**31.36**	**394.44**	**30.62**	**0.43**
			Panel B: Tests of means (t-statistics)					
Common vs German	−1.52	2.27**	−0.13	1.17	−0.96	−1.10	2.23**	−0.77
Common vs Scandinavian	1.25	1.58	0.97	1.96*	−2.85***	2.37**	1.64	−1.30
Common vs Socialist	0.38	2.57	−1.47	1.14	2.21**	0.07	0.62	2.76***
Common vs French	−0.78	−0.89**	−3.08***	−0.34	3.20***	−2.59***	−0.84	2.30**
Common vs French (other)	−1.02	−2.00**	−2.92***	−0.51	2.96***	−2.28**	−1.25	1.91*
Common vs French (LAC)	−0.25	1.99*	−2.23**	0.17	2.08***	−2.68***	0.64	1.74*

Notes:
* significant at 10%
** significant at 5%
*** significant at 1%

time it takes to register a property's title and the associated costs. Columns 3, 4 and 5 present measures of the time and costs to shut down a firm and the recovery rate for secured creditors of their claim after closing. Intuitively, a better set of credit institutions (especially those under the control view) should lead to a more expeditious process and a higher recovery rate when firms need to close down. Columns 6 and 7 show the measures for the time required to enforce the collection of an overdue claim and the legal costs of the process. Finally, column 8 shows what is probably the best measure of credit access: the size of private credit in the country through banks and capital markets, as a proportion of the size of the economy.[9] In accordance with the idea of the importance of legal families as an exogenous component of credit access institutions, the data shows that compared to common law countries, French legal origin countries consistently show more lengthy and costly processes for registering property and closing a business, as well as a lower size of private credit as a proportion of the economy.

The crucial question is if institutions matter for credit access or not. Following the work of La Porta et al. (1997 and 1998) and Djankov et al. (2007) we relate a large set of credit access institutions to each of the measures of outcomes presented in Table 1.6. We prepared several tables of regressions of each measure of credit market development, explained by country characteristics and testing for different combinations of indices of credit access institutions.[10] The time and cost to register property or shut down a business speak of the inefficiency of the process, but they may be regarded as intermediary measures. For these reasons, as well as due to space constraints, we only present results on the size of private credit as a proportion of the economy.[11]

Results on the size of credit are shown in Table 1.7. This table shows that the size of private credit through banks and markets is larger in more devel-

---

[9]   All these measures of outcomes in the credit market come from different data-sets with different methodologies and address different areas of the market. The correlations amongst these variables are very high and statistically significant at 1 percent in all cases (results not shown for space reasons).

[10]   Regressions control for GDP per capita and contract enforcement measures. Results are robust to changes in enforcement proxies and to the inclusion of other control variables such as ethnolinguistic fractionalization. All of these regressions are not shown for space reasons but they are available from the author.

[11]   In all of these regressions poorer countries and those with worse enforcement measures have higher times and costs of registering assets. The number of procedures to register property, as well as the lack of information sharing and control rights institutions, have a negative impact, although they are not statistically significant in all specifications.

Table 1.7 Size of credit markets

	Private credit to GDP				
Log GDP per capita	0.142	0.144	0.134	0.144	0.134
	(0.013)***	(0.015)***	(0.016)***	(0.018)***	(0.021)***
GDP growth	0.013	0.016	0.014	0.017	0.017
	(0.011)	(0.011)	(0.011)	(0.011)	(0.011)
Inflation	−0.000	−0.000	−0.000	−0.000	−0.000
	(0.001)	(0.001)	(0.001)	(0.001)	(0.001)
Procedures for reg. a prop.	−0.010	−0.014	−0.014	−0.014	−0.013
	(0.006)	(0.006)**	(0.006)**	(0.006)**	(0.006)**
Log (procedures for enforcing)	−0.094	−0.126	−0.115	−0.121	−0.102
	(0.051)*	(0.051)**	(0.053)**	(0.053)**	(0.056)*
Information sharing	0.131	0.116			
	0.040***	(0.040)***			
Public registry			0.028		
			(0.047)		
Private registry			0.131		
			(0.056)**		
Max. reg. coverage, credit					0.002
					(0.001)
Credit information index				0.013	
				(0.013)	
Creditor collateral index	0.034				
	(0.012)***				
Creditor rights index		0.047	0.040	0.037	0.039
		(0.021)**	(0.021)*	(0.020)*	(0.020)*
Constant	−0.554	−0.342	−0.262	−0.293	−0.286
	(0.227)**	(0.207)	(0.213)	(0.228)	(0.220)
Observations	128	128	128	128	128
R-squared	0.67	0.66	0.66	0.65	0.66

Notes: Robust standard errors in parentheses
  * significant at 10%
 ** significant at 5%
*** significant at 1%

oped countries and in those with a higher level of contract enforcement. These results match those found previously in the literature. The first two regressions show that there is a positive impact of less onerous procedures for registering property and of the existence of information sharing institutions. The impact is also positive for control rights institutions (creditor rights and collateral rules). The evidence in these two regressions can be interpreted to say that there is a complementary role of both of these sets of institutions in credit access.

The last three regressions in Table 1.7 analyse further the impact of information sharing institutions. In regressions 4 and 5 of the Table, we test if the coverage or the quality of the information by credit bureaus has a significant impact. The results show that although the coefficients have the right signs, there is no statistical significance once we control for the institutions of control rights. Finally, the third regression splits the information sharing institutions into public registries and private bureaus to see if there is any differential impact. The results show that only the existence of private credit bureaus has a positive and statistically significant impact on the size of the credit markets across countries.

To summarize, the results in this section show a large and significant role in the protection of creditors through legal rules and contract enforcement. The existence of information sharing institutions also has a positive effect on credit access, but the results are not as robust as with those measures of control rights and there is uncertainty about the benefits of public registries.

1.5   REFORMS AND POLICY IMPLICATIONS

1.5.1   Do Institutions have the Same Effect in Poor and Rich Countries?

In Table 1.8, we sort countries by per capita income into the top 75 percentile and the bottom 25 percentile, to present the average of the measures of credit access institutions for these two sub-groups, as well as the t-statistics comparing the two groups. The least developed countries consistently show lower levels of all credit-supporting institutions. The statistical differences are more pronounced for information sharing institutions. Creditor rights and collateral rules are also lower in the poorest nations, but these are not the indices where the largest differences exist. Although an explicit comparison of contract enforcement measures does not appear in this table, the regressions in previous sections show very large differences in the efficiency of contract enforcement between poor and rich nations.

The implication for developing countries is clear: the creation of information sharing mechanisms and legal reform in the areas of creditor rights and collateral law need to take into account the poor enforcement environment and be complemented with judicial reform itself. Table 1.9 runs the same regressions as Table 1.7 but splits the sample according to income levels. Panel A has as a sample the top 75 percentile of countries based on

Table 1.8 *Institutions for credit access, top and bottom GDP per capita*

	Procedures for reg. a prop.	Public registry	Private registry	Information sharing	Credit information index	Pub. reg. coverage	Priv. reg. coverage	Creditor rights index	Creditors collateral index
				Panel A: Means					
Top 75% of GDP pc	5.82	0.51	0.55	0.85	3.24	4.72	22.85	1.94	5.07
Bottom 25% of GDP pc	6.85	0.59	0.08	0.65	1.27	0.64	0.08	1.43	4.28
Sample average	**6.09**	**0.53**	**0.42**	**0.80**	**2.72**	**3.63**	**16.79**	**1.80**	**4.86**
			Panel B: Tests of means (t-statistics)						
Top 75% vs Bottom 25%	−2.00 **	−0.87	5.41 ***	2.69 ***	5.39 ***	2.29 **	4.51 ***	2.31 **	2.10 **

Notes:
* significant at 10%
** significant at 5%
*** significant at 1%

Table 1.9 Institutions for credit access and level of development (controlling by Log GDP)

	Panel A: Top 75% Private credit to GDP				
Log GDP	0.107	0.109	0.105	0.110	0.109
	(0.014)***	(0.016)***	(0.016)***	(0.018)***	(0.020)***
GDP growth	0.010	0.018	0.017	0.020	0.022
	(0.011)	(0.012)	(0.012)	(0.013)	(0.013)*
Inflation	−0.002	−0.002	−0.002	−0.002	−0.002
	(0.001)*	(0.001)**	(0.001)**	(0.001)**	(0.001)**
Procedures for reg. a prop.	−0.022	−0.030	−0.030	−0.030	−0.029
	(0.009)**	(0.009)***	(0.009)***	(0.009)***	(0.009)***
Log (Procedures for enforcing)	−0.082	−0.155	−0.145	−0.150	−0.136
	(0.072)	(0.075)**	(0.078)*	(0.078)*	(0.080)*
Information sharing	0.248	0.212			
	(0.064)***	(0.066)***			
Public registry			0.035		
			(0.063)		
Private registry			0.156		
			(0.070)**		
Max. reg. coverage, credit					0.001
					(0.001)
Credit Information Index				0.024	
				(0.017)	
Creditors collateral index	0.063				
	(0.014)***				
Creditors rights index		0.091	0.085	0.082	0.084
		(0.027)***	(0.028)***	(0.028)***	(0.028)***
Constant	−2.246	−1.815	−1.678	−1.765	−1.745
	(0.440)***	(0.499)***	(0.506)***	(0.545)***	(0.551)***
Observations	91	91	91	91	91
R-squared	0.63	0.62	0.61	0.60	0.59

Notes: Robust standard errors in parentheses
  * significant at 10%
 ** significant at 5%
*** significant at 1%

GDP per capita, while Panel B's sample is the poorest 25 percentile. The two panels show interesting results in terms of the institutions that work best. For both rich and poor countries, collateral rules and creditor rights lead to more credit access. Similarly, the existence of information sharing agencies is also positively and significantly related to the size of credit markets. Yet,

Table 1.9 (continued)

	Panel B: Bottom 25% Private credit to GDP				
Log GDP	0.033	0.029	0.028	0.028	0.030
	(0.007)***	(0.008)***	(0.008)***	(0.010)***	(0.010)***
GDP growth	0.011	0.011	0.011	0.011	0.011
	(0.008)	(0.008)	(0.008)	(0.008)	(0.008)
Inflation	−0.000	−0.000	−0.000	−0.000	−0.000
	(0.000)	(0.000)	(0.000)	(0.000)	(0.000)
Procedures for reg. a prop.	−0.008	−0.010	−0.010	−0.009	−0.010
	(0.005)	(0.005)**	(0.005)**	(0.004)**	(0.004)**
Log (Procedures for enforcing)	0.016	0.020	0.014	0.016	0.027
	(0.034)	(0.033)	(0.035)	(0.039)	(0.039)
Information sharing	0.045	0.058			
	(0.028)	(0.027)**			
Public registry			0.060		
			(0.029)**		
Private registry			0.023		
			(0.020)		
Max. reg. coverage, credit					0.015
					(0.008)*
Creditor collateral index				0.010	
				(0.012)	
Creditors rights index	0.016				
	(0.007)**				
Credit Information Index		0.038	0.040	0.025	0.035
		(0.010)***	(0.011)***	(0.014)*	(0.011)***
Constant	−0.689	−0.588	−0.545	−0.524	−0.602
	(0.192)***	(0.196)***	(0.206)**	(0.265)*	(0.279)**
Observations	37	37	37	37	37
R-squared	0.47	0.53	0.53	0.48	0.50

Notes: Robust standard errors in parentheses
   * significant at 10%
  ** significant at 5%
*** significant at 1%

when we split the registries in public and private bureaus, public registries only have a positive impact on credit access in the lowest income group.

Table 1.10 explores this fact further trying to disentangle what information sharing agencies bring to the table. The countries included in this Table are those that already have any of the two types of credit bureaus. For these 102 countries, results show that access to credit is not at all

Table 1.10   *Institutions for credit access for countries with an information*
              sharing facility

	Private credit to GDP		
Log GDP per capita	0.145	0.161	0.143
	(0.018)***	(0.023)***	(0.023)***
GDP growth	0.016	0.019	0.017
	(0.013)	(0.013)	(0.013)
Inflation	−0.002	−0.002	−0.002
	(0.001)**	(0.001)**	(0.001)**
Procedures for reg. a prop.	−0.019	−0.019	−0.019
	(0.007)**	(0.007)***	(0.007)**
Log (Procedures for enforcing)	−0.124	−0.127	−0.132
	(0.070)*	(0.069)*	(0.070)*
Public registry	−0.047		
	(0.068)		
Max. reg. coverage, credit			0.001
			(0.001)
Credit Information Index		−0.020	
		(0.021)	
Creditor rights index	0.048	0.056	0.048
	(0.023)**	(0.024)**	(0.023)**
Constant	−0.173	−0.258	−0.180
	(0.292)	(0.309)	(0.292)
Observations	102	102	102
R-squared	0.67	0.67	0.67

Notes: Robust standard errors in parentheses
   * significant at 10%
  ** significant at 5%
*** significant at 1%

improved where public registries are the only kind of credit bureau that
exists. The coefficient is in fact negative. The last two regressions in the
Table also find little evidence that the coverage or the quality of information of the bureaus gives an additional boost to credit access. Across
all three regressions though, both kinds of measures of contract enforcement are positively related to bigger credit markets. In other words, better
creditor protections in bankruptcy and reorganization procedures, as
well as a more streamlined civil procedure to resolve disputes, are both
linked to more credit access. These results suggest that information
sharing facilities are no substitute for poor legal protection of creditors
(through creditor rights and collateral law) and uncertain enforcement
process.

Table 1.11   Size of credit markets by creditor rights index

	Panel A: Higher creditors rights Private credit to GDP			
Log GDP per capita	0.199	0.175	0.173	0.182
	(0.042)***	(0.051)***	(0.041)***	(0.040)***
GDP growth	0.014	0.001	0.011	0.012
	(0.010)	(0.010)	(0.011)	(0.010)
Inflation	−0.000	0.000	−0.000	−0.000
	(0.001)	(0.001)	(0.001)	(0.001)
Procedures for reg. a prop.	−0.003	0.003	−0.003	0.001
	(0.017)	(0.015)	(0.014)	(0.013)
Log (Procedures for	−0.221	−0.183	−0.223	−0.191
enforcing)	(0.131)	(0.129)	(0.125)*	(0.143)
Information sharing	0.027			
	(0.153)			
Public registry		−0.087		
		(0.133)		
Private registry		0.248		
		(0.152)		
Max. reg. coverage, credit				0.002
				(0.002)
Credit Information Index			0.045	
			(0.031)	
Constant	−0.324	−0.359	−0.251	−0.364
	(0.557)	(0.640)	(0.564)	(0.580)
Observations	37	37	37	37
R-squared	0.64	0.69	0.66	0.66

Notes: Robust standard errors in parentheses
 * significant at 10%
 ** significant at 5%
 *** significant at 1%

Finally, Table 1.11 splits the sample of countries according to creditor rights score. Panel A includes those countries with creditor rights above the mean for the sample, while Panel B's sample is formed by countries with poor creditor rights, of which there are over twice as many as those in Panel A. The purpose of the table is to analyse the impact of information sharing institutions in both kinds of settings. The results show that the impact of the existence of an information sharing institution of any kind does not have any significant effect on the size of credit markets among the high creditor rights countries. It is only in the case of poor creditor protection countries that

Table 1.11   (continued)

	Panel B: Lower creditors rights Private credit to GDP			
Log GDP per capita	0.134	0.129	0.137	0.125
	(0.018)***	(0.018)***	(0.021)***	(0.028)***
GDP growth	0.028	0.028	0.031	0.030
	(0.013)**	(0.013)**	(0.013)**	(0.012)**
Inflation	0.000	0.000	0.000	0.000
	(0.001)	(0.001)	(0.001)	(0.001)
Procedures for reg. a prop.	−0.012	−0.014	−0.014	−0.013
	(0.006)*	(0.007)**	(0.007)**	(0.007)*
Log (Procedures for enforcing)	−0.113	−0.109	−0.098	−0.090
	(0.051)**	(0.056)*	(0.053)*	(0.053)*
Information sharing	0.088			
	(0.038)**			
Public registry		0.044		
		(0.050)		
Private registry		0.076		
		(0.055)		
Max. reg. coverage, credit				0.001
				(0.002)
Credit Information Index			0.003	
			(0.014)	
Constant	−0.262	−0.212	−0.269	−0.222
	(0.217)	(0.222)	(0.246)	(0.245)
Observations	91	91	91	91
R-squared	0.64	0.64	0.63	0.63

Notes: Robust standard errors in parentheses
   * significant at 10%
  ** significant at 5%
*** significant at 1%

credit bureaus have an impact. Nonetheless, when we split the bureaus into private and public, the statistical significance disappears for both sub-groups. We get similar results if we split the sample according to high and low collateral rules. In that case, only private credit bureaus have a positive and statistically significant impact (tables not included).

There seem to be marked differences in the effect of public and private credit bureaus. The different characteristics of these two types of information gathering institutions may explain part of their differential impact on credit access.[12] Table 1.12 illustrates an important characteristic of countries which rely on public credit registries. Countries with public registries have lower creditor protection, worse collateral rules, more formalistic regulation of court procedures and higher levels of government ownership of banks (based on the data of La Porta et al., 2002). The correlation between public registries and government ownership of banks is statistically significant for 1970 and 1995, after the privatization wave. One interpretation of these findings is that public registry of banks is another manifestation of a regulatory style that relies more on state intervention than on market mechanisms. As other papers have shown (Botero et al. 2004, Djankov et al. 2003a, La Porta et al. 2002 and 2008), the pattern of institutions across countries suggests that there are different regulatory styles. French civil law nations seem to rely more on government intervention than on market forces in the regulation of business activities. This data may partially explain the econometric results in previous tables showing that exclusive reliance on public registries is not connected with more credit access. The policy implications of this section suggest that developing nations would be well advised to avoid complete reliance on government intervention to solve their low credit access problem.

1.5.2 Feasible Reforms in Emerging Markets

The previous section suggests that there may be large pay-offs to reforming the framework for access to credit in developing countries. But before moving in that direction, one would like to know if there is any empirical support for the view that reforms do pay off. In a recent paper, Djankov et al. (2007) do such a test for several of the institutions of credit access that we have been analysing in this chapter. In line with other studies on the effect of institutional reforms in other areas, they show that changes in control rights

---

[12] Public credit registries are databases created by government authorities that are typically managed by the central bank of the country. Lenders are compelled to send the data to the central authority, which in exchange sends additional data to credit institutions. In the typical country with public credit registries, all financial intermediaries are required to send information to the central bank. In contrast, private credit bureaus tend to contain data provided only by the institutions that are part of it. Private credit bureaus are typically voluntary and act as information brokers operating under reciprocity condition. The timeliness and accuracy of the information reported is typically enforced by the threat that institutions that fail to commit to the requirements will be expelled from the bureau. For all of these reasons, and the fact that public registries typically have a size cut-off rate and do not care much for consumer loans, private credit bureaus' information tends to be more accurate and to have a wider coverage.

Table 1.12 Correlation among different styles of credit access institutions

	Government ownership of banks (1995)	Government ownership of banks (1970)	Procedures for reg. a prop.	Public registry	Private registry	Information sharing	Credit Information Index	Pub. reg. coverage	Priv. reg. coverage	Creditor rights index	Creditors collateral index	Formalism index (check collection)
Government ownership of banks (1970)	0.765 0.000 ***											
Procedures for reg. a prop.	0.235 0.028 **	0.311 0.003										
Public registry	0.246 0.024 **	0.347 0.001 ***	0.001 0.988									
Private registry	−0.352 0.001 ***	−0.363 0.001 ***	−0.183 0.035 **	−0.272 0.002								
Information sharing	−0.206 0.061 *	−0.195 0.075 *	−0.179 0.040 **	0.540 0.000 ***	0.430 0.000							
Credit Information Index	−0.378 0.000 ***	−0.340 0.001 ***	−0.139 0.087 *	0.123 0.160	0.759 0.000 ***	0.660 0.000						
Pub. reg. coverage	−0.089 0.412	0.131 0.226	−0.006 0.943	0.373 0.000 ***	0.194 0.026 **	0.198 0.023 **	0.328 0.000					
Priv. reg. coverage	−0.363 0.001 ***	−0.433 0.000 ***	−0.226 0.005 ***	−0.217 0.013 **	0.706 0.000 ***	0.311 0.000 ***	0.652 0.000 ***	0.018 0.825				

Creditor rights index	−0.161 0.145	−0.238 0.029**	0.047 0.592	−0.219 0.011**	0.165 0.058*	−0.106 0.224	0.248 0.004***	−0.048 0.587	0.183 0.036**		
Creditors collateral index	−0.384 0.000***	−0.482 0.000***	−0.171 0.035**	−0.420 0.000***	0.253 0.003***	−0.087 0.318	0.175 0.030**	−0.088 0.277	0.320 0.000***	0.559	
Formalism Index (check collection)	0.280 0.011**	0.413 0.000***	0.135 0.203	0.420 0.000***	−0.067 0.531	0.166 0.120	0.116 0.272	0.281 0.007***	−0.266 0.011**	−0.255 0.016**	−0.517 0.000***
Log (Procedures for enforcing)	0.343 0.001***	0.234 0.030**	0.150 0.067*	0.249 0.004***	−0.280 0.001***	−0.057 0.515	−0.218 0.007***	0.004 0.964	0.337 0.000***	−0.227 0.009***	−0.385 0.000*** 0.551 0.000***

Notes:
* significant at 10%
** significant at 5%
*** significant at 1%

institutions as well as information sharing institutions are related with improvements in the development of markets, and in this case, in credit access.

Most emerging markets suffer from many deficiencies across most parts of the credit institutional framework and, as a result, have the lowest debt penetration levels in the world. The evidence presented in the previous two sections suggests there is a connection between credit institutions and credit access both at the cross-country and time-series levels. The available empirical evidence suggests that a sound credit institutional framework would result in faster and less costly title registration and bankruptcy procedures, and ultimately larger credit markets. Developing nations should find a way to push for reforms that help them improve their credit institutions. But reforms typically face challenges and opposition (Lopez-de-Silanes 2002).

1.5.3   The Forces of Legal Reform

For most developing countries, the improvement of credit institutions would require radical changes in the legal system and court procedures, as well as a serious effort to improve the functioning of information sharing institutions. Additionally, the evidence presented here also suggests that the country's judicial system plays a key role in shaping access to credit.

But there are large political obstacles to effective institutional reforms. Perhaps the most important objections come from the controllers at the top of large corporations. From the point of view of the controlling investors, an improvement in creditor rights and the introduction of more transparent mechanisms to gather borrower information may be reflected in more access to credit for the rest of the corporate sector, and thus less preference for them. Under the status quo, many existing firms can finance their own investment projects through internal cash flows, as well as relationships with captive or closely tied banks (La Porta et al. 2003). As a consequence, large firms not only get the finance they need, but also the political influence that comes with the access to such finance. Opposition to reform also includes banks, who are supposed to be the main beneficiaries of credit markets' reforms. They may be uninterested in reforming credit institutions, particularly bankruptcy law, if they have to write down the value of bad loans and inject fresh capital. Opposition may also come from labor interests since they are also receiving some rents from the existing arrangements.[13] Objections from labor groups make it more difficult to get reforms

---

[13]   The losers in the existing arrangements are the new entrepreneurs who cannot raise external funds to finance new investment, and the parts of the labor force that do not have access to the privileged jobs.

through Congress. Congress itself may not be interested in reforms, as different groups represent different interests. Finally, politicians in charge of reforms may not have the right incentives to push them through if they enjoy rents from current status quo arrangements.

Yet there are some countervailing political interests as well, including foreign (institutional) shareholders and creditors who have recently begun insisting on the need to improve credit institutions and their rights as creditors. In some countries, these outside investors are beginning to have influence. Their influence becomes particularly great in times of financial crisis, such as the one the emerging world experienced in 1997–98, when companies were in desperate need of funds. Successful reforms have mostly occurred when the special interests could be destroyed or appeased. In this respect, institutional reform is no different from most other reforms in developing or developed countries (Hirschman 1963). Slow and difficult as it is, real legal reform needs to take place in most developing countries. But what parameters should reforms follow?

Although there are many reforms at work around the world, our understanding of the principles of reform of credit access institutions remains limited. There is no checklist of what needs to be done. However, the available evidence presented here and in other studies indicates that to foster credit access in developing countries, reforms must take into account two things: (1) enforcement of legal rules is deeply connected with the rules themselves; and (2) since institutional reform is slow and complicated, complementary market-based mechanisms should be adopted to help create the necessary pressures for more reforms to take place.

The implications of the previous sections are important for the design of feasible institutional reforms. Many times, the failure of reforms is due to underestimating the politics behind and to the strong opposition that these changes encounter through the process of approval. Let us illustrate this process in the area of bankruptcy law. When a business is insolvent and its assets need to be liquidated to pay back its creditors (secured and unsecured), there are two basic realization procedures: (1) public auctions; and (2) structured private bargaining. In practice, both types of procedures have serious problems. Under perfect and complete capital markets, public auctions would sell the firm's assets to the highest bidder and guarantee an efficient outcome. However, if capital markets are not efficient, the best managers may not be able to raise the cash necessary to buy the firm's assets. Capital market imperfections may have dire consequences if firms are inefficiently dismantled and their assets sold off cheaply at fire sale prices.

There are also inherent problems with structured bargaining processes. First, they require sophisticated legal systems to function properly. Second, it is difficult to know what fraction of the firm should be allocated to each class of creditors because there is no objective valuation for the firm. Third, different types of creditors have different objectives. Senior creditors prefer rapid liquidation, while junior creditors may prefer more orderly liquidation or even reorganization. These conflicts have pushed most countries to opt for slow, reorganization-focused bankruptcy schemes rather than liquidations (Hart 1995).

In addition to these conflicts, developing nations face additional problems, ranging from less developed capital markets to ineffective and corrupt judicial systems, all of which lead to lower expected outcomes of liquidation and reorganization procedures. The failure of judicial-based bankruptcy reforms observed in Latin America and East Asia in the last 15 years suggests that court-intensive bankruptcy procedures may impose substantial deadweight losses as assets are dissipated throughout the process. For this reason, the search for alternative bankruptcy procedures to reduce reliance on the judiciary may be of particular appeal for developing countries.

There are two alternative reorganization procedures that could be considered. A first alternative is to allow creditors (for example secured creditors) the right to appoint an administrative receiver, in charge of both running the firm in default and disposing of its assets piecemeal or as an ongoing operation. This method would parallel the UK administration procedure. Once the assets of the firm had been disposed of, the receiver would distribute the proceeds in accordance with creditors' priority ranking, marking the end of the process. The advantage of this mechanism is that it can be implemented quickly, therefore minimizing the firm's loss of value.[14] Unfortunately, there is no reason to believe that a creditor-appointed receiver would be interested in maximizing the firm's value. Not only may he favor some creditors over others, but he may also fail to act in the interest of shareholders when the firm is still economically viable. Another suggestion departing from court-intensive procedures is to leave the decision to restructure or liquidate to market forces. Introducing market forces in bankruptcy proceedings requires steps akin to those in a privatization. Hart et al. (1997) develop such a bankruptcy procedure using auctions. Specifically, both firm insiders and outsiders are invited to place cash and non-cash offers for the *assets* of the firm. In other words, the assets of the bankrupt firm are auctioned off to the highest bidder and the proceedings are used towards paying the existing claims according to priority ranking. Although

---

[14]   In addition, the immediate transfer of control to creditors minimizes intervention from the court whose main role is to police the procedure to avoid fraud.

the firm is stripped of its assets, in preparation for the auction, creditors retain control and cash flow rights ('bankruptcy rights') over the firm's assets. The holders of bankruptcy rights decide among the competing offers made by bidders and retain all the proceeds from the auction. To eliminate conflicts of interests among different classes of claimants, this procedure transforms the capital structure of the firm into an all-equity firm through a mechanism that preserves absolute priority of claims. The way to achieve this goal is to cancel all debts, allocate all bankruptcy rights to the most senior class of claimants, and allow more junior classes to acquire these rights if, and only if, they are willing to retire all senior claims to them.[15]

There is a lot of work to do designing enforceable laws in most of the developing countries, particularly those with a history of poor enforcement. Blindly copying principles or inserting some investors' rights into the laws is not likely to lead to effective legal reform. The new mechanisms just outlined could be offered to firms allowing them to opt into a more protective creditor regime by specifying irrevocably in their charters whether the new creditor-friendly rules apply in the event of financial distress. If the new rules are superior to the old ones, firms should voluntarily adhere to higher standards enticed by the prospect of lower interest rates which creditors would be likely to offer them.

Based on the large impact of the quality of enforcement shown in the previous empirical sections, it is imperative to try to complement the reform of rules with reforms that will improve the judicial system. Legal rules are

---

[15]   The introduction of market forces into bankruptcy through this procedure has several advantages. First, the ability for firm insiders and outsiders to make offers in cash and/or non-cash securities, for the firm as a whole or for parts of it, makes it more likely that the assets of the firm will be put to their most productive use. Second, it eliminates conflicts between different classes of claimants regarding the future of the firm since all holders of bankruptcy rights are equal and have only one objective: to maximize the value of the firm. Third, this procedure, while increasing creditor rights, allows for debtor protection by giving shareholders and management the opportunity to propose offers for the firm, which may include reorganization plans, and by allowing them first priority to exercise their right to acquire the bankruptcy rights from creditors. Fourth, the procedure is simple and quick, reducing uncertainty and minimizing the loss of value created by financial distress and the depletion of assets which usually follows the declaration of bankruptcy and reorganization. The preservation of the firm's value increases the probability of a successful reorganization and is translated into higher cash flows for the claimants entitled to the assets. And finally, the procedure minimizes the reliance on and room for discretion of the judicial system, yet it achieves the 'fair outcome' in terms of absolute priority. An additional advantage of this procedure over existing options is that contentious claims need not hold up the reorganization process. This feature makes the proposal particularly attractive for emerging markets with a poor registry of property and/or lengthy court proceedings.

only one element of investor protection; the enforcement of these rules may be equally or even more important.[16] A quick analysis of all of the reforms of judicial systems across countries sheds four common threads:

1. reforms that increase resources need to address incentives;
2. reforms should increase accountability;
3. reforms should institute competition and choice;
4. reforms should streamline procedure.

Some emerging markets rank amongst the lowest in contract enforcement, which is a key ingredient in any successful combination of measures to promote credit access. Based on the available evidence on judicial reform, and considering the current stage of judicial development in most developing countries, the reforms that show most promise are those that try to increase accountability, institute competition and choice, and streamline procedures.

1.6   CONCLUSION AND POLICY IMPLICATIONS

Access to credit in many emerging economies has been claimed to be too low to promote further investment and growth. Indeed, this chapter showed that there are severe credit problems in many developing countries and that credit access institutions have a strong influence. Several developing nations offer investors a rather unattractive institutional and legal environment, which results in exceedingly small credit markets and difficult credit access, costly registration of property, long and costly claim enforcement, long and costly bankruptcy procedures and lower recovery rates. The econometric results have shown that the establishment of credit bureaus, particularly private ones, stronger creditor rights and simpler civil procedure rules have a large economic impact on credit access. Reforms should

---

[16]   Judicial systems in most developing countries are perceived to be in crisis: cases take too long, cost too much and are littered with dishonest judges. Litigants are dissatisfied with the process and creditors never use bankruptcy laws, feeling it would be impossible to win. As a result, several countries have opted to implement judicial reform hoping to improve the efficiency of the judicial system. Judicial reform has taken many shapes, but according to Botero et al. (2003), one could divide them into six groups based on: (1) the enhancement of the judiciary's managerial capabilities; (2) incentives to judges; (3) incentives to the parties and other actors of the judicial process; (4) structural modification of the judicial system; (5) modification of rules of procedures; and (6) simplification of substantive rules (for a classification and analysis of these reforms see Botero et al. 2003).

thus aim at improving the interrelated institutional areas that foster credit access.

But additional lessons can be drawn from the two sets of credit supporting institutions analysed in this chapter. The first set of recommendations pertains to information sharing institutions. For property registries, the prescription is simple: make sure they are established and improve their working. The vast majority of countries have managed to establish credit bureaus, but some of them need to be restructured to provide the valuable information that is needed to take more informed credit decisions. Their coverage should also be increased. As the econometric results here show, the promotion of private credit bureaus may be a priority, as they tend to be associated with higher levels of information quality, coverage and credit penetration.

A second set of recommendations involves control rights institutions. The evidence shows that developing nations have weak collateral and creditor rights laws and inefficient judicial systems. Therefore, an improvement in creditor rights and the establishment of mechanisms that will increase the efficiency of the legal system are urgent. Additionally, the evidence suggests that the use of market mechanisms to avoid rigidities of the court system may be a powerful strategy of reform, particularly in developing countries. Finally, more efficient rules for the enforcement of claims is also of vital importance.[17] The poor quality of courts and the backlog in the system in many countries may well be due to a poor set of rules of the system itself. Contract enforcement is a key ingredient in the framework for secured transactions in credit markets, but more generally in all property rights issues.

REFERENCES

Aghion, Philippe and Patrick Bolton (1992), 'An incomplete contracts approach to corporate bankruptcy', *Review of Economic Studies*, **59**, 473–94.

Banfield, Edward (1958), *The Moral Basis of a Backward Society*, New York: Free Press.

Botero, Juan Carlos, Rafael La Porta, Florencio Lopez de Silanes, Andrei Shleifer and Alexander Volokh (2003), 'Judicial reform', *World Bank Research Observer*, **18**(1), 61–88, Spring.

Botero, Juan, Simeon Djankov, Rafael La Porta, Florencio López de Silanes and Andrei Shleifer (2004), 'The regulation of labor', *Quarterly Journal of Economics*, November.

---

[17]   In this area, a reform of civil procedure rules could include the creation of small claims court, as in New Zealand, South Africa, and Brazil, and the simplification of civil procedure across the board.

Coase, Ronald (1960), 'The problem of social costs', *Journal of Law and Economics*, **3**, 1–44.

Damaska, Mirjan R. (1986), 'The faces of justice and state authority: A comparative approach to the legal process', New Haven: Yale University Press.

Djankov, Simeon, E. Glaeser, R. La Porta, F. Lopez-de-Silanes and A. Shleifer (2003a), 'The new comparative economics', *Journal of Comparative Economics*, **31**, 595–619.

Djankov, Simeon, R. La Porta, F. Lopez-de-Silanes and A. Shleifer (2003b), 'Courts', *Quarterly Journal of Economics*, **118**, 453–517.

Djankov, Simeon, C. McLiesh and A. Shleifer (2007), 'Private credit in 129 countries', *Journal of Financial Economics*, Elsevier, **84**(2), May, 299–329.

Djankov, Simeon, Rafael La Porta, Florencio Lopez-de-Silanes and Andrei Shleifer (2008), 'The law and economics of self-dealing', *Journal of Financial Economics*, forthcoming.

Dotsey, Michael and Robert G. King (1986), 'Informational implications of interest rate rules', *American Economic Review*, American Economic Association, **76**(1), March, 33–42.

Easterbrook, Frank and Daniel Fischel (1991), *The Economic Structure of Corporate Law*, Cambridge, MA: Harvard University Press.

Grossman, Sanford and Oliver Hart (1986), 'The costs and benefits of ownership: a theory of vertical and lateral integration', *Journal of Political Economy*, **94**, 175–202.

Hart, Oliver and J. Moore (1994), 'A theory of debt based on the inalienibility of human capital', *Quarterly Journal of Economics*, **109**, 841–79.

Hart, Oliver (1995), 'Firms, contracts and financial structure', Oxford: Oxford University Press.

Hart, Oliver, R. La Porta, F. Lopez-de-Silanes and J. Moore (1997), 'A new bankruptcy procedure that uses multiple auctions', *European Economic Review*, **41**, 461–3.

Hart, Oliver and J. Moore (1998), 'Default and renegotiation: a dynamic model of debt', *Quarterly Journal of Economics*, **113**, 1–42.

Hirschman, Albert O. (1963), *The Strategy of Economic Development*, New Haven and London: Yale University Press.

Jaffee, Dwight M. and Thomas Russell (1976), 'Imperfect information, uncertainty, and credit rationing', *The Quarterly Journal of Economics*, MIT Press, **90**(4), November, 651–66.

Jappelli, Tullio and Marco Pagano (1999), 'The welfare effects of liquidity constraints', *Oxford Economic Papers*, **51**.

Jappelli, Tullio and M. Pagano (2002), 'Information sharing, lending, and defaults: cross-country evidence', *Journal of Banking and Finance*, **26**, 2017–45.

Johnson, Simon, R. La Porta, F. Lopez-de-Silanes and A. Shleifer (2000), 'Tunneling', *American Economic Review Papers and Proceedings*, **90**(2), 22–7.

Landis, James (1938), *The Administrative Process*, New Haven, CT: Yale University Press.

La Porta, Rafael, F. Lopez-de-Silanes and A. Shleifer (2008), 'The economic consequences of legal origins', *Journal of Economic Literature*, forthcoming.

La Porta, Rafael, F. Lopez-de-Silanes and A. Shleifer (2002), 'Government ownership of banks', *Journal of Finance*, **LVII**(1)(February), 265–302.

La Porta, Rafael, F. Lopez-de-Silanes, A. Shleifer and R.W. Vishny (1997), 'Legal determinants of external finance', *Journal of Finance*, **52** (July), 1131–50.

La Porta, Rafael, F. Lopez-de-Silanes, A. Shleifer and R.W. Vishny (1998), 'Law and Finance', *Journal of Political Economy*, **106**, (December), 1113–55.

La Porta, Rafael, F. Lopez-de-Silanes, A. Shleifer and R.W. Vishny, (1999), 'The quality of government', *Journal of Law Economics and Organizations*, **15**, 222–79.

La Porta, Rafael, F. Lopez-de-Silanes, A. Shleifer and R.W. Vishny (2000), 'Investor protection and corporate governance', *Journal of Financial Economics*, **58**(1), (October), 1–25.

La Porta, Rafael, F. Lopez-de-Silanes and G. Zamarripa (2003), 'Related lending', *Quarterly Journal of Economics*, **118**(1), (February), 231–68.

La Porta, Rafael, F. Lopez-de-Silanes and A. Shleifer (2006), 'What works in securities laws?', *Journal of Finance*, **LXI**(1), February 1–32.

Lopez-de-Silanes, Florencio (2002), 'The politics of legal reform', *Economia*, **2**(2), (Spring).

Manove, Michael, J. Padilla and M. Pagano (2001), 'Collateral versus project screening: a model of lazy banks', *RAND Journal of Economics*, **32**(4), 726–44.

Modigliani, Franco and Merton Miller (1958), 'The cost of capital, corporation finance, and the theory of investment', *American Economic Review*, **48** (June), 261–97.

Pagano, Marco and T. Jappelli (1993), 'Information sharing in credit markets', *Journal of Finance*, **43**, 1693–1718.

Putnam, Robert (1993), *Making Democracy Work: Civil Traditions in Southern Italy*, Princeton, NJ: Princeton University Press.

Stigler, George (1964), 'Public regulation of the securities market', *Journal of Business*, **37**, 117–42.

Stiglitz, Joseph and A. Weiss (1981), 'Credit rationing in markets with imperfect information', *American Economic Review*, **71**, 393–410.

Townsend, Robert (1979), 'Optimal and competitive markets with costly state verification', *Journal of Economic Theory*, **21**, 265–93.

Vives, Xavier (1990), 'Information and competitive advantage,' *International Journal of Industrial Organization*, Elsevier, **8**(1), 17–35.

Weber, Max (1958), *The Protestant Ethic and the Spirit of Capitalism*, New York: Charles Scribner's Sons.

World Bank (2003–2007), *Doing Business Reports*, Washington, DC: Oxford University Press.

World Bank (1995–1996), *World Development Report*, Washington, DC: Oxford University Press.

APPENDIX

Table A1.1   Variable definition and sources

Variable name	Definition and source
	Due to space constraints, this table provides a simple definition of all the variables used in this chapter and their original source. For the exact definitions of the variables, please refer to the original source.
	1) Credit access information sharing institutions
Procedures for registering a property	Number of different procedures for registering a property. It is the full sequence of procedures necessary when a business purchases land and a building to transfer the property title from another business so that the buyer can use the property for expanding its business, as collateral in taking new loans or, if necessary, to sell to another business. Every procedure required by law or necessary in practice is included, whether it is the responsibility of the seller or the buyer or must be completed by a third party on their behalf. Local property lawyers, notaries and property registries provide information on procedures as well as the time and cost to complete each of them. *Source: World Bank, Doing Business Report.*
Public registry	The variable equals one if a public credit registry operates in the country in 2003, and zero otherwise. A public registry is defined as a database owned by public authorities (usually the central bank or banking supervisory authority) that collects information on the standing of borrowers in the financial system and makes it available to financial institutions. *Source: Djankov et al. (2007).*
Private registry	The variable equals one if a private credit bureau operates in the country in 2003, and zero otherwise. A private bureau is defined as a private commercial firm or nonprofit organization that maintains a database on the standing of borrowers in the financial system, and its primary role is to facilitate exchange of information amongst banks and financial institutions. Private credit reporting firms, which collect information from public sources but not banks and financial institutions, operate in several other countries but are not considered here. *Source: Djankov et al. (2007).*

Information sharing
The variable equals one if either a public registry or a private bureau operates in the country, and zero otherwise. *Source: Djankov et al. (2007).*

Credit information index
The depth of credit information index measures rules affecting the scope, accessibility and quality of credit information available through either public or private credit registries. A score of 1 is assigned for each of the following 6 features of the public registry or the private credit bureau (or both): (1) Both positive credit information (for example, loan amounts and pattern of on-time repayments) and negative information (for example, late payments, number and amount of defaults and bankruptcies) are distributed; (2) Data on both firms and individuals are distributed; (3) Data from retailers, trade creditors or utility companies as well as financial institutions are distributed; (4) More than 2 years of historical data are distributed. Registries that erase data on defaults as soon as they are repaid obtain a score of 0 for this indicator; (5) Data on loans below 1% of income per capita are distributed (a registry must have a minimum coverage of 1% of the adult population to score a 1 for this indicator); (6) By law, borrowers have the right to access their data in the largest registry in the country. The index ranges from 0 to 6, with higher values indicating the availability of more credit information, from either a public registry or a private bureau, to facilitate lending decisions. If the registry is not operational or has coverage of less than 0.1% of the adult population, the score on the depth of credit index is 0. *Source: World Bank, Doing Business Report.*

Public registry coverage
The public credit registry coverage indicator reports the number of individuals and firms listed in a public credit registry with current information on repayment history, unpaid debts or credit outstanding. The number is expressed as a percentage of the adult population. If no public registry operates, the coverage value is 0. *Source: World Bank, Doing Business Report.*

Private registry coverage
The private credit bureau coverage indicator reports the number of individuals and firms listed by a private credit bureau with current information on repayment history, unpaid debts or credit outstanding. The number is expressed as a percentage of the adult population. A private credit bureau is defined as a private firm or nonprofit organization that maintains a database on the creditworthiness of borrowers (persons or businesses) in the financial system and facilitates the exchange of credit information among banks and financial institutions. Credit investigative bureaus and credit reporting firms that do not directly facilitate information exchange among banks and other financial institutions are not considered. If no private bureau operates, the coverage value is 0. *Source: World Bank, Doing Business Report.*

Table A1.1 (continued)

Variable name	Definition and source
	2) Credit access control rights and enforcement institutions
Restrictions for reorganization	This variable equals one if the reorganization procedure imposes restrictions, such as creditors' consent, to file for reorganization. It equals zero if there are no such restrictions. *Source: La Porta et al. (1998) and Djankov et al. (2007).*
No automatic stay on assets	This variable equals one if the reorganization procedure does not impose an automatic stay on the assets of the firm upon filing the reorganization petition. Such a restriction would prevent secured creditors gaining possession of their security quickly. It equals zero if such restriction exists in the law. *Source: La Porta et al. (1998) and Djankov et al. (2007).*
Secured creditors first	This variable equals one if secured creditors are ranked first in the distribution of the proceeds that result from the disposition of the assets of a bankrupt firm. Equals zero if non-secured creditors, such as the Government and workers, are given absolute priority. *Source: La Porta et al. (1998) and Djankov et al. (2007).*
Management does not stay	This variable equals one when an official appointed by the court, or by the creditors, is responsible for the operation of the business during reorganization. The variable equals zero when the debtor keeps the administration of its property pending the resolution of the reorganization process. *Source: La Porta et al. (1998) and Djankov et al. (2007).*
Creditors rights index	Creditor rights index is an index that aggregates the score of: (1) restrictions for reorganization; (2) no automatic stay on assets; (3) secured creditors first; and (4) management does not stay. A score of one is assigned when each of the following rights of secured lenders is defined in laws and regulations: First, there are restrictions, such as creditor consent or minimum dividends, for a debtor to file for reorganization. Second, secured creditors are able to seize their collateral after the reorganization petition is approved, i.e., there is no automatic stay or asset freeze. Third, secured creditors are paid first out of the proceeds of liquidating a bankrupt firm, as opposed to other creditors such as government or workers. Finally, if management does not retain administration of its property pending the resolution of the reorganization. The index ranges from 0

(weak creditor rights) to 4 (strong creditor rights) and is constructed as at January for every year from 1978 to 2003. The index aggregates creditor rights, following La Porta, Lopez-de-Silanes, Shleifer, and Vishny (1998). *Source: La Porta et al. (1998) and Djankov et al. (2007).*

Creditors collateral index	The index measures the degree to which collateral and bankruptcy laws protect the rights of borrowers and lenders and thus facilitate lending. The index includes 7 aspects related to legal rights in collateral law and 3 aspects in bankruptcy law. A score of 1 is assigned for each of the following features of the laws: (1) General rather than specific description of assets is permitted in collateral agreements; (2) General rather than specific description of debt is permitted in collateral agreements; (3) Any legal or natural person may grant or take security in the property; (4) A unified registry operates that includes charges over movable property; (5) Secured creditors have priority outside of bankruptcy; (6) Secured creditors, rather than other parties such as government or workers, are paid first out of the proceeds from liquidating a bankrupt firm; (7) Secured creditors are able to seize their collateral when a debtor enters reorganization; there is no 'automatic stay' or 'asset freeze' imposed by the court; (8) Management does not stay during reorganization. An administrator is responsible for managing the business during reorganization; (9) Parties may agree on out-of-court enforcement by contract; and (10) By law, and without the need for a contract, creditors may both seize and sell collateral out of court without restriction. The index ranges from 0 to 10, with higher scores indicating that collateral and bankruptcy laws are better designed to expand access to credit. *Source: World Bank, Doing Business Report.*
Formalism index	The index measures substantive and procedural statutory intervention in judicial cases at lower-level civil trial courts (check collection), and is formed by adding up the following sub-indices: (i) professionals vs. laymen, (ii) written vs. oral elements, (iii) legal justification, (iv) statutory regulation of evidence, (v) control of superior review, (vi) engagement formalities, and (vii) independent procedural actions. The index ranges from 0 to 7, where 7 means a higher level of control or intervention in the judicial process. *Source: Djankov et al. (2003b).*
Procedures for enforcing	Number of procedures for enforcing a contract (check collection). An independent procedural action is defined as a step of the procedure, mandated by law or court regulation, that demands interaction between the parties or between them and the judge or court officer (e.g., filing a motion, attending a hearing, mailing a letter, or seizing some goods). We also count as an independent procedural action every judicial or

Table A1.1 (continued)

Variable name	Definition and source
	administrative writ or resolution (e.g., issuing judgment or entering a writ of execution) which is legally required to advance the proceedings until the enforcement of judgment. Actions are always assumed to be simultaneous if possible, so procedural events that may be fulfilled in the same day and place are only counted as one action. To form the index, we: (1) add the minimum number of independent procedural actions required to complete all the stages of the process (from filing of lawsuit to enforcement of judgment); and (2) normalize this number to fall between zero and one using the minimum and the maximum number of independent procedural actions among the countries in the sample. The index takes a value of zero for the country with the minimum number of independent procedural actions, and a value of one for the country with the maximum number of independent procedural actions. *Source: Djankov et al. (2003b) and World Bank, Doing Business Report.*
	3) Other variables
Private credit to GDP	Ratio of credit from deposit taking financial institutions to the private sector (International Financial Statistics lines 22d and 42d) to GDP (International Financial Statistics line 99b), expressed as a percentage. Line 22d measures claims on the private sector by commercial banks and other financial institutions that accept transferable deposits such as demand deposits. Line 42d measures claims on the private sector given by other financial institutions that do not accept transferable deposits but that perform financial intermediation by accepting other types of deposits or close substitutes for deposits (e.g., savings and mortgage institutions, post office savings institutions, building and loan associations, certain finance companies, development banks, and offshore banking institutions). *Source: International Monetary Fund, International Financial Statistics.*
Buddhist	A dummy variable equal to one if the largest proportion of the population practices the Buddhist religion, and zero otherwise. *Source: La Porta et al. (1999).*
Catholic	A dummy variable equal to one if the largest proportion of the population practices the Catholic religion, and zero otherwise. *Source: La Porta et al. (1999).*

Muslim	A dummy variable equal to one if the largest proportion of the population practices the Muslim religion, and zero otherwise. *Source: La Porta et al. (1999).*
Orthodox	A dummy variable equal to one if the largest proportion of the population practices the Orthodox religion, and zero otherwise. *Source: La Porta et al. (1999).*
Protestant	A dummy variable equal to one if the largest proportion of the population practices the Protestant religion, and zero otherwise. *Source: La Porta et al. (1999).*
Common law legal origin	A dummy variable equal to one if the origin of the company law or commercial code of the country is English common law, and zero otherwise. *Source: La Porta et al. (1998), (1999) and (2008).*
French legal origin	A dummy variable equal to one if the origin of the company law or commercial code of the country is French civil law, and zero otherwise. *Source: La Porta et al. (1998), (1999) and (2008).*
German legal origin	A dummy variable equal to one if the origin of the company law or commercial code of the country is German civil law, and zero otherwise. *Source: La Porta et al. (1998), (1999) and (2008).*
Scandinavian legal origin	A dummy variable equal to one if the origin of the company law or commercial code of the country is Scandinavian civil law, and zero otherwise. *Source: La Porta et al. (1998), (1999) and (2008).*
Socialist legal origin	A dummy variable equal to one if the origin of the company law or commercial code of the country is socialist civil law, and zero otherwise. *Source: La Porta et al. (1998), (1999) and (2008).*
Log GDP	Logarithm of gross domestic product (constant 2000 U.S. Dollars), average 2001–2003. *Source: World Development Indicators.*
Log GDP per capita	Logarithm of gross domestic product per capita, (constant 2000 U.S. Dollars), average 2001–2003. *Source: World Development Indicators.*
GDP growth	Average annual growth in gross domestic product per capita from 1979–2003. *Source: World Development Indicators.*
Inflation	Annual percentage inflation, GDP deflator, average 1999–2003. *Source: World Development Indicators.*

Table A1.2   Summary statistics

Variable	Obs.	Mean	Median	Std. Dev.	Min	Max
Procedures for registering a property	153	6.09	6.00	2.82	1.00	21.00
Public registry	133	0.53	1.00	0.50	0.00	1.00
Private registry	133	0.42	0.00	0.50	0.00	1.00
Information sharing	133	0.80	1.00	0.40	0.00	1.00
Credit Information Index	155	2.72	3.00	2.18	0.00	6.00
Public registry coverage	154	3.63	0.00	9.92	0.00	64.30
Private registry coverage	154	16.79	0.00	29.42	0.00	100.00
Restrictions for reorganization	133	0.31	0.00	0.46	0.00	1.00
No automatic stay on assets	133	0.38	0.00	0.49	0.00	1.00
Secured creditors first	133	0.62	1.00	0.49	0.00	1.00
Management does not stay	133	0.49	0.00	0.50	0.00	1.00
Creditors rights index	133	1.80	2.00	1.15	0.00	4.00
Creditors collateral index	154	4.86	5.00	2.08	0.00	10.00
Formalism Index (check collection)	109	3.53	3.52	1.08	0.73	6.01
Procedures for enforcing	153	31.54	28.00	12.36	11.00	69.00
Private credit to GDP	129	0.43	0.27	0.40	0.01	1.64
Buddhist	133	0.08	0.00	0.26	0.00	1.00
Catholic	133	0.32	0.00	0.47	0.00	1.00
Muslim	133	0.27	0.00	0.45	0.00	1.00
Orthodox	133	0.08	0.00	0.28	0.00	1.00
Protestant	133	0.14	0.00	0.35	0.00	1.00
English legal origin	133	0.27	0.00	0.45	0.00	1.00
French legal origin	133	0.48	0.00	0.50	0.00	1.00
French (Latin American and Caribbean) legal origin	133	0.16	0.00	0.17	0.00	1.00
French (Rest of the countries) legal origin	133	0.32	0.00	0.34	0.00	1.00
German legal origin	133	0.14	0.00	0.28	0.00	1.00
Scandinavian legal origin	133	0.03	0.00	0.47	0.00	1.00
Socialist legal origin	133	0.08	0.00	0.36	0.00	1.00
Log GDP	163	23.37	23.06	2.36	17.74	29.94
Log GDP per capita	161	7.58	7.44	1.59	4.45	10.73
GDP growth	133	1.19	1.12	2.64	−4.93	20.85
Inflation	133	13.31	4.10	36.54	−4.73	280.37

2. Policy choices for an efficient and inclusive financial system

Thorsten Beck*

2.1 FINANCE: PRO-GROWTH AND PRO-POOR

Market frictions such as transaction costs, uncertainty and asymmetric information prevent the smooth flow of society's savings into investment projects. Financial institutions and markets arise to overcome these market frictions. Specifically, they arise to help ease the exchange of goods and services by providing payment services; mobilize and pool savings from a large number of investors; acquire and process information about enterprises and possible investment projects, thus allocating society's savings to its most productive use; monitor investments and exert corporate governance; and diversify and reduce liquidity and intertemporal risk (Levine 1997, 2005). However, there is large variation across countries in the efficiency with which financial institutions and markets reduce transaction costs and information asymmetries and reach out to households of different income levels and enterprises of different sizes. Private credit to GDP was 228 per cent in the United States in 2005, but only 2 per cent in Congo.[1] While in most Western European countries more than 90 per cent of the population has access to a financial account, less than 20 per cent of the population has in most of Sub-Saharan Africa (Honohan 2007). While interest rate spreads (the difference between lending and deposit rates) vary typically between 2 and 4 per cent in developed financial systems, they are over 30 per cent in Brazil (Laeven and Majnoni 2005).

* I am grateful to Edward Al-Hussainy for research assistance and Agnes Yaptenco for assistance with the manuscript. This chapter's findings, interpretations and conclusions are entirely those of the author and do not necessarily represent the views of the World Bank, its Executive Directors, or the countries they represent.
[1] Private credit to GDP is a standard measure of financial intermediary development and is the ratio of claims by deposit money banks and other financial institutions on the private, domestic non-financial sector to GDP.

Countries with better developed financial systems, that is, financial markets and institutions that more effectively channel society's savings to its most productive use, experience faster economic growth.[2] Figure 2.1 summarizes a well-established body of empirical evidence: countries with higher levels of credit to the private sector relative to GDP experienced higher average annual real GDP per capita growth rates over the period 1980 to 2003. This relationship is not only robust to controlling for other factors that are associated with economic growth, such as macroeconomic stability, human capital accumulation, demographic traits and trade openness, but is also robust to controlling for the reverse causation from faster economic growth to financial development and to the relationship being driven by a third factor. While Figure 2.1 shows the relationship between private sector lending and GDP per capita growth, other measures of financial development yield similar results and these findings are confirmed by cross-country, panel and by time-series estimation techniques (Levine 2005).

Financial development is not only pro-growth, but also pro-poor. Recent cross-country evidence has shown that it is the lowest income quintile that stands to gain most from financial development. In countries with better developed financial systems, the share of the lowest income quintile grows at a faster rate and income inequality, as measured by the Gini coefficient, falls more rapidly (Beck et al. 2007). Further, countries with higher levels of private credit to GDP experience faster reductions in poverty rates as measured by the headcount, the proportion of the population living on less than a dollar per day (Figure 2.2). While the empirical literature on the links between finance, income inequality and poverty reduction is still in its early days, these initial findings suggest that there is no trade-off between pro-growth and pro-poor in the case of policies that enhance a sound and efficient financial system.

There is also evidence on the micro-level about the link between access to and use of financial services, especially credit, and firm growth and household wellbeing. Firms grow faster than predicted by their cash flow constraints and the relationship between financing constraints and growth is relaxed in countries with better developed financial systems (Demirgüç-Kunt and Maksimovic 1998; Beck et al. 2005). Firms whose financing constraints are exogenously alleviated, increase their sales accordingly (Banerjee and Duflo 2004). Similarly, on the household-level, several studies have shown the positive impact that access to and use of financial services can have on household welfare (World Bank 2007a).

---

[2] To be sure, there is *also* a feedback of faster economic growth on the development of the financial system.

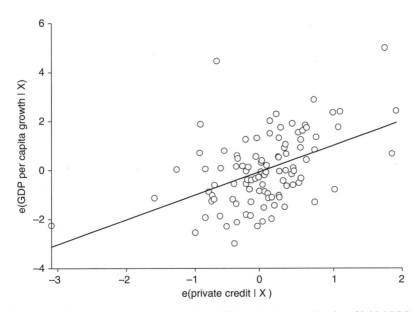

Notes: This graph illustrates a regression of real GDP per capita growth on log of initial GDP per capita, government consumption as share of GDP, trade as share of GDP, black market premium, average years of schooling, inflation and private credit. Specifically, this figure represents the two-dimensional representation of the regression plane in GDP per capita growth – private credit space. To obtain this figure, we regress GDP per capita growth on all explanatory variables except private credit, collect the residuals, and call them (GDP per capita growth | X). Next, we regress private credit against all other explanatory variables, collect the residuals, and call them e(private credit | X). Then, we plot e(GDP per capita growth | X) against e(private credit | X). All data for the regressions are averaged over the period 1980–2003. Private credit is the claims of financial institutions on the private non-financial sector to GDP.

Source: Beck et al. (2007)

Figure 2.1   GDP per capita growth and financial depth

While the academic and policy debate has for a long time focused on deep and efficient financial systems, the debate has recently been broadened towards broad and inclusive financial systems. The next section will therefore discuss these two different concepts, present measures of both depth and breadth, and show correlations between the two. Given the importance of financial development for economic growth and poverty reduction, policy makers and academics alike are interested in the building blocks for an effective and inclusive financial system. Section 2.3 will therefore discuss three important policy areas for financial sector development and cross-country experience in these areas: macroeconomic stability and effective and reliable contractual and informational frameworks. What, however, is the

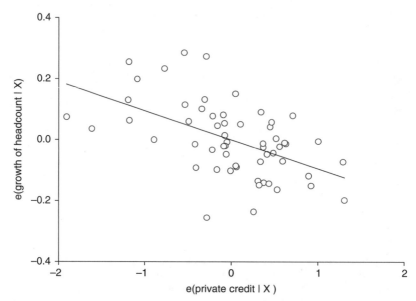

Notes: This graph illustrates a regression of growth of headcount against log of initial headcount, GDP per capita growth and private credit. Specifically, this figure represents the two-dimensional representation of the regression plane in growth of headcount – private credit space. To obtain this figure, we regress growth of headcount on log of initial headcount and GDP per capita growth, collect the residuals, and call them (growth of headcount | X). Next, we regress private credit against log of initial headcount and GDP per capita growth, collect the residuals, and call them e(private credit | X). Then, we plot e(growth of headcount | X) against e(private credit | X).

Source: Beck et al. (2007)

Figure 2.2   Poverty alleviation and financial depth

role of government in the financial sector, if any? Section 2.4 describes different approaches to government involvement in the financial sector, discussing the limitation of both laissez-faire and the activist views and proposing a new approach, the market-enabling view. Section 2.5 concludes.

2.2   FINANCIAL DEVELOPMENT: DEPTH VERSUS BREADTH

Financial systems have different functions, which result in the distinction of different specific services that financial institutions and markets provide. Specifically, a common distinction is between payments, deposit or savings, lending and insurance services.

The literature has developed different measures to gauge the depth and efficiency with which financial systems provide these services. For several reasons, however, these indicators are mostly based on institution- or market-specific data, rather than referring to specific services. First, institutions and markets often offer several services and it is often difficult to disentangle the institution- or market-specific data to measure these specific services. Second, institutions sell packages of services to their clients and again it is difficult to disentangle the cost and benefits of individual services to the customers. Finally, it is very difficult to aggregate data from different providers of the same service in a consistent manner. Economists have therefore focused on institution- or market-specific indicators.

The most traditional measure of financial, or rather monetary, depth has been M2 or M3 as ratio of GDP (Goldsmith 1969). While this is a very broad indicator of monetization, it is not necessarily a measure of financial depth or intermediation. Recently, researchers have therefore focused on private credit to GDP, the outstanding claims of financial institutions on the domestic non-financial sector relative to GDP. While not a perfect measure of the extent to which financial institutions screen potential borrowers and projects and monitor borrowers after credit approval, this is a proxy variable for the extent to which financial institutions channel society's savings into private sector loans, thus fulfilling a key function of financial systems.[3]

These aggregate indicators of financial depth and intermediation have the advantage that they are available for a broad cross-section of countries over a 30- or 40-year period, and they have formed the basis for the cross-country finance and growth literature and a literature on the determinants of financial sector development. More micro-level indicators on the efficiency of banks or insurance companies and the market structure of specific financial markets or segments are more difficult to obtain and are typically available for fewer countries over shorter time periods.

While there are thus reasonably good data to assess and compare the financial depth of countries, much less is known on who has access to which financial services. In other words, how inclusive are financial systems: how many borrowers are behind the total outstanding loans of a country's banking system, how many depositors are represented by the statistic on total deposits? Or taking the perspective from the demand side: what share

---

[3] For stock markets, economists have focused on the turnover ratio, which is the ratio of stocks traded to stocks listed, as an indicator of liquidity, as research has shown that it is the liquidity or activity rather than the size of stock markets, which is associated with economic development (Levine and Zervos 1998). Insurance penetration, insurance premiums relative to GDP, has often been used as indicator of the depth of the insurance sector (Beck and Webb 2003).

of the population uses deposit accounts, what share of the population has taken out a loan? Unlike financial depth data, no accurate statistics are handily available to answer these questions.

Among the complications in measuring who is served by the financial sector is the fact that unlike in the case of financial depth measures, where data from individual institutions can be added up to obtain aggregate measures, data on financial use cannot be constructed this way, as households and enterprises might have business with several institutions. Further, regulatory entities traditionally do not collect data on individual accounts or account holders (unless they are large ones), as this information is not considered necessary input for stability analysis.

Another challenge is to distinguish between access to and use of financial services. Even in the most developed financial systems we do not observe penetration ratios of 100 per cent, that is, every household having a deposit account, and the share of households with loan accounts is typically far below 100 per cent. To which extent do usage ratios of less than 100 per cent constitute a problem of access? The challenge is to distinguish between voluntary and involuntary self-exclusion, between lack of demand and lack of the possibility to access, and between different dimensions of exclusion. Some recent data compilation efforts have made progress towards measuring access and use of financial services.

2.2.1 Indicators of Use of Financial Services

First, take the use of financial services by households. One would ideally like to have census data on the share of households using different financial services. In the absence of census data, one would at least like to have survey-based measures that are representative of the whole population. However, such survey-based representative indicators are very costly to collect and currently only exist for a few countries. Therefore proxy measures have been developed, such as the number of loan or deposit accounts. One such effort was recently undertaken by Beck et al. (2007) who compiled loan and deposit account data for a broad cross-section of countries for the period 2003/04 and documented the large variation in these indicators across countries. While in Austria there are three deposit accounts for every inhabitant, there are only 14 for 1000 inhabitants in Madagascar. While in Greece there are 0.77 loan accounts for every inhabitant, there are only four for every 1000 inhabitants in Albania.[4]

---

[4]   These account-based indicators are subject to certain caveats, though, such as the non-linear relationship between the number of accounts and the share of population holding these accounts; people might have several accounts with one

Based on account data from Beck et al. (2007) for commercial banks, from Peachey and Roe (2006) for savings banks, and Christen et al. (2004) for microfinance institutions, Honohan (2007) constructs a synthetic estimator of the share of population that uses a financial account. He finds a large cross-country variation in the breadth of financial systems, ranging from over 90 per cent in many European countries to less than 20 per cent of the population in many Sub-Saharan African countries.

Second, to measure enterprises' access to and use of financial services, firm-level surveys over the past decade have provided us with a better picture of financing patterns and constraints of firms of different sizes, ownership, legal forms and sectors. These sources include the Regional Program on Enterprise Development (RPED) studies for Sub-Saharan Africa in the 1990s, World Bank–EBRD Business Environment and Enterprise Performance Survey for the transition economies, the World Business Environment Survey (WBES) across 80 countries in 1999/2000 and the Investment Climate Assessment (ICA) surveys over the past five years and available for almost 100 countries. Similar to household-based indicators, cross-country comparisons have found a positive link between economic and financial development and the use of external finance by firms. Research based on these firm-level surveys has also found that institutional development helps close the financing gap between large and small firms (see Safavian, Chapter 4, this volume). Further, financing obstacles as reported by firms are lower in economically, financially and institutionally more developed economies and financial development helps close the growth gap between large and small firms.[5]

2.2.2 Indicators of Access to Financial Services

Recent efforts have also been directed at developing cross-country indicators of access to financial services, along different dimensions, including geography, eligibility and affordability. Take first geographic access. Branches have been the traditional bank outlet and geographic distance to the nearest branch or density of branches relative to the population can

---

institution or accounts with several institutions, with the ratio of the number of accounts per account holder varying across countries. Further, there might be a number of dormant accounts, particularly common in many postal savings banks with free pass-book savings accounts and inefficient documentation systems. Nevertheless, Beck et al. (2007) and Honohan (2007) show that such aggregate indicators of loan and deposit accounts are highly correlated with the actual proportion of households using financial services in countries for which this information is available from household surveys.

[5] See Beck and Demirgüç-Kunt (2006) for an overview of this literature.

provide a first crude indication of geographic access or lack of access barriers (Beck et al. 2007). As in the case of usage, we can observe large variations in geographic access across countries. In Ethiopia, there is less than one branch per 100 000 people, while in Spain, there are 96. Similarly, Spain has 79 branches for every 1000 square kilometres, while in Botswana there is one branch for every 10 000 square kilometres. These indicators are only crude proxies for geographic access though, since branches are never distributed equally across the country. The high and positive correlation of these indicators with the usage ratios discussed above, however, suggest that they are good proxies for geographic access to financial services.

Second, documentation requirements can be another important barrier to access, limiting eligibility. While banks in Albania, Czech Republic, Mozambique, Spain and Sweden demand on average only one document to open a bank account, banks in Bangladesh, Cameroon, Chile, Nepal, Sierra Leone, Trinidad and Tobago, Uganda and Zambia require at least four documents, including ID card or passport, recommendation letter, wage slip and proof of domicile (Beck et al. 2008). Given the high degree of informality in many developing countries, only a small proportion of the population can produce these documents. Sixty per cent of the population in Cameroon works in the informal sector and is thus not able to produce a wage slip. People in rural areas in Sub-Saharan Africa (61 per cent of the overall population) are often unable to provide a formal proof of domicile. Limiting banking services to customers with links to the formal economy and society thus automatically excludes a large share, if not the majority, of people in many low-income countries.

Third, affordability barriers form another important dimension of access to financial services. Customers in Cameroon need over US $700 to open a checking account, that is, an account which can be used both for savings and payment services, an amount higher than the GDP per capita of this country; and to maintain a checking account in Uganda, one needs 30 per cent of annual income (Beck et al. 2008). Customers in Brazil, on the other hand, do not face any minimum amount when opening a checking or savings account and pay no annual fee on these accounts. Perhaps not surprising, in Brazil there are 630 deposit accounts per 1000 people, while in Uganda there are only 47.

Fourth, lack of appropriate products and services for low-income households and micro-enterprises are another important barrier to accessing financial services. In Nepal, the minimum amount a consumer can borrow is ten times GDP per capita, whereas in many other countries it is possible to borrow amounts of less than 10 per cent of GDP per capita. Mortgage loans with a maturity of 40 years have been recently introduced in the United States; in contrast borrowers in many developing countries cannot

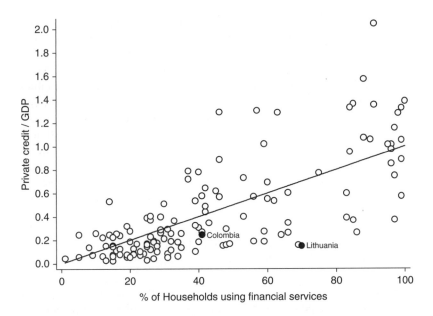

Notes: This graph plots private credit against the share of households using financial services. Private credit/GDP is the claims of financial institutions on the private non-financial sector to GDP. Share of households using financial services is an estimate of the proportion of households in a country that uses financial services.

Source: Honohan 2007

Figure 2.3 Financial depth and breadth

secure loans for a maturity of more than five years. While these statistics give an imperfect picture of appropriate product features and convenience of services, they give an indication of the cross-country variation in this dimension of access.

As noted before, financial depth and breadth are positively and significantly correlated, but this correlation is far from perfect. Figure 2.3 presents a scatter plot of private credit to GDP and the share of households using deposit services, as estimated by Honohan (2007). While clearly showing a positive correlation, there is a dispersion that increases with higher depth and breadth. Take Colombia and Lithuania as examples. Both countries have similar levels of private credit to GDP of around 20 per cent, but in Colombia 40 per cent of households have accounts, whereas this ratio is 70 per cent for Lithuania. Using other indicators of financial sector breadth yields similar positive but imperfect correlations with financial sector depth.

Unlike financial depth data, data on the use of and access to financial services are not available over long time-periods, which prevents their use to rigorously assess the impact of financial breadth on outcome variables such as economic development or poverty alleviation. As of now, the link between financial breadth and desirable outcome variables can thus not be established with cross-country comparisons, although initial work considering partial correlations finds that enterprises report lower financing obstacles in countries with higher geographic outreach of the banking system and higher deposit and loan account penetration (Beck et al. 2007). As time-series data become available over time, more rigorous analysis of the impact of financial sector breadth will be possible.

2.3　BUILDING AN EFFICIENT AND INCLUSIVE FINANCIAL SYSTEM

Given the importance of financial development for economic growth and poverty reduction, policy makers and academics alike are interested in identifying policies and features that are associated with efficient and inclusive financial systems. Cross-country analysis and specific country examples have shown the importance of macroeconomic stability and of the contractual and informational framework for a deep and efficient financial system. Recent research, however, has also linked these fundamental building blocks of financial development to measures of breadth, as we will discuss below.[6] The market structure and the regulation and supervision of institutions and markets are important for financial deepening and broadening; the discussion of these areas, however, will be left to the next section where I discuss the role of government.

Financial contracts consist of an exchange of money today for the promise of money tomorrow, thus an enormous leap of faith into an uncertain future. The intertemporal nature of the contract and several market frictions make financial contracts critically different from other contracts in a market-based economy. First, there is uncertainty whether today's contracted or expected repayment (be it in the form of interest, insurance payout, dividends or capital gains) will be the same in terms of tomorrow's consumption units due to inflation. Second, information asymmetries between borrowers and lenders lead to principal-agent problems, resulting

---

[6] There is also an extensive literature on historic determinants of financial sector development, such as the colonial experience, and the impact of political institutions on finance. See Beck and Levine (2005) for an overview.

in adverse selection and moral hazard problems (Stiglitz and Weiss 1981) (see Fleisig, Chapter 3, this volume).[7]

These market frictions give rise to financial institutions and markets. Financial institutions take on the role of 'delegated monitors' (Diamond 1984) for savers vis-à-vis borrowers. On behalf of their depositors, financial institutions acquire and process information about borrowers and the success probabilities of their investment projects; their efficiency critically depends on the macroeconomic stability and an effective contractual and informational framework.

2.3.1 Macroeconomic Stability

The intertemporal character of financial contracts makes macroeconomic stability a prerequisite for financial development and a first building block for an effective financial system. Theory has shown that inflation can exacerbate credit market frictions, resulting in even higher credit rationing (Huybens and Smith 1998, 1999). A low and stable rate of inflation provides incentives for financial rather than non-financial forms of savings. It is also conducive to long-term contracting and thus long-term savings and investment by providing monetary certainty. Savers are more likely to entrust their savings for a given interest rate if they can be ensured the expected return in terms of real consumption units. Similarly, monetary stability allows investors to adequately compute the return on projects and commit to payments in real terms.

Empirical studies have confirmed these predictions. Countries with lower and more stable inflation rates experience higher levels of banking and stock market development (Boyd et al. 2001). This is illustrated in Figure 2.4, which plots private credit to GDP over the period 1980 to 2003 against the average annual inflation rate for the same period.

2.3.2 Informational Framework

Financial markets and institutions arise due to information asymmetries that prevent direct interaction between multiple savers and investors (see above), and effective financial intermediation depends on tools to reduce these information asymmetries. The informational framework is thus a second fundamental requirement for effective financial intermediation.

Proper accounting and auditing standards can help deepen and broaden financial systems. Financial statements that give an accurate picture of

---

[7] See Levine (1997, 2005) for an overview over theoretical models discussing these market frictions.

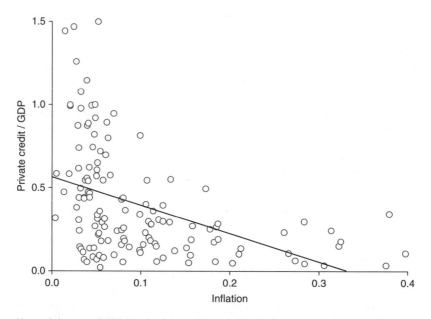

Note: Private credit/GDP is the claims of financial institutions on the private non-financial sector to GDP. Inflation is the log of (1 + average annual CPI inflation). Data averaged for 1980–2003.

Figure 2.4   Financial depth and inflation

a firm's financial situation reduce screening and monitoring costs for financial institutions and increase the efficiency of resource allocation. Here again, cross-country comparisons have shown a positive association of more transparent and comprehensive accounting standards with higher levels of banking sector and stock market development (Levine et al. 2000; La Porta et al. 1997).

International experience has shown that the sharing of credit information about borrowers is important to reduce adverse selection problems, foster competition and thus deepen and broaden the financial system (Jappelli and Pagano 2002; Brown et al. 2007; Djankov et al. 2007; see Miller 2003, for an overview).[8] Credit registries that give easy and reliable access to clients' credit history and both negative and positive information can dramatically reduce the time and costs of obtaining such information

---

[8]   Djankov et al. (2007) also find that credit registries seem to be particularly important for financial deepening in low-income countries, while their analysis suggests a higher priority for creditor rights protection through contractual framework in middle-income countries.

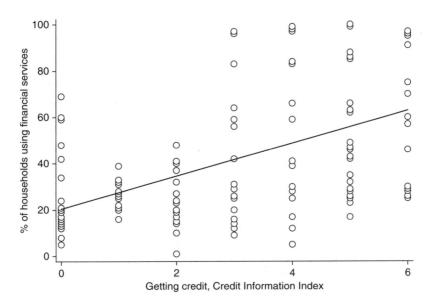

Notes: Share of households using financial services is an estimate of the proportion of households in a country that uses financial services (Honohan 2007). Credit Information Index measures rules affecting the scope, accessibility and quality of credit information available through either public or private bureaus; the index ranges from 0 to 6, with higher values indicating that more credit information is available from either a public registry or a private bureau to facilitate lending decisions (World Bank 2007b).

Figure 2.5   Financial breadth and creditor information sharing

from individual sources and therefore reduce the total costs of financial intermediation. Credit reporting makes borrower quality much more transparent, which benefits good borrowers and increases the cost of defaulting on one's obligations. It helps borrowers build up a credit history ('reputation collateral') and thus eases access to credit. Credit registries are especially important for SMEs as their creditworthiness is harder to evaluate and they have less visibility and transparency relative to large enterprises. Consumer rights to access their information and challenge erroneous information have to be effectively protected to make such a system a widely acceptable part of the financial system infrastructure and balance consumer rights with efficiency considerations.

Empirical evidence has not only shown the importance of credit information sharing for financial depth, but also for firms' access to finance. Figure 2.5 illustrates this evidence by showing the positive relationship between the effectiveness of credit information sharing and the estimate of the share of households with a financial account.

2.3.3　Contractual Framework

Financial contracts depend on the certainty of legal rights of borrowers, creditors and outside investors and the predictability and speed of their fair and impartial enforcement. Private property rights (the legally recognized and opposable right of someone over some property) and enforcement of contracts – both vis-à-vis other private parties and vis-à-vis the government – are thus the third crucial pillar of an effective financial system. Savers will be only willing to relinquish control over their funds if they are ensured repayment including the contracted return. Creditor rights are therefore crucial for a functioning financial system. Even more important, however, is their effective and swift enforcement.

Recent cross-country comparisons have shown the importance of the contractual framework for the depth of the financial system. Countries with better creditor rights protection and more efficient judicial systems experience higher levels of financial development (La Porta et al. 1997; Levine et al. 2000; Djankov et al. 2007). Cross-country comparisons have shown that financial systems that can rely on more effective legal systems have lower interest rate spreads and are more efficient (Demirgüç-Kunt et al. 2004; Laeven and Majnoni 2005).

The efficiency of the contractual framework, that is to say, flexible, adaptable and rapid conflict resolution rather than rigid, lengthy, statutorily-based processes, is also critical for the breadth of financial systems (Djankov et al. 2003; Beck et al. 2005). Countries with higher cost of contract enforcement have lower levels of deposit account and branch penetration, higher affordability barriers and higher documentation requirements for bank customers (Beck et al. 2007, 2008). Interestingly, the laws on the books, such as the legal provisions underpinning creditor rights, are not robustly associated with the breadth of financial systems. Figure 2.6 illustrates these results and shows a strong negative correlation between the cost of contract enforcement and the estimated share of households with a financial account.

Regional and country specific studies have given us additional insights into the importance of the contractual framework for the breadth of the financial system and specific channels through which this relationship works. Some of these studies exploit the introduction of new legal mechanisms at different times across different sub-national entities. For example, the introduction of an expedited mechanism for loan contract enforcement – specialised debt recovery tribunals for loans over one million rupees – had a positive impact on repayment delays and helped reduce interest rates for eligible borrowers in states where it was introduced (Visaria 2006). The transition economies offer a good laboratory to

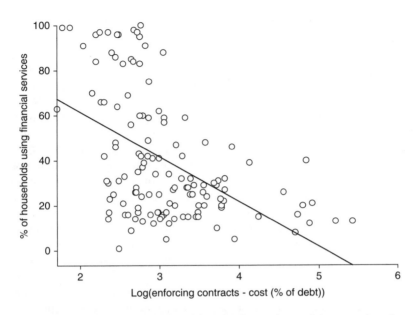

Notes: Share of households using financial services is an estimate of the proportion of households in a country that uses financial services (Honohan 2007). Cost of contract enforcement is an indicator that measures the cost of the judicial (or administrative) system in the collection of overdue debts relative to Gross National Income (World Bank 2007b).

Figure 2.6   Financial breadth and contract enforcement

assess the effect of legal system characteristics since all of these countries had to start building new market-compatible institutions after the start of transition, but did so at different speeds and with different priorities. Haselmann et al. (2006) show for a sample of 12 transition economies that secured transactions laws that regulate creditor rights outside bankruptcy are more important than creditor rights inside bankruptcy for private sector lending. This suggests that institutional reforms focused on enabling the lender to recover collateral have been more important for these countries than reforms focused on resolving claims between multiple claimants, such as in bankruptcy. Haselmann and Wachtel (2006) show that banks in transition economies whose managers have more trust in the country's legal system also provide more SME and mortgage lending and less lending to consumers, large enterprises and government. And in Brazil, banks provided payroll loans, that is, loans whose repayment is allowed by law to be deducted directly from the borrower's payroll check, at significantly lower rates than regular consumer loans, which

were subject to the slow and inefficient recovery procedures of the
Brazilian legal system (Costa and de Mello 2006).

2.4   ROLE OF GOVERNMENT

The different policy areas discussed in the previous section seem to call for
an important role of government in the deepening and broadening of
financial systems. But what exactly government's role should be, is still
subject to discussion. Least controversial is the role of government in providing the contractual and informational framework (credit registries,
secured transactions laws, etc.) and ensuring a stable macroeconomic
environment. Government is the natural provider of key institutions
such as legislation and court systems. Similarly, given the government's
monopoly over the issue of monetary instruments, ensuring macroeconomic stability is a natural government task. However, governments
in most developed and developing countries have taken a much more
active approach to financial sector policies over the past 50 years,
going beyond the provision of basic 'institutional infrastructure'. This
section briefly discusses different approaches to government's involvement in financial systems, before focusing on three specific policy areas:
competition, supervision and regulation, and market-friendly activist
policies.

2.4.1   Laissez-faire versus Activist Approach

The laissez-faire approach to financial sector policy sees the role of government limited to providing for this basic institutional framework and
sees any wider ranging government involvement in the financial sector as
damaging rather than helping. Related to this, a modernist approach
draws lessons from the development of financial systems in North
America and Western Europe and tries to apply them to today's developing and emerging economies. Both approaches, however, have been
criticized for ignoring market failures and blindly transplanting successful models from developed countries and imposing them on developing
economies without taking into account the more challenging socio-
economic and political reality of these countries (Honohan and Beck
2007).

The activist approach, on the other hand, takes market failures as starting points and defines a very active role for government in financial sector
policy. Accordingly, governments in many developed and emerging
economies took a very active if not interventionist role in the financial

system in the 1960s and 1970s.[9] Through ownership of financial institutions governments hoped to enhance savings mobilization, direct credit to priority sectors and make financial services affordable to larger parts of the population. Through ceilings on lending interest rates governments hoped to reduce lending costs for borrowers, while floors for deposits interest rate were to provide incentives to savers. Credit quotas imposed even on private providers were supposed to guarantee that financial resources flowed to priority and underserved sectors, such as agriculture and small-scale enterprises. Through specialized institutions, such as agricultural banks or housing finance companies, governments hoped to provide more financial resources to these sectors.

Most of these attempts to overcome market failures with government interventions, however, have failed. Not only are bureaucrats poor bankers, lacking the skills and incentives to secure sustainable financial service provision, but the lack of appropriate governance structures has condemned most of these efforts to failure. The public interest view that governments maximize social welfare has been proven wrong by the overwhelming evidence across the developed and developing world.[10] Bureaucrats have turned out to have limited knowledge and expertise to run financial institutions and systems and they do not maximize society's welfare, but are rather subject to political and regulatory capture, that is, influenced by the political sphere and the regulated entities, as hypothesized by the private-interest view.

Bureaucrats as bankers have failed almost everywhere, but especially in developing countries; economies with a higher share of government-owned banks experience lower levels of financial development, more concentrated lending and lower economic growth and are more likely to suffer systemic fragility (La Porta et al. 2002; Barth et al. 2004). Moreover, government-owned banks are often used by politicians to finance commercially unviable government projects or state-owned enterprises. Politicians use government-owned banks for electoral purposes; experience across developing countries has pointed to increased lending in election years and especially to contested districts (Cole 2005; Dinc 2005; Khwaja and Mian 2005). The resulting non-performing loans have resulted in large fiscal costs and often in banking crises (Barth et al. 2004).

While empirical work has provided a clear picture of the negative association of government-owned banking with the depth and stability of financial systems, proponents of government ownership often point to the

---

[9] See Fry (1988) for a discussion of these policies and numerous examples.
[10] For an in-depth discussion on the public and private interest views in the context of financial regulation and supervision, see Barth et al. (2006).

positive impact that government-owned banks might have on the breadth of financial systems. Beck et al. (2007), however, find no significant relationship of the share of government-owned banks with deposit or loan account penetration and a negative association with branch penetration. Similarly, while Beck et al. (2008) find some evidence of lower barriers to accessing deposit services in countries with higher shares of government-owned banks, they find higher barriers to loan services in countries with predominantly government-owned banking systems.

Interventionist policies, however, have gone beyond government provision of financial services. Credit quotas and interest caps and floors have impeded the efficient allocation of society's savings to its most productive uses and have especially hurt 'smaller' depositors and borrowers (Fry 1988). In case of binding ceilings, banks are prevented from charging adequate risk premiums for riskier and more opaque borrowers or from recovering fixed transaction costs through a mark-up on smaller loan amounts. Subsidized credit schemes have often failed to reach their targeted clientele (Zia 2007) Credit quotas have resulted in fragmentation of credit markets and higher costs for non-priority sectors. Further, competition between credit institutions is hampered as financial institutions have no incentives to become more efficient or to attract more deposits if they cannot finance more marginal customers. Similarly, given fixed transaction costs in financial intermediation, floors on deposit interest rates make savers with small transaction amounts unattractive for financial institutions. In many cases, financial institutions have found ways around these restrictions, but at high costs and with consequent efficiency losses.

The failure of market-substituting financial sector policies together with the realization that long-term institution building and macroeconomic stability will not be enough to deepen and broaden the financial system in most developing countries, has led economists to explore a more active role for governments than the laissez-faire view would allow, while avoiding the pitfalls of direct market-substituting government interventions ('activist approach'). This market-enabling approach relies on private institutions to provide financial services efficiently but takes into account their incentive structure. This approach foresees a government that works with the market, but does not leave it to the market.

The market-enabling approach starts from the observation that financial institutions and markets might not maximize the constrained optimum given by the fundamentals such as the macroeconomic environment and the contractual and informational frameworks (Beck and de la Torre 2007). It tries to push financial institutions and markets to this constrained optimum through an array of measures, including competition policies, the regulatory and supervisory framework and even market-friendly interventionist approaches. We will discuss each in turn.

2.4.2 Competition Policies

Competitive financial markets can have a positive impact on financial sector depth and breadth. Cross-country comparisons have shown that countries with lower entry barriers into the financial system, fewer restrictions on banking and a higher share of foreign-owned banks have more competitive, more efficient and more stable banking systems (Claessens and Laeven 2004; Demirgüç-Kunt et al. 2004). Allowing or even encouraging entry by sound and prudent new institutions, whether they be domestic or foreign, is important to maintain contestability. While theory and some empirical work suggest that market power might entice banks to invest in long-term relationships with small and opaque enterprises, as they know that they can regain the initial investment in the relationship at a later stage (Petersen and Rajan 1995; Bonaccorsi di Patti and Dell'Ariccia 2004), other empirical papers point to the healthy effect of competition on availability of lending to SMEs (Cetorelli and Strahan 2004; Beck et al. 2004).[11] Depositors and borrowers face lower barriers to accessing financial services in economies with more competitive and contestable banking systems (Beck et al. 2008).[12]

Further, state variables such as the contractual and informational frameworks can influence the competitiveness of a financial system through the ability to transfer collateral easily from one lender to another and the ability of SMEs to build up reputation capital through a credit registry. On the one hand, the lack of a credit registry can reduce the contestability of a financial system by raising the cost of entry; on the other hand, the lack of credit information sharing can have negative effects on the stability of financial institutions in a competitive environment as the recent experience of competing microfinance institutions in Uganda shows (McInstosh et al. 2005).

2.4.3 Supervision and Regulation

Given the maturity transformation – using deposits withdrawable at short notice to finance medium-to-long-term loans – and given the limited

---

[11] See Berger et al. (2004) for an overview.
[12] Complicating the debate on the effect of competition on financial market depth and breadth is that market structure, as for example measured by concentration ratios, is not the same as competitiveness, which is also influenced by the segmentation and contestability of a market (Claessens and Laeven 2004).

transparency of financial institutions, banks have been subject to special regulation and supervision not applied to non-financial corporations. Given the put-option character of bank equity, bank shareholders participate only in the up-side risk of the bank business and have therefore strong incentives to take too aggressive risks, ignoring sound and prudent risk management. Effective bank regulation and supervision, as well as market discipline exercised by large depositors and creditors, can keep bank owners and managers in check. The question is, as before, what measures are appropriate to take without running the risk of negative effects on financial system depth and breadth.

Take first deposit insurance, which has often been seen as an instrument to reduce bank fragility by limiting the possibilities of bank runs (Diamond and Dybvig 1983). Research for the United States and across countries, however, has shown that the moral hazard risk stemming from generous and poorly designed deposit insurance schemes more than outweighs its positive effects. By bailing out not only small, but also large depositors and creditors, poorly designed deposit insurance schemes can reduce market discipline, which in the absence of effective bank supervision has often resulted in imprudent and unchecked risk taking by banks with subsequent fragility (Demirgüç-Kunt and Detragiache 2002; Demirgüç-Kunt and Huizinga 2004). This negative effect is even stronger in weak regulatory and supervisory environments, as is the case in many developing countries. Further, cross-country comparisons have not confirmed the assertion that deposit insurance is crucial for financial sector development; to the opposite, countries with more generous deposit insurance schemes tend to have lower levels of financial savings and private sector lending (Cull et al. 2005).

Second, regulatory and supervisory approaches might also have a critical impact on financial sector breadth. Enterprises face higher financing obstacles in economies with more restrictive regulatory policies, such as restrictions on banks' activities, entry barriers for foreign banks, deposit insurance and a large share of government-owned banks, while both depositors and borrowers face higher barriers to accessing financial services (Beck et al. 2004; Beck et al. 2008).

Supervisory approaches that rely on powerful supervisors that can intervene in banks in good and bad times are not associated with higher financial sector development and there is even evidence that it might result in higher barriers for firms to access bank finance, while firms in countries where supervisors rely more on market signals and market discipline are less likely to report major obstacles due to corruption in lending (Beck et al. 2006). Similarly, borrowers face lower barriers to accessing financial services in banking systems where supervisors rely more on private sector monitoring, while depositors face higher barriers to accessing financial services in economies with powerful bank supervisors (Beck et al. 2008).

Third, there are also very specific regulations that can help make a financial system more or less inclusive. On the negative side, high compliance costs with unduly complicated 'Know Your Customer' (KYC) and anti-money laundering (AML) regulations may prevent financial institutions from reaching out to marginal customers (Claessens 2006). On the positive side, relaxing branching restrictions by allowing financial institutions to offer limited services through non-financial correspondents can significantly reduce the fixed cost element of financial service provision and thus help overcome the lack of scale economies in remote and small market places.[13] A further step would be to allow the use of public post office networks as platforms for service provision by different financial institutions, as in India and South Africa (see World Bank 2004a, 2004b). This can, not only help overcome problems of scale economies, but address concerns of competition, compared to the situation where only one institution is allowed to use post offices as correspondents, as in Brazil, or a situation where one financial institution dominates service provision in remote areas, as is the case in large parts of Sub-Saharan Africa.

2.4.4 Market-friendly Activist Policies

The role of the government might have to go beyond competition and regulatory policies in order to create competitive and inclusive financial systems. The setting up of credit reference bureaus, for example, often requires involvement of the government to overcome resistance by financial institutions since sharing positive information diminishes information rents of incumbent banks. Avoiding segmentation in the financial sector through expanding access to the payment system or the credit information sharing system beyond the commercial banks to bank-like institutions such as cooperatives or regulated microfinance institutions can help the financial system cater to marginal customers in all financial services. Sometimes, government action takes the form of 'affirmative regulatory' policy, such as the moral suasion exercised by authorities to make South African banks introduce the Mzansi (basic transaction) account or make British banks introduce the Basic Bank Account (BBA). Government authorities might also have an important role in defining the border between cooperation and competition across financial institutions: inducing banks to share or ensure

---

[13]   In Brazil for instance some of the largest banks have expanded their network through correspondent agreements with the Post Office, lottery shops and supermarkets (Kumar 2005).

interoperability of payments infrastructures (including ATM networks) can help avoid undesirable competition on access to infrastructure while enhancing desirable competition on price and quality of service.

Governments have also tried to move the financial system to be more inclusive by addressing hindrances such as coordination failures, first mover disincentives[14] and obstacles to risk distribution and sharing. While not easy to define in general terms, given their variety, these government interventions tend to share a common feature: to create incentives for private lenders and investors to step in, without unduly shifting risks and costs to the government (De la Torre et al. 2006). Three examples illustrate this approach. One is the creation by NAFIN (a Mexican development bank) of an Internet-based market, which allows small suppliers to use their receivable from large credit-worthy buyers in order to secure working capital financing (Klapper 2006). Another example is the Chilean programme (FOGAPE) to promote lending to SMEs via the auctioning of partial government guarantees (Benavente et al. 2006). Finally, the Mexican development fund FIRA has brokered a variety of structured finance packages to finance agricultural production (for example shrimp, corn) to realign credit risks with the pattern of information between financial institutions and different participants in the supply chains of these agricultural products. While intriguing examples, it is not certain whether risk is really not being shifted to government and taxpayers through such interventions and whether these interventions have sunset clauses that will allow the government to withdraw once its engagement is not needed any longer. There are also governance concerns stemming from a government intervention in a private market. Finally, from a political economy viewpoint, such schemes might take away the pressure to implement the long-term institution building to create effective contractual and informational frameworks. Overall, it is too early to pass a general judgment on these efforts and more research is needed in this area.

2.5   CONCLUSIONS

This chapter discussed the policy choices for building efficient and inclusive financial systems. While measures of financial depth have been compiled for a long time period and have formed the basis for an extensive literature assessing the determinants and implications of financial sector depth, it is

---

[14]   Stemming from high set-up costs whose benefits cannot be completely reaped by the first mover due to externalities.

only recently that measures of financial breadth, that is, access to and use of financial services, have been designed and constructed. Initial results show a positive but imperfect correlation of financial breadth with financial depth. Many policies that are fundamental for creating a deep, efficient and stable financial system, however, are also associated with financial breadth. Macroeconomic stability and effective contractual and informational frameworks are definitely important for creating inclusive financial systems. A more expansive role for government in financial sector policy, however, is still controversial and subject to debate. On the one hand, government solutions such as state-owned commercial banks, directed credit and interest rate regulations have proven to be not only ineffective but damaging for financial depth and breadth; on the other hand, governments might have an important role in enabling financial markets beyond long-term institution building. We discussed it in three areas – competition, supervision and regulation, and interventionist but market-friendly approaches. This role is still subject to debate and more research is certainly needed. Especially in the case of government interventions, which imply subsidies and thus taxpayer's money, a careful cost-benefit analysis, including a comparison to other non-financial sector interventions, is paramount.

REFERENCES

Banerjee, A.V. and E. Duflo (2004), 'Do firms want to borrow more? Testing credit constraints using a directed lending program', CEPR Discussion Paper 4681.

Barth, J., G. Caprio and R. Levine (2004), 'Bank regulation and supervision: What works best?', *Journal of Financial Intermediation*, **13** (2), 205–48.

Barth, J., G. Caprio and R. Levine (2006), *Rethinking Bank Regulation: Till Angels Govern*, New York, NY: Cambridge University Press.

Beck, T. and A. De la Torre (2007), 'The basic analytics of access to finance', *Financial Markets, Institutions and Instruments*, **17** (2), 79–117.

Beck, T. and A. Demirgüç-Kunt (2006), 'Small and medium-size enterprises: Access to finance as a growth constraint', *Journal of Banking and Finance*, **30** (11), 2931–43.

Beck, T., A. Demirgüç-Kunt and R. Levine (2005), 'Law and firms' access to finance', *American Law and Economics Review*, **7** (1), 211–52.

Beck, T., A. Demirgüç-Kunt and R. Levine (2006), 'Bank supervision and corruption in lending', *Journal of Monetary Economics*, **53** (8), 2131–63.

Beck, T., A. Demirgüç-Kunt and R. Levine (2007), 'Finance, inequality and the poor', *Journal of Economic Growth*, **12** (1), 27–49.

Beck, T., A. Demirgüç-Kunt and V. Maksimovic (2004), 'Bank competition and access to finance: International evidence', *Journal of Money, Banking, and Credit*, **36** (3), 627–48.

Beck, T., A. Demirgüç-Kunt and V. Maksimovic (2005), 'Financial and legal constraints to firm growth: Does firm size matter?', *Journal of Finance*, **60** (1), 137–77.

Beck, T., A. Demirgüç-Kunt and M. Martinez Peria (2007), 'Reaching out: Access to and use of banking services across countries', *Journal of Financial Economics*, **85** (1), 234–66.

Beck, T., A. Demirgüç-Kunt and M. Martinez Peria (2008), 'Banking services for everyone? Barriers to bank access and use around the world', *World Bank Economic Review*, forthcoming.

Beck, T. and R. Levine (2004), 'Stock markets, banks and growth: Panel evidence', *Journal of Banking and Finance*, **28**, 423–42.

Beck, T. and R. Levine (2005), 'Legal institutions and financial development', in C. Menard and M. Shirley (eds), *Handbook of New Institutional Economics*, The Netherlands: Kluwer Dordrecht.

Beck, T. and I. Webb (2003), 'Economic, demographic, and institutional determinants of life insurance consumption across countries', *World Bank Economic Review*, **17**, 51–88.

Benavente, J.M., A. Galetovic and R. Sanhueza (2006), 'Fogape: An economic analysis', World Bank mimeo.

Berger, A.N., A. Demirgüç-Kunt, R. Levine and J.G. Haubrich (2004), 'Bank concentration and competition: an evolution in the making', *Journal of Money, Credit, and Banking*, **36** (3), 433–654.

Bonaccorsi di Patti, E. and G. Dell'Ariccia (2004), 'Bank competition and firm creation', *Journal of Money, Credit, and Banking*, **36** (2), 225–51.

Boyd, J.H., R. Levine and B.D. Smith (2001), 'The impact of inflation on financial sector performance', *Journal of Monetary Economics*, **47** (2), 221–48.

Brown, M., T. Jappelli and M. Pagano (2007), 'Information sharing and credit: Firm-level evidence from transition countries', Swiss National Bank mimeo.

Cetorelli, N. and P.E. Strahan (2004), 'Finance as a barrier to entry: Bank competition and industry structure in local U.S. markets', Federal Reserve Bank of Chicago working paper.

Christen, R.P., V. Jayadeva and R. Rosenberg (2004), 'Financial institutions with a double bottom line: Implications for the future of microfinance', Occasional Paper No. 8, Washington DC: CGAP.

Claessens, S. (2006), 'Access to financial services: a review of the issues and public policy issues', *World Bank Research Observer*, **21**, 207–40.

Claessens, S. and L. Laeven (2004), 'What drives bank competition? Some international evidence', *Journal of Money, Credit, and Banking*, **36** (3), 563–82.

Cole, S. (2005), 'Fixing market failures or fixing elections? Elections, banks, and agricultural lending in India', Harvard Business School mimeo.

Costa, Ana Carla and Joao de Mello (2006), 'Judicial risk and credit market performance: micro-evidence from Brazilian payroll loans', NBER working paper 12252.

Cull, R., L. Senbet and M. Sorge (2005), 'Deposit insurance and financial development', *Journal of Money, Credit, and Banking*, **37** (1), 43–82.

De Haas, R. and I. Naaborg (2005), 'Does foreign bank entry reduce small firms' access to credit: Evidence from European transition economies', working paper 50, Dutch National Bank.

De la Torre, A., J.C. Gozzi and S. Schmukler (2006), 'Innovative experiences in access to finance: Market friendly roles for the visible hand', Latin America Regional Study, World Bank.

Demirgüç-Kunt, A. and E. Detragiache (2002), 'Does deposit insurance increase banking system stability? An empirical investigation', *Journal of Monetary Economics*, **49** (7), 1373–406.

Demirgüç-Kunt, A. and H. Huizinga (2004), 'Market discipline and deposit insurance', *Journal of Monetary Economics*, **51**, 375–99.

Demirgüç-Kunt, A., L. Laeven and R. Levine (2004), 'Regulations, market structure, institutions, and the cost of financial intermediation', *Journal of Money, Credit, and Banking*, **36**, 593–622.

Demirgüç-Kunt, A. and V. Maksimovic (1998), 'Law, finance and firm growth', *Journal of Finance*, **53**, 2107–37.

Diamond, D. (1984), 'Financial intermediation and delegated monitoring', *Review of Economic Studies*, **51**, 393–414.

Diamond, D. and P. Dybvig (1983), 'Bank runs, liquidity and deposit insurance', *Journal of Political Economy*, **91**, 401–19.

Dinc, S. (2005), 'Politicians and banks: Political influences on government-owned banks in emerging countries', *Journal of Financial Economics*, **77** (August), 453–79.

Djankov, S., R. La Porta, F. Lopez-de-Silanes and A. Shleifer (2003), 'Courts: the lex mundi project', *Quarterly Journal of Economics*, **118**, 453–517.

Djankov, S., C. McLiesh and A. Shleifer (2007), 'Private credit in 129 countries', *Journal of Financial Economics*, **84** (2), 299–329.

Fry, M.J. (1988), *Money, Interest, and Banking in Economic Development*, Baltimore, MD: John Hopkins University Press.

Goldsmith, R.W. (1969), *Financial Structure and Development*, New Haven, CT: Yale University Press.

Haselmann, R., K. Pistor and V. Vig (2006), 'How law affects lending', Columbia Law and Economics working paper 285.

Haselmann, R. and P. Wachtel (2006), 'Institutions and bank behavior', NYU Stern Economics working paper 06-16.

Honohan, P. (2007), 'Cross-country variation in household access to financial services', World Bank mimeo.

Honohan, P. and T. Beck (2007), *Making Finance Work for Africa*, Washington, DC: World Bank.

Huybens, E. and B. Smith (1998), 'Financial market frictions, monetary policy, and capital accumulation in a small open economy', *Journal of Economic Theory*, **81**, 353–400.

Huybens, E. and B. Smith (1999), 'Inflation, financial markets, and long-run real activity', *Journal of Monetary Economics*, **43**, 283–315.

Jappelli, T. and M. Pagano (2002), 'Information sharing, lending and defaults: Cross-country evidence', *Journal of Banking and Finance*, **26** (10), 2017–45.

Khwaja, A.I. and A. Mian (2005), 'Do lenders favor politically connected firms? Rent provision in an emerging financial market', *Quarterly Journal of Economics*, **120**, 1371–1411.

Klapper, L. (2006), 'The role of "reverse factoring" in supplier financing of small and medium sized enterprises', *Journal of Banking and Finance*, **30**, 3111–30.

Kumar, A. (2005), *Access to Financial Services in Brazil*, Washington, DC: World Bank.

La Porta, R., F. Lopez-de-Silanes and A. Shleifer (2002), 'Government ownership of commercial banks', *Journal of Finance*, **57**, 265–301.

La Porta, R., F. Lopez-de-Silanes and A. Shleifer (2006), 'What works in securities laws?', *Journal of Finance*, **61**, 1–32.

La Porta, R., F. Lopez-de-Silanes, A. Shleifer and R.W. Vishny (1997), 'Legal determinants of external finance', *Journal of Finance*, **52**, 1131–50.

Laeven, L. and G. Majnoni (2005), 'Does judicial efficiency lower the cost of credit?', *Journal of Banking and Finance*, **29**, 1791–812.

Levine, R. (1997), 'Financial development and economic growth: Views and agenda', *Journal of Economic Literature*, **35**, 688–726.

Levine, R. (2005), 'Finance and growth: Theory and evidence', in P. Aghion and S. Durlauf (eds), *Handbook of Economic Growth*, The Netherlands: Elsevier Science.

Levine, R., N. Loayza and T. Beck (2000), 'Financial intermediation and economic growth: Causes and causality', *Journal of Monetary Economics*, **46**, 31–77.

Levine, R. and S. Zervos (1998), 'Stock markets, banks and economic growth', *American Economic Review*, **88**, 537–58.

McIntosh, C., A. De Janvry and E. Sadoulet (2005), 'How rising competition among microfinance lenders affect incumbent village banks', *Economic Journal*, **115**, 987–1004.

Miller, M. (2003), *Credit Reporting Systems and the International Economy*, Cambridge, MA: MIT Press.

Peachey, S. and A. Roe (2006), 'Access to finance: measuring the contribution of savings banks', World Savings Banks Institute.

Petersen, M. and R. Rajan (1995), 'The effect of credit market competition on lending relationships', *Quarterly Journal of Economics*, **110**, 407–43.

Stiglitz, J. and A. Weiss (1981), 'Credit rationing in markets with imperfect information', *American Economic Review*, **71**, 393–410.

Visaria, S. (2006), 'Legal reform and loan repayment: The microeconomic impact of debt recovery tribunals in India', IED working paper No. 157, Boston University.

World Bank (2004a), 'India: Scaling-up access to finance for India's rural poor', Washington, DC.

World Bank (2004b), 'South Africa: Technology and access to financial services', World Bank mimeo.

World Bank (2007a), *Finance for All? Policies and Pitfalls in Expanding Access*, Policy Research Report, Washington, DC.

World Bank (2007b), *Doing Business*, Washington, DC.

Zia, B. (2007), 'Export incentives, financial constraints, and the (mis)allocation of credit: Micro-level evidence from subsidized export loans', *Journal of Financial Economics*, **87**, 498–527.

PART 2

Secured transactions law to support access to credit: a case for reform

3. The economics of collateral and of collateral reform

Heywood Fleisig

Developing countries face daunting problems in funding the investment they need for growth. Private funding, domestic and foreign, will play the most important roles. Donor funding will supply a small fraction of these needs. These savings alone, though, cannot guarantee that domestic investment opportunities will be funded. Rather, funding investment successfully also requires a financial sector – bank and non-bank – that mobilizes these savings and delivers them to the highest return domestic investment opportunities. If industrial country experience is a guide, the most important funding instrument will be lending, not capital market equity.

In mobilizing loans and directing them to their most efficient use, secured transactions play an important part. The importance of collateral arises from how well it addresses key features and risks in financial markets. Financing movable property is essential to growth, as it amounts to more than half of the enterprise capital stock (see Figure 3.5 below). Obsolete laws and legal institutions, however, sharply restrict the use of movable property as collateral for loans. The remedy lies in reforming the laws and institutions that govern using property as collateral for loans. This reform costs little and delivers large benefits. Therefore, a simple economic model of social change that imagines governments and donors gravitating toward reforms with large net benefits would predict its wide acceptance. This has not happened. While the reform has progressed slowly over the past 15 years, many factors continue to impede its adoption. The outlook is for continued slow progress, possibly becoming more rapid as successful reform examples multiply and if international opinion coalesces in support.

3.1 FINANCING INVESTMENT: HOW MUCH AND BY WHOM?

In 2005, developing countries invested about US$2.8 trillion (Figure 3.1). Where did this money come from? Donors often focus on donor efforts.

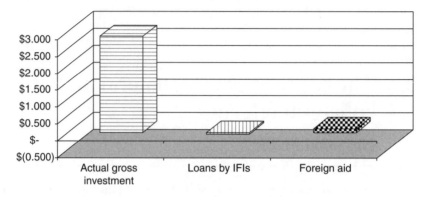

Source: Industrial and developing country GDP and investment taken from World Bank, Key Data, 2007. Net lending by multilateral financial institutions (multilateral development banks and the International Monetary Fund) are taken from Joint BIS-IMF-OECD-WB External Debt Hub, 2007. Foreign aid disbursements from OECD, DAC, Final ODA Data, 2007.

Figure 3.1   Gross domestic investment in developing countries, compared with aid and multilateral lending (US$ billion, 2005)

However, developing countries largely financed this investment with private resources, their own and foreign. Against this US$2.8 trillion investment, foreign aid amounted to US$117 billion. International financial institutions (IFIs) (the multilateral development banks and the International Monetary Fund) could also have funded part of this investment. However, net disbursements by IFIs in 2005 were negative, that is, developing countries repaid about US $36 billion more to the IFIs than they borrowed (Figure 3.1).

Even these enormous levels of gross domestic investment, however, will not close the per capita income gap between developed and developing countries. For developing countries to support per capita incomes equal to those of today's industrial countries, gross investment in developing countries must rise to about US$48 trillion annually (Figure 3.2).

Donors and multilateral development banks cannot finance these investment needs. Nor will domestic public entities. Domestic public funding of commercial investment, both loans and loan guarantees, is being discontinued all over the world because of its poor track record in funding good investments. For well-documented reasons, they have not been a solution in the past and for the same reasons are unlikely to be a solution in the future. Consequently, private sources, both domestic and foreign, will likely have to fund most private domestic investment in developing countries.

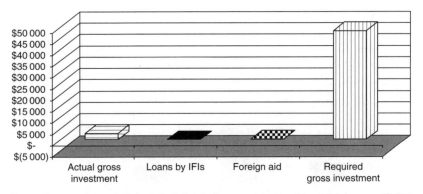

Note: Investment required for today's developing countries to achieve high-income OECD Countries per capita incomes is estimated by the author. It assumes that developing countries will have to increase investment so that investment/GDP ratio equals the same 21.7 percent of GDP as today's high income OECD countries. It estimates high-level GDP for developing countries by multiplying their present population by the present per capita income levels of the high income OECD countries. Investment ratio for the industrial countries taken from World Bank, Key Data, 2007.

Source: Industrial and developing country GDP and investment taken from World Bank, Key Data, 2007. Net lending by multilateral financial institutions (multilateral development banks and the International Monetary Fund) are taken from Joint BIS-IMF-OECD-WB External Debt Hub, 2007. Foreign aid disbursements from OECD, DAC, Final ODA Data, 2007.

Figure 3.2   Required and actual gross domestic investment in developing countries, compared with aid and multilateral lending ($ billion, 2005)

3.2   FINANCING INVESTMENT: WHAT INSTRUMENTS?

Some enterprises will have more funds than they need for their own investments and some consumers will be saving for future consumption. Other enterprises will be unable to fund all their profitable investments. Effective financial markets transfer these savings from savers to their highest return uses of investors.

Will that transfer take the form of lending or equity issued in capital markets? The experience of the United States is instructive. There, the government and the private sector have invested enormous amounts in the infrastructure for equity finance, starting with the Securities and Exchange Act of 1934[1] and continuing with the expansion of the Securities and

---

[1]   Available at www.sec.gov/divisions/corpfin/34act/index1934.shtml. September 2007.

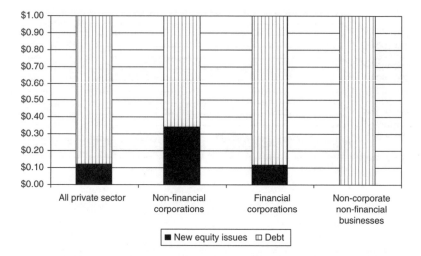

Source: *Statistical Supplement to the Federal Reserve Bulletin*, various issues. New stock issues of US private firms appears in Table 1. 46, 'New Security Issues, U.S. Corporations' while borrowing by US firms appears in Table 1. 59, 'Summary of Credit Market Debt Outstanding'.

Figure 3.3   Debt versus equity financing: share of new equity issues and new borrowing in external finance of US private firms, 2001–2005

Exchange Commission, which regulates public exchanges. Despite this support for equity finance, US private business raised only about 10 cents in equity capital for every US$1.00 in debt capital (Figure 3.3). Even non-financial US corporations, who rely most heavily on stock markets, raised only about 35 cents in equity capital for every US1.00 in debt capital. Non-corporate businesses (microenterprises and many SMEs) depend entirely on debt capital.

In developing and transitional economies, where the infrastructure for equity capital is less developed than in the United States, it seems safe to assume that an even smaller fraction of private business investment funding will take the form of equity rather than debt.

3.3   INCREASING PRIVATE DEBT FINANCING

When firms in developing countries, therefore, seek outside funds for investment, they will rely largely on private debt. How can the legal environment encourage such lending?

Any successful private lending system must respond to the lender's central concern: 'How do I get my money back?' Financial markets have developed two systems for addressing this concern: secured lending and unsecured lending. How do these systems compare?

We can see the difference reflected in the loan terms of the credit union of the employees of the International Monetary Fund (IMF) and of the World Bank. This credit union operates in Washington, DC, where the legal framework governing debt collection is well developed. When the borrowers offer collateral for a loan instead of only a signature, the credit union offers better terms: it will, lend at interest rates that are about half as high, make loans that are five to ten times larger relative to income and give the borrower as much as five times longer time to repay (Figure 3.4). These differences are true whether the collateral consists of movable or immovable assets, but these differences are even more marked for immovable assets.

Collateral improves the terms for loans because it deals efficiently with important features of the market for loans. Collateral addresses *adverse selection*. Lenders cannot bring their supply of loans into line with greater borrower demand simply by raising interest rates to select the borrowers. As lenders raise interest rates, some honest borrowers will find that returns on their projects fall below the interest rate and will leave the market. Remaining in the borrower pool are honest borrowers with high-return projects, fools who do not understand the risks they are taking, and knaves who conceal risk from the lender or who have no intention of repaying either loan or interest. With each increase in the interest rate, good borrowers drop out of the pool while fools and knaves remain. As a result, the pool gets worse – hence, 'adverse selection'. In unsecured loans, lenders manage adverse selection by reducing the size of their loans (as seen in the terms of the WB-IMF credit union (Figure 3.4)) and by lending to a larger number of borrowers. In taking these steps, lenders hope to reduce their overall risk by diversification, reducing the impact of any single default. In secured loans, however, lenders take collateral and, thereby, can address adverse selection more powerfully. The lender can supplement the assessment of the borrower's character and capacity to pay with the more easily determined value of the collateral. The collateral provides a route to payment that is an alternative to the borrower's project, about which the lender may be misinformed.

Collateral also addresses *moral hazard*. Suppose a lender knows from a borrower's payment history that a borrower has reliably paid back earlier, smaller loans. Can the lender reasonably infer from this history that the borrower will repay a new, larger loan? Stripped to its economic fundamentals, borrowers can be seen as weighing the benefits of payment:

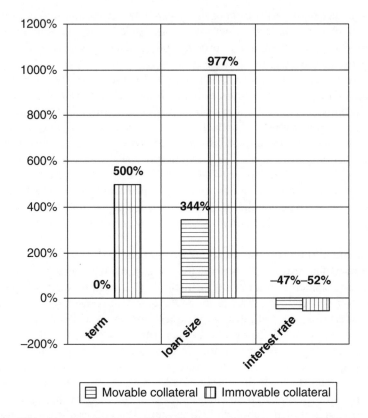

☐ Movable collateral ☐ Immovable collateral

Note: Table shows how the terms of loans for the same borrower change when the borrower offers different collateral compared to the terms the same borrower faces when not offering collateral (unsecured or signature loan). The time for repayment of a secured loan is up to five times greater, the amount of the loan is three to ten times greater, while the rate of interest is about half as great.

Source: Author's computations using lending terms taken from the World Bank/ International Monetary Fund Staff Federal Credit Union, available at http://bfsfcu.org/ consumer_loan_rates_161.html, September 2007. Personal loans are capped at six months pay. Total debt service is set at 36% of income, using the 'back-end' ratio at the low end of the range followed in the guidelines of US Government-sponsored enterprise mortgage lenders (Federal National Mortgage Association ('Fannie Mae'), Federal Home Loan and Mortgage Corporation ('Freddie Mac'), cited at www.mortgageunderwriters.com/debtto. html, September 2007). Given the interest rate and term of loan, setting loan payments at the back-end ratio determines the loan size relative to income. For each type of loan, the table uses fixed rate loans with the maximum maturity.

Figure 3.4   *Power of collateral: terms of loans at WB-IMF staff credit union, comparing secured to base-line unsecured, September 2007*

access to future loans, against the benefits of default: absconding with today's loan. The larger is today's loan relative to possible future loans, the more that balance weighs in favor of default. Moral hazard is the risk that the borrower's behavior will change with the size of the loan. In unsecured loans, lenders manage moral hazard by increasing loan size slowly, always holding out to the borrower the prospect of larger loans should the smaller loan be repaid. However, this is an imperfect way of managing moral hazard. Even though past behavior may point toward debt repayment, circumstances may change and the borrower may not repay the loan in the future. This system also carries a high social cost. Since good borrowers remain underfunded during the adjustment period to higher loans, they and society lose the returns on the high-return but unfunded projects. In secured loans, collateral addresses moral hazard better because the amount of the collateral can be adjusted to the size of the loan.

Finally lenders face the prospect of *uninsurable risk.* For some adverse outcomes, no insurance is available or easily acquired, for example insurance against an illness that disables a key employee[2] or a mistaken business decision. In unsecured lending, lenders adjust to the prospect of uninsurable risk by giving many small loans to many different borrowers. In secured lending, collateral addresses this problem, however, by giving the lender a different route to payment whose value is independent of the uninsured risk and which the lender can verify accurately and inexpensively.

Because of the ways in which collateral addresses the problems of adverse selection, moral hazard and uninsurable risk, all but the largest borrowers will get better terms on a secured loan than on an unsecured loan:[3] lower interest rates, larger loans relative to income, and longer periods in which to repay. Modern lending relies on borrower's credit history, capacity to repay and the quality of the collateral. As the WB-IMF

---

[2] Illustrating the uneven way in which insurance covers risks facing firms, firms cannot easily get disability insurance for key employees but can easily get life insurance on them. In part, that is because it is easier to determine when a key employee is dead than when a key employee is disabled.

[3] That does not mean that secured loans, as a group, are less risky than unsecured loans. A US$20,000 unsecured loan to a billionaire may be less risky than a US$20,000 loan secured by the house trailer of a poor person. However, for any given borrower, a loan with collateral will always be less risky than a loan without collateral. Moreover, securitization choices can dramatically change risk-return configurations. For example, a portfolio of sub-prime loans may be more risky than a portfolio of prime first mortgages. However, a US$1 million loan with a first priority claim on a US$10 million portfolio of sub-prime may be less risky than a US$1 million loan with a first priority claim on US$1 million in prime mortgages.

credit union example indicates, the first two alone have much less impact on access to credit than do the first two combined with good collateral. Collateral is an efficient social institution for reducing risk and transactions costs in financial markets.

3.3.1   Unsecured versus Secured Lending

These features of secured lending do not mean that unsecured lending is generally inferior to secured lending. Rather, these different lending systems serve different purposes. Loans that take collateral are more expensive to set up than loans that are unsecured (see also the need for collateral system to be efficient, Dahan and Simpson, Chapter 5, this volume). Consequently, small loans or loans to buyers with long histories of timely debt servicing are often made without supporting collateral. In modern financial markets, secured and unsecured lending coexist happily.

A modern framework for secured lending builds on this complementarity, playing a key role in integrating secured and unsecured lending. Modern securitization takes portfolios of unsecured loans (credit card, micro credit, accounts receivables and chattel paper from merchants selling on credit) and uses these portfolios of smaller loans as collateral for asset-backed securities.[4] This permits refinancing small unsecured loans in capital markets or with private investors, thereby transmitting the cost-reducing effects of collateral to the unsecured loans. In advanced financial systems like that of the United States, about one-third of credit is unsecured and about two-thirds is secured. Both forms of credit have important places in modern systems. The legal framework for secured lending is a central feature of both secured and unsecured lending in modern financial systems.

3.4   IMPORTANCE OF MOVABLE PROPERTY FOR PRODUCTION AND GROWTH

For a modern economy as a whole, about half of the enterprise assets are movable property; about half are immovable (Figure 3.5). This statistic represents the average for the economy, including enterprises such as railroads, electrical and gas utilities that use immovable property more intensively than the average. At the other extreme, the vast majority of micro, small,

---

[4]   Of course, securitization can also use as collateral secured loans, such as mortgage loans.

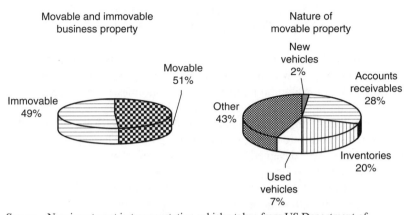

Movable and immovable business property

Nature of movable property

Source: New investment in transportation vehicles taken from US Department of Commerce, Bureau of Economic Analysis, *National Economic Accounts*, National Income and Product Accounts Tables, Table 5.5.5. 'Private Fixed Investment in Equipment and Software by Type', available at www.bea.gov/national/nipaweb/SelectTable.asp?Selected= N#S5, September 2007. US inventories from US Department of Commerce, Bureau of Economic Analysis, *National Economic Accounts*, National Income and Product Accounts Table, Table 5.7.5B. 'Private Inventories and Domestic Final Sales by Industry', available at www.bea.gov/national/nipaweb/TableView.asp#Mid, September 2007, accounts receivable data appear in Federal Reserve Board, statistical release Z.1, *Flow of Funds Accounts of the United States; Flows and Outstandings*, Second Quarter 2007, Table L.101 'Nonfinancial Business', available at www.federalreserve.gov/releases/z1/current/z1.pdf, September 2007. Remaining stocks of capital by type are taken from US Department of Commerce, Bureau of Economic Analysis, *National Economic Accounts*, Fixed Asset Table, Table 2.1. 'Current-Cost Net Stock of Private Fixed Assets, Equipment and Software, and Structures by Type', available at www.bea.gov/national/FA2004/ TableView.asp? SelectedTable=18&FirstYear= 2001&LastYear=2006&Freq=Year, September 2007.

Figure 3.5   *In modern economies, most enterprise assets are movable: shares of different capital in the US private business capital stock, 2005*

and medium scale enterprises, as well as many farms, often operate out of rented immovable property. For them, the share of movable property in total enterprise assets can reach 100 per cent. The same holds for key growth areas in the service sectors, including private medical and law practice, computer software and equipment sales and maintenance.

Movable assets include a diverse variety of property that can serve as collateral in modern legal frameworks: inventories; accounts receivable; any debt instrument, secured or unsecured; leases; intellectual property rights; equipment; and transport vehicles (Figure 3.5). For producers, when property can serve as collateral, two advantages follow: first, they can borrow using their existing assets as collateral for loans; second, they can buy this property on credit.

3.5   PROBLEM: WHEN MOVABLE PROPERTY CANNOT SERVE AS COLLATERAL

Collateral is important to lenders. Movable property is important to producers. Nonetheless, most movable property cannot effectively serve as collateral in most developing countries and economies in transition.[5] Even when laws nominally permit taking movable property as collateral, the rules for taking it are so cumbersome, inefficient and awkward that collateral loses its economic function of mitigating risk for lenders. This failure arises from poorly designed secured transactions laws; from badly run, badly designed legal institutions; and from weak enforcement. It has no significant causal roots in the economy or, typically, in regulations issued by banking and capital market supervisory authorities.

Of these problems, the most serious follows from poorly designed laws. Modern laws can circumvent many of the constraints presented by poorly designed legal institutions. Good laws can mandate more efficient institutions, replacing obsolete registry systems with Internet-based filing archives that have greater private participation. Good laws can bypass weak enforcement by permitting creditor-administered repossession and sale.

The problems in the law's design arise at each crucial stage of a right to use property as collateral: creation, priority, publicity, enforcement. These issues are ably discussed elsewhere in this volume by several legal contributors (see Mathernová, Chapter 9 and de la Peña, Chapter 11, this volume).

3.6   SOLUTION: REDRAFT LAWS, REFORM INSTITUTIONS

The solution is straightforward: introduce a modern secured transactions law and an Internet-based filing archive.

The results of some past reforms are encouraging. In the Romanian reform (see Lupulescu, Chapter 10, this volume), cumulative filings surpassed 1 000 000 by 2006 in a reform begun in 2000. This volume of filings represents an economic gain more than 10 percent of Romanian GDP (Figure 3.6). Other reforms have not fared so well, some apparently stagnating, and others indicating some progress. Other rumored reforms, disturbingly, have not generated publicly available statistics by which to

---

[5]   Sometimes the legal framework for selling new registered transport vehicles (motor vehicles, ships, planes) on credit and using them as collateral does function. However, this property amounts to only about 2 percent of the movable business capital stock.

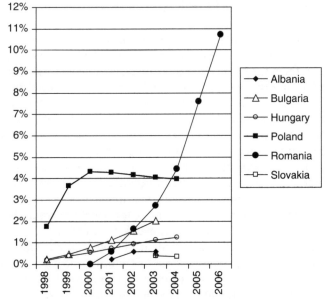

Note: The source document explains the derivation of the chart and data sources. The relative quality of reforms can be shown with simple estimating procedures. It assumes that individual loans will have a size proportionate to per capita income that is similar across countries, a plausible but untested assumption. The demonstration of the size of the gain relative to GDP requires an additional assumption about the difference in interest rates on secured and unsecured loans. The calculation shown here assumes that interest rates on secured loans will be about 6% (600 basis points) lower than those on unsecured loans, other characteristics of the borrower being the same. These issues are explored more fully in the source document.

Source: Heywood Fleisig (2006), *Indicators of Success in Secured Transactions Reform*, Washington, DC: Center for the Economic Analysis of Law, CEAL Issues Brief, June (rev. May 2007), available at www.ceal.org, September 2007.

Figure 3.6   Details matter: estimated economic impact of different reforms of secured transactions

judge them that are available on the Internet or easily available by email contact with responsible parties: Guyana, India, Ukraine, Trinidad and Tobago, Sri Lanka, Viet Nam, Mexico and Peru. With a well-designed online filing archive, gathering the data shown in the figure is simple. So the unavailability of data already indicates some problem in the 'reformed' system.

3.7   REFORM: SUPPORT AND OBSTACLES

A simple economic model of any reform would compare the cost of under-taking a reform with the benefit from the reform. The greater the economic return from the reform, the more quickly the government will move ahead on it. Reforming the law of secured transactions seems to meet this test easily. It costs less than US$1 million per country, but has a considerably greater economic return. As noted earlier, the gain from the Romanian reform is estimated conservatively at 10 percent of Romanian GDP[6] after seven years of operation and is still rising. This gain amounts to about US$12 billion. The annual rate of return on this project is several hundred percent per year. So a simple economic model of reform that predicts that donors and government officials will do what is most economically beneficial for the country would predict that this reform would be high in the list of desirable projects for governments and donors.

However, such a model fails to explain what we observe. Governments, on the whole, are not enthusiastic about this reform. And when they do pass new laws, they tend to remove features that require that they actually change legal and institutional features that are major barriers to access to credit. These adjustments reduce or nullify the economic impact of the legal reform.

What explains the minimal support for an important reform with a low cost and huge impact?

3.7.1   Lawyers versus Economists?

This reform requires both lawyers and economists. Lawyers must lay out drafting options and write the law. Economists must assess the costs and benefits of different ways of adapting foreign legal principles to the laws and institutions of the country undertaking the reform. Perhaps lawyers and economists have difficulty communicating (see Dahan and Simpson, Chapter 5, this volume). Lawyers are often averse to considering the eco-nomic implications of their laws or of economic aspects of alternative legal formulations. Compounding this, local lawyers in the reforming countries, even when they have been foreign-educated, typically do not study the debt collection systems of developed countries. So foreign education, which often can help disseminate new techniques, tends not to disseminate infor-mation about modern debt collection systems.

---

[6]   Romania's GDP in 2006 was US$121.6 billion. World Bank, 'Key develop-ment data and statistics', available at http://worldbank.org, September 2007.

On the other side, economists often do not understand that some obscure laws can have important economic implications.[7] Some economists seem to have resisted this reform because the economic function of collateral is typically something they have not learned about in graduate school.

Since the vast majority of government policymakers are lawyers and economists, this gap in communication could explain some of the reluctance of governments to act.

However, this argument cannot be pushed too far. Certainly, our group at the Center for the Economic Analysis of Law (CEAL) includes economists and lawyers who have worked together toward a common goal for years. CEAL staff members have, moreover, been in touch with John Simpson and other EBRD-lawyers since the beginning of the EBRD-sponsored secured transactions reforms. Similarly, CEAL staff members have worked with lawyers at UNIDROIT, UNCITRAL and the American Bar Association on different aspects of the reform of the law of secured transactions.

Moreover, lawyers specializing in secured transactions have published hundreds of articles conjecturing about the economic gain from systems of secured lending, both pro and con. Certainly they have published far more articles exploring these issues than have economists and have reached out to the community of economists. Economists, for their part, have not devoted as many resources to analysing secured transactions law and almost none to implementing such reforms in a developing country context. However, they have to some degree; and that literature largely points to the same conclusions set out here. In addition, economists have certainly analysed other laws embodying economic principles. So communication problems between lawyers and economists could explain some of the slowness of adoption of this reform, but it is not my impression that it explains very much of the slowness.

---

[7]   In the author's experience, economists do understand that clearly labeled laws, such as 'capital markets law', 'labor law', 'the tax code', 'competition law' or 'banking law' have important economic implications. However, they do not seem generally aware that the background codes (the civil code, the Companies Act, and the commercial code) can have equally important implications. Many economists, in addition, delegate not just the legal drafting to lawyers, but the content of the laws. IMF-sponsored banking laws, drafted by the IMF legal department, for example, sometimes regulate 'financial activities', and other times regulate 'financial institutions' or 'deposit-taking institutions'. These are large differences, insofar as the first broad definition could include (and discourage) economic agents such as fertilizer dealers selling on credit. Despite this, the pros and cons of regulating just deposit-taking institutions are rarely discussed in World Bank or IMF financial sector documents.

3.7.2   Opposition and Support within the Country

Governments of developing countries have not strongly supported this reform. Donor assistance is more tolerated than sought. Only a few governments have hired teams of experts in developed country legal systems to evaluate their own secured transactions laws. Nor have they convened national commissions or task forces to redraft them[8]. Since governments are largely composed of lawyers and economists, it could be argued that this lack of enthusiasm could be another manifestation of economists and lawyers failing to communicate.

However, this explanation will not suffice. Governments, alas, often pass laws or take actions where they do not fully understand the merits of the case. They do that because of pressure from interest groups. What is striking about this reform is that, despite the large potential gain, no group of stakeholders systematically supports it. At the same time, different interest groups emerge under different circumstances who strongly oppose it. Governments, consequently, are slow to act and, when they do act, they pass laws with limited effectiveness.

Banks and banking associations[9]
While individual bankers are often the most aware of the issues surrounding collateral, few banking associations have formally supported this reform. In some cases, the banking associations have opposed it. I know of no country where a banking association has actively pushed forward a strong reform. Lawyers of banking associations often oppose the reform ostensibly on grounds of legal principle. This opposition can continue long after exhaustive presentation of legal arguments and even, in one case, where the president of the Supreme Court stated that the reform was consistent with local law. Nor is the unchecked opposition of bank lawyers consistent with observed support from lawyers from other chambers. Typically, bank lawyers report to a hierarchy of bank managers who consider overall business needs of the bank.

In some cases, this management structure simply instructs the bank lawyer to support the reform. Typically, though, bank management does not issue such instructions to its lawyers or to the banking association. Where banks and their associations have supported reforms, they have

---

8   Peru convened such a commission as, apparently, has Hungary.
9   This section draws on work prepared for the Inter-American Development Bank, Fleisig and de la Peña (2007), 'How weak property rights limit finance, and supervision and regulation' in Carolin Crabbe, (ed), *Banking on Small Business* (Washington, DC: Inter-American Development Bank, 2007).

done so only after removing key economic features of the law that permit non-bank lenders and credit sellers to compete with banks. Where they have actively opposed reform, they have specifically mentioned these key economic features as points of objection.

These features are crucial to the economic success of the reform. Non-bank lenders, such as equipment dealers, can manage the risk of repossession and sale of specialized equipment, located in remote places. The huge expansion of credit occurs because banks can then refinance such non-bank activities. The banks can then take as collateral the debt instruments created by the sales of the dealer. Banks have an advantage in evaluating the financial condition of such dealers – a considerably greater advantage than they have in making final loans for equipment and inventories in businesses and areas they may not know well, especially when the dealers' clients have no long-term relationship with the bank.

As a result of this broader granting of credit, banks operating in modern secured transactions systems account for a smaller fraction of total credit granted. In the typical developing countries, banks account for more than 90 percent of credit. In the United States, that number is closer to 40 percent. Banks in the United States, however, do more business than banks in developing countries relative to GDP. Banks in the United States have 40 percent of credit amounting to 220 percent of GDP, or 88 percent of GDP. Banks in developing countries have 90 percent of credit amounting to at most 50 percent of GDP, for a total market of 45 percent of GDP; that is, about half as much business relative to GDP as their US counterparts.

However, for banks to voluntarily cede monopoly powers may require taking a deep breath and overcoming childhood fears based on hearing the national equivalent of 'a bird in the hand is worth two in the bush'. There is ample economic literature supporting the view that low-income farmers resist experimentation more than do middle-income farmers because for a low-income farmer, failure can be disastrous. Perhaps bankers are more like farmers than we think.

More darkly, it has been suggested that poorly regulated and under-capitalized banks that are concealing uncollectible debts and banks with many related-party loans on their books have no underlying interest in improving legal framework for collecting either secured or unsecured loans. CEAL has worked in only one country where the banks insisted that any improvement in the legal framework for secured lending would not apply to the existing portfolio of secured loans. However, this is an interesting logical possibility and we should be alert for evidence for and against.

Chambers of commerce and of industry

These typically, but not invariably, support the reform. The reason for support is apparent: their members can finance a larger amount of profitable business opportunities and can safely expand their sales on credit. Opposition is more idiosyncratic. Sometimes the issue is self-interest. In one country, the chamber of commerce controlled the filing archive for the commercial pledge and the officers of the private company operating the archive and of the chamber were the same. Their opposition to reform of the filing archive was ferocious. However, in other countries, where membership in the chamber seems to represent a broader group of businesses, chambers of commerce who received revenues from existing filing activities supported the reform.

Chambers of commerce seem far more likely to support the reform than are chambers of industry. One systematic difference that may contribute to this is that, compared to commercial enterprises, industries often have more real estate that they can use as collateral. By contrast, commercial enterprises in chambers of commerce have larger holdings of movable property such as inventory and accounts receivables on their balance sheets. Another difference may arise from the often greater ability of large industries to get state-directed subsidized credits and, thereby, avoid the credit constraint imposed by the weak framework for collateral. However, the support of these chambers is typically less strong than is the opposition of the banks. A group whose members perceive large individual losses may oppose a reform more forcefully than another group, perceiving small individual gains, will support the reform. This can occur even when the total of these gains to the supporting group is far greater than the loss to the opposing group.[10]

Key government agencies: Ministry of Finance, supervisors and regulators of financial institutions, Central Bank

Ministries of Finance rarely support the reform. Task managers of multilateral development banks routinely report that their government counterparts, typically the Ministry of Finance, do not request collateral reform to

---

[10] Consider US protection of domestically produced sugar, ongoing since the early 1800s. This policy imposes costs on consumers in every congressional district. These costs typically exceed the gains to producers in those districts. Moreover, the total cost of the program to consumers exceeds its total gain to domestic producers. However, in the few congressional districts receiving net gains, representatives work ferociously to protect the arrangement. They do this by swapping votes on many issues for the few votes of other congressmen necessary to preserve the sugar tariff.

be included in reform programs and, when such projects are suggested, frequently actively oppose them. With few exceptions,[11] no reform has been championed by a Ministry of Finance and pushed through the legislative process. This may not be surprising given the lack of support from the banks, typically a powerful lobby and the most visible representatives of the financial sector in most countries.

Similarly, with few exceptions, Central Banks have not supported this reform. In one presentation at the IMF to an audience of about 50 developing country central bank lawyers, the speaker asked for show of hands on what country was considering reforming the secured transactions laws. Not a single hand went up.

Sometimes Central Banks oppose the reform. In one country, at a large public meeting presenting a draft secured transactions law, both the head of the Central Bank and the head of supervision and regulation took the opportunity of their presentations to oppose the reform, dismissing the economic problem as insignificant and the proposed legal solution as inappropriate.

Agencies in charge of financial sector supervision and regulation

These would seem to have a natural interest in supporting this reform: after all, the reform permits the supervised financial institutions to expand lending at the same time that they reduce the riskiness of the portfolio. Nonetheless, in our experience, supervisors and regulators divide about evenly in supporting and opposing this reform, with the majority sitting out the reform. Reasons given for failure to support or even oppose the reform have included a desire to avoid the political process of passing a law, not wishing to spend political influence on a reform they see the financial institutions as opposing, and recitals of supervisor bromides like 'good collateral doesn't make a good loan' and 'bankers are not pawnbrokers'. On the other hand, one head of supervision and regulation overruled his skeptical staff and demanded immediate action on reform; another convened a large international seminar and announced that the superintendency's full support of the reform would go beyond the more narrow requests of the sponsoring donor; and another supervisor attempted ushering the law though a complex ratification process in a difficult political environment that included, inexplicably, the strong opposition of the chamber of commerce.

---

[11]   One interesting exception to this is the IADB's Peru program, which eventually overcame the opposition of the Ministry of Finance by supplying extensive documentation of the need for reform and its likely economic impact and then patiently urging reconsideration by the Ministry of Finance.

Registries
Before reform, if they exist at all, security interests in movable property in the possession of the debtor are made public with a registration process that verifies and files key documents. After reform, publicity should rely on a notice filing system; a database that does not verify documents and files only a notice of the existence of these documents. The new system requires far fewer employees. The registration systems of some small countries operate with hundreds of employees. In contrast, the notice filing system of the state of California, whose GDP is eighth among the countries of the world, employs about seven employees.[12] The super-modern notice filing system of Romania is supervised by one state employee.[13] Not surprisingly, public registrars often oppose this reform. Poorly designed efforts by donors to strengthen national registration systems have actually worsened this problem in recent years. The efforts have often supported national registry laws and funded institutions that turn the registries into enormous organizations with monopoly powers. Typically, the reform fares better when the existing filing archive is in an economic ministry or a chamber of commerce that is responsive to the broad concerns of its members. In two such cases, the registry operators were strong proponents of reform and of decentralized registration with private participation.

Courts and Ministries of Justice
These differ considerably among countries in their roles in legal reform. In some countries, the Ministry of Justice is the gate-keeper for all laws. In other countries, the economic ministries have the main responsibility for economic laws. These differences seem uncorrelated with the region or whether the legal regime is based on civil code or common law. Sometimes, courts and Ministries of Justice have principled legal concerns that can only be met by extensive discussions with international experts and trusted local lawyers. Sometimes their objections are not so principled. Ministries of Justice and court systems may get a large portion of their budget

---

12   Presentation by the head of the California filing archive, 1996. Ranked by GDP, California was eighth in the world in 2006 behind the remaining United States, Japan, Germany, China, United Kingdom, France and Italy. GDP data from US Department of Commerce, Bureau of Economic Analysis, 'Gross Domestic Product (GDP) by state, 2006', Table 1. Real GDP by State, 2003–2006, available at www.bea.gov/newsreleases/regional/gdp_state/2007/pdf/gsp0607.pdf. GDP for other countries taken from International Monetary Fund, World Economic and Financial Surveys, 'World economic outlook' Database, April 2007, available at www.imf.org/external/pubs/ft/weo/2007/01/data/index.aspx, September 2007.

13   Correspondence with Paul Stanescu, Ministry of Justice, Romania, March 2007.

revenues from the fees charged by the registries, as well as from the auction and appraisal fees arising from the obsolete recovery processes mandated in current laws. In every country where the courts or the Ministry of Justice have such an interest, they have opposed reform of these key features.

3.7.3   International Peer Guidance: Inner Circle[14]

Most of us like to think of ourselves as operating by right reason, but who among us is not susceptible to the voice of authority whispering in our ear, 'It is so! It is so!!' Who could be these voices of international authority for national decisionmakers to push for collateral reform?

International financial institutions and bilateral donors
The 'front line' agencies in the effort to convince national decisionmakers of the importance of any reform are the bilateral donors and the international financial institutions: the multilateral development banks (MDBs) and the IMF.

Among the MDBs and the donors' support for reform has increased steadily since the early 1990s and more sharply over the past five years. The EBRD was the first MDB to officially endorse this reform, with its Model Law. It remains the only institution to have continuously supported the reform since 1994 (see details at www.ebrd.com). Developments in the other MDBs have also become more positive. Hits for the word 'collateral' on the websites of MDBs, for example, have risen sharply between 2000 and 2006. The World Bank's widely-quoted 'Doing Business Indicators' now feature several indicators of the state of secured transactions. The World Bank has now published two guides to reform.[15]

While this MDB endorsement is promising and lends credibility to the reform, the MDBs have done little to raise the reform of the framework of secured transactions to the policy dialogue state, where the MDB offers the short list of actions that the country should take. The reform typically receives no attention in the MDB reviews of the financial sector. The majority of MDB credit line, banking, micro-credit and financial sector lending operations, as well as credit line operations, contain no proposals for reform of the legal framework. And, typically, when they do contain such proposals, they are not implemented.

---

[14]   This section draws on Fleisig and de la Peña (2007).
[15]   See Fleisig et al. (2006) and Baranes et al. (2001) available at http://rru.world-bank.org/Toolkits/Collateral/.

This inattention is a key reason why Ministers of Finance often do not take this reform seriously. The reform of secured transactions suffers because it is not on the list of actions that MDBs recommend. Not surprisingly, a policymaker confronted with a long list of tasks for which a large loan will be disbursed will pay little attention to an additional task such as 'reform secured transactions' that is not on that list. Moreover, because the time and power of most policymakers is limited, the reform suffers because other actions are present on the list. Policymakers ask, not unreasonably: if secured transactions reform is so important, why is it not on the list?

MDBs also have some trouble managing effective legal reform projects within their lending programs. For the small amounts of money required for the reform, the administrative costs of loan preparation and loan supervision typically exceed the amounts the MDBs routinely budget for such activities. Such actions require particularly great dedication when the government does not want to borrow for the reform at all. It is possible but difficult to get around this budget constraint by including the reform component in a larger policy based loan. However, since such a loan disburses fast, linking a reform with an uncertain schedule to loan tranches can force surrendering of key legal details if the rest of the loan is to be kept intact. It takes a cool task manager with solid backing from his superiors to delay disbursement of US$100 million tranche for a year, as the World Bank's task manager did on a loan to the Government of Romania, pending agreement on the organization of the filing archive. Most managers find this prospect too daunting. As one Division Chief explained, 'I can't afford to do secured transactions. I have a division to feed'.

MDBs are making some progress in reform implementation, mainly by moving the reform outside the lending program. The IADB is partnering with its Multilateral Investment Fund grant program for secured transactions reform; the World Bank has organized some stand-alone projects and also offers technical assistance from its International Finance Corporation trust funds; and the ADB has made substantial use of its grant-based technical assistance funds. The EBRD has long given such technical assistance. It remains to be proved whether such projects, divorced from loan conditions, can achieve a solid economic impact.

Among the donors, USAID was an early champion of this reform, about contemporaneous with EBRD efforts in the transitional economies. It has now expanded its support to other regions. Nonetheless, like the lending operations of the MDBs, most USAID solicitations ('requests for proposals') on access to credit, micro-credit, rural finance or financial sector activities do not include components aimed at reforming the law of secured transactions. Without such instructions, bidding contractors have little incentive to propose the inclusion of such elements. Another US donor, the Millennium Challenge Corporation, has made reform of secured transactions part of its compact in several countries. It is too early to assess their impact on the reform.

All of these efforts have produced reforms of widely varying quality. The enormous performance spread between the impact of the best and worst reforms shows that considerably more attention needs to be paid to the economic impact of legal details before we can get consistently good results.

Altogether, though, awareness today is much higher than ten years ago. In 1996, the staff of the International Labor Organization presented a competent survey of the work on collateral and development to assembled donors. It polled the donor representatives on the importance of collateral. The representatives of all donors present (except for those of USAID and one from the World Bank) stated that further work on the laws governing collateral was not a central concern.[16]

Perhaps the single most influential donor on issues of reforming the laws governing finance is the International Monetary Fund. Support for the reform of secured lending, unfortunately, has not yet arrived at the IMF. In 1997, the G-10, concerned about financial instability in developing countries, set out a broad agenda of 'Key elements of robust financial systems' that gave primary emphasis to the 'creation of an institutional setting and financial infrastructure necessary for a sound credit culture and effective market functioning. To this end, it is necessary to create a legal environment where the terms and conditions of contracts are observed and where legal recourse, including the taking possession of collateral, is possible without undue delay'.[17] It emphasized the reponsibilities of the IMF and MDBs in supporting this reform.[18] Following up on this detailed G-10 directive, the G-22 instructed the IMF to support the reform of secured transactions.[19]

---

[16] Bernd Balkenhol and Haje Schütte (1996). See, especially Annex: Survey responses by members of the Donors' Working Group, responses to question 9. 'What do you think are the implications of the collateral problem for donors interested in the development of the financial sector in developing countries?'

[17] Group of Ten, 'Financial stability in emerging market economies: A strategy for the formulation, adoption and implementation of sound principles and practices to strengthen financial systems', April 1997, available at www.bis.org/publ/gten02.htm. See p. 3, but also pp. 15, 25–7, 37, 66 and 74.

[18] Ibid. pp. 2, 6, 7, 52, 61, 62, 64.

[19] The Working Group on International Financial Crises noted 'debtor-creditor regimes were identified as important means of limiting financial crises and facilitating rapid and orderly workouts from excessive indebtedness. The report outlines the key principles and features of such regimes (p. iii)'. The report sets out in 'Annex B: Key Features of Effective Debtor-Creditor Regimes, key elements of 1.

These ministerial urgings notwithstanding, an IMF review of its Financial Sector Advisory Program[20] prepared in 2006, which studied 25 countries in depth, mentions the legal framework for secured transactions in only one of the countries examined. In the Letters of Intent and Memoranda of Understanding,[21] the IMF's principal record of IMF agreement with borrowing member countries, a brief study of those for Latin America indicates that only Ecuador and Peru mention the reform of their systems for taking collateral or registering security interests. (For more details on how the region is in dire need of reform, see de la Peña, Chapter 11, this volume). The remaining Latin American countries either do not mention collateral or mention it only in the context of central bank operations and security for debt swaps and transactions with the IMF. The IMF's lack of interest in this reform will remain a heavy burden on its public acceptance.[22]

Creation of Security Interest; 2. Priority; 3. Registration of Security Interests; 4. Enforcement. It stated that 'technical assistance from both the IMF and the World Bank should help encourage and facilitate improvements in existing insolvency and debtor-creditor regimes' (p. 18). Group of 22 'Report of the working group on international financial crises', October 1998 available at www.imf.org/external/np/ g 22/#crises. The G-22 Working group on Strengthening Financial Systems similarly emphasized the role of good collateral in resolving financial, restating the old advice 'to maintain incentives for good management, liquidity assistance should be provided only for short periods; the loan should be fully collateralised, and granted at a penalty rate' (p. 22 and again at p. 25 and p. 26). It noted 'For these purposes, the existence and strict implementation of applicable laws on liquidation, bankruptcy, the assumption of collateral and seniority rules for claims are crucial.' (p. 26). It recommended the use of conditionality to achieve these ends: 'The use of conditionality in IMF and World Bank programmes is a powerful means of fostering the implementation of standards and sound practices directly' (Group of 22, Working Group on Strengthening Financial Systems, 'Report of the working group on strengthening financial systems', October 1998 p. 42, available at www.imf. org/external/np/g 22/ sfsrep.pdf).

20   International Monetary Fund (2006), p. 119.

21   Letters of Intent are prepared by the member country. They describe the policies that a country intends to implement in the context of its request for financial support from the IMF. Memoranda of Economic and Financial Policies are prepared by the member country. They describe the policies that a country intends to implement in the context of its request for financial support from the IMF. These documents were searched using the term 'collateral'. Available at www.imf.org/

22   This discussion draws on a paper prepared for the Inter-American Development Bank and non-Latin American countries were not studied. See Fleisig and de la Peña (2007).

3.7.4 International Peer Groups: the Outer Circle[23]

Other important institutions influence both the views of the IFIs and those of developing country decisionmakers. Among the more important are bank regulators such as the Federal Reserve, the Comptroller of the Currency and the Bank for International Settlements. These influences are transmitted partly through the extension of supervisory standards, partly through the example they set throughout the world, and partly through their staff who are often hired by the IFIs.

Shortly after leaving the presidency of the Federal Reserve Bank of New York, a position with enormous responsibilities for national and international bank supervision and regulation, Gerald Corrigan stated that: 'it is a total myth to suggest that Latin American and Caribbean banking problems will be solved by improved banking supervision, even if it is clear that improved supervision is needed' (p. 13) 'the problems associated with the credit life cycle are severely complicated by the historic lack of a credit culture that firmly establishes in law, tradition and custom, the relationships, duties and responsibilities between creditors and debtors. One particular and very costly aspect of this lack of a well-established credit culture is the enormously complex set of issues surrounding the collection process for bad loans. These problems tend to ensure that ultimate losses on bad loans will be very high, if for no other reason than the fact that the passage of time usually means larger ultimate losses' (p. 17).[24] That point extends far beyond Latin America and remains true for today's developing countries.

Sadly, Corrigan's view is the exception. The importance of the property rights regime and its bearing on the financial sector remains largely ignored by industrial country bank regulators. By law, the Federal Reserve and the Comptroller of the Currency assess the riskiness of Latin American banking systems in order to regulate branches of Latin American banks operating in the United States. However, the analyses of foreign financial systems available on their websites or described in their supervision manuals show no awareness of how problems in property rights affect the debt collection system in Latin America. They do not discuss the greater riskiness of both secured and unsecured loans in countries without reformed systems.[25] Yet these problems are central in any appraisal of the

---

[23] This section draws in the discussion set out in Fleisig and de la Peña (2007).

[24] Corrigan (1997) available at http://www.iadb.org/sds/doc/ifm-107e.pdf.

[25] Federal Reserve examination procedures dwell heavily on collateral and collateral adequacy. Hundreds of references in their examination manuals address different aspects of collateral and the link between the taking of collateral and the legal foundation of collateral in the Uniform Commercial Code, Article 9. The manual

soundness of any loan by a US-based banking institution to a Latin American client or using collateral located in Latin America, or assessing the soundness of the dealings of a US branch of a Latin American bank with its parent bank.

Nor has the link between risk mitigation and its legal foundation been given much attention by the Basel Committee on Bank Supervisors, who are issuing international standards on bank supervision. The Basel II standards show a considerable advance since the 1998 agnosticism of Basel I about collateral, which stated that: 'it has not been found possible to develop a basis for recognising collateral generally in the weighting system'.[26] However, even the Basel II standards steer clear of generalizations at the country level about the quality of laws governing collateral. Instead, they leave these judgments to a bank-by-bank assessment and to the national supervisor's review.[27] Curiously, hundreds of hits show that the BIS has focused on the use of collateral for cross-border transactions for banks, but not examined the legal frameworks for secured lending and debt collection in the systems of the countries whose risk they hope to assess.

---

repeatedly emphasizes the need to comply with that law and other laws. However, the taking of foreign collateral and the evaluation of bank branches of banks that depend on foreign collateral is largely glossed over. Here is the Federal Reserve's only treatment of foreign collateral in its examiner's manual: 'The branch [of the foreign bank] should have policies for taking foreign collateral as security for a loan to assure adherence with the local [foreign] required procedures. For example, liens on fixed assets in many countries must be registered with the local government'. Board of Governors of the Federal Reserve System (1997), available at www.federalreserve.gov/boarddocs/supmanual/us_branches/usbranch.pdf.

[26] 'In view of the varying practices among banks in different countries for taking collateral and different experiences of the stability of physical or financial collateral values, it has not been found possible to develop a basis for recognising collateral generally in the weighting system. The more limited recognition of collateral will apply only to loans secured against cash, and against securities issued by OECD central governments, OECD noncentral government public sector entities, or specified multilateral development banks'. Basel Committee on Banking Supervision, *International Convergence of Capital Measurement and Capital Standards*, July 1988, updated to April 1998, (iv) Collateral and guarantees, para. 39, p. 11. Available at www.bis.org/publ/bcbsc111.pdf39.

[27] 'the additional credit risk mitigation permitted under Basel II . . . will depend on which additional eligible instruments are used as collateral in a particular jurisdiction, whether the legal basis for the enforcement of collateral is effective, the existence of liquid markets to obtain reliable collateral valuations and the availability of a larger range of guarantors, including providers of credit derivatives'. Basel Committee on Banking Supervision, *Implementation of Basel II: Practical Considerations*, Basel: Basel Committee on Banking Supervision, July 2004, p. 10, available at www.bis.org/publ/bcbs 109.htm.

There is no evidence from the public documents or websites of these institutions that they themselves understand how much the success of their own regulatory policies rests on the advanced systems for property rights in their own countries. However, when banks and regulators in developed countries follow the myth that the success of their financial systems arises from their regulatory efforts alone and is independent of the legal framework for debt collection in the industrial countries, it is a harmless vanity. The progress of laws, property rights and legal institutions continues in these countries independent of the view of these regulators.

Nonetheless by ignoring these problems, these institutions indirectly promulgate the myth that developing countries can develop their financial sectors only by improved financial institutions supervision and regulation and by improved banking techniques. Many supervisors and regulators, including those from industrial countries, have questioned the points set out in this chapter simply because they are not reflected in the concerns of the BIS, the Fed or the Comptroller. The argument from authority is alive and well. By this silence, these agencies make the task of reform harder.

In contrast to these institutions, several other international agencies have taken steps that recognize the importance of the legal framework for secured transactions. UNIDROIT has issued an international convention on international mobile equipment financing (aircraft, railway stock, satellite). UNCITRAL has issued an international convention on accounts receivable financing, though the optional registration requirements will limit its importance as a security device. UNCITRAL has also issued a legislative guide on secured transactions reform. And the OAS has issued a model secured transactions law for Latin America. These efforts all contribute to the respectability of the reform and, thereby, to its support. However, their effect is limited because economic policymakers know little about them, as do international economic agencies. Curiously, those efforts aimed largely at advising (the OAS model law and the UNCITRAL legislative guide) have so far had little effect on the judicial and legal communities who presumably do recognize their authority.

3.7.5 General Obstacles

Finally, over and above issues peculiar to secured transactions, are some general features that inhibit all successful reform.

No measurement of impact
Neither MDBs nor donors measure the impact of their programs. In the face of past concerns about over-reliance on rates of return, they have abandoned such measurement almost entirely. MDBs and donors,

therefore, typically have no idea what the gain is from the programs they support. Sometimes they are even unsure whether countries undertake the actions that loans and grants are supposed to support. In such an environment, where only a loose intellectual link exists between resource input and economic output, the high potential return from the reform of the framework for secured transactions simply attracts no attention.

Slowly changing paradigms

MDBs, donors and policymakers have paradigms – ways of viewing and understanding reality – about the development process. These paradigms change only slowly. For many years, MDBs supported the development of government finance agencies in developing countries that would lend directly to 'underserved' business and agriculture (see Beck, Chapter 2, this volume). Even though billions of dollars were lost by these institutions, MDBs never asked why developing countries needed state-run lenders to handle 'underserved' lenders when private lenders in developed countries would make exactly the same loans to the same clients. After years of failure and billions in losses, the paradigm shifted to a mix of credit line operations, some of which disbursed through private banks in order to ensure efficiency. But, especially when efficient, these disbursements tended to be slow and these operations did not seem to reach target borrowers. Once again, MDBs did not ask why private lenders did not onlend these credit lines in order to make loans in developing countries that their equivalents in developed countries were happy to make. The paradigm again shifted, this time to micro-credit: small unsecured loans. These programs did appear to exploit a significant market niche. However, since these projects were also undertaken with no attention to the legal framework for collecting either unsecured loans or secured loans, they too seem to have reached the limits of their utility (on micro-finance, see Engelhardt and Regitz, Chapter 6 and Holtmann, Chapter 7, this volume). The time may be ripe for a new paradigm. Some MDB managers support taking a step backward and advocate once again funding government-run credit lines, which will make loans despite the absence of a reformed legal framework for secured lending. But others may be prepared to look at reforming the underlying legal framework that prevents the private sector from making these loans in the first place.

General resistance to change

People resist change, even when it is good for them. Hybrid corn was introduced in the United States in the second half of the nineteenth century. Planting hybrid corn is a simple horticultural decision: all inputs – plowing, harrowing, weeding, seed drilling – remain the same. Only the seed changes.

A hybrid corn seed, however, produces about three times as much corn as an ordinary seed. Tripling your income for the same effort seems simple to explain and quite attractive. Nonetheless, it took American farmers 50 years to fully adopt hybrid corn.

Change can be risky

American sharecroppers (poor farmers who reimbursed the landowner with part of their harvest) knew that growing cotton yielded more income than does growing corn. Nonetheless, sharecroppers devoted a large fraction of their effort to growing corn, not cotton. Because they were poor and had no cash reserves, poor sharecroppers risked starvation if their cash crop failed. So they must always plant some food. For poor countries, embracing the future may be similarly scary. They will require not just a consensus among their international peer group, but many successful adoptions by other developing countries before they take a step forward.

3.8   REFORM: THE OUTLOOK

The outlook for reform is guardedly optimistic. The number of legal reform projects is rising and the MDBs and US donors are wheeling more resources into play. Disturbingly, many projects implement financial reforms that do not address the economic fundamentals of secured lending. Consequently, many reforms have had to be redone, sometimes more than once. However, donors seem willing to finance these duplicative efforts until success is achieved. This push, together with a rising volume of supporting research from MDBs, will increase the respectability of the reform and push it higher on the agendas of MDB task managers and country policymakers. Adoption of successful reforms should spur interest, though this will be a slow process since criteria for a successful reform do not yet seem to be of interest to those funding the reform. If it occurs, endorsement of the reform by the IMF and other international organizations influential in the financial sector will accelerate adoption. Remembering the experience with hybrid corn, this hopeful outlook should be guarded.

REFERENCES

Balkenhol, Bernd and Haje Schütte (1996), *Collateral, Collateral Law and Collateral Substitutes*, International Labour Organization, April, available at www.ilo.org/public/english/employment/ent/papers/collat.htm#N_1_, September 2007.

Baranes, Yair and Ronald C.C. Cuming (2001), *Handbook on the Albanian Collateral Law*, International Bank for Reconstruction and Development and International Finance Corporation, Washington, DC.

Basel Committee on Banking Supervision (1988), *International Convergence of Capital Measurement and Capital Standards*, July 1988, updated to April 1998, (iv) Collateral and guarantees, available at www.bis.org/publ/bcbsc111.pdf39.

Basel Committee on Banking Supervision (2004), *Implementation of Basel II: Practical Considerations*, Basel: Basel Committee on Banking Supervision, July, available at www.bis.org/publ/bcbs 109.htm.

Board of Governors of the Federal Reserve System (1997), *Examination Manual for U.S. Branches and Agencies of Foreign Banking Organizations*, Washington, DC: Board of Governors of the Federal Reserve System, September, available at www.federalreserve.gov/boarddocs/supmanual/us_ branches/usbranch.pdf.

Corrigan, Gerald (1997), Building Effective Banking Systems in Latin America and the Caribbean: Tactics and Strategy Washington, DC: IDB, May, available at www.iadb.org/sds/doc/ifm-107e.pdf.

Federal Reserve Board, statistical release Z.1, 'Flow of funds accounts of the United States; flows and outstandings, second quarter 2007', Table L.101 'Nonfinancial Business', available at www.federalreserve.gov/releases/z1/current/z1.pdf, September 2007.

Federal Reserve Board, 'Statistical Supplement' to the Federal Reserve Bulletin, available at www.federalreserve.gov/pubs/supplement/2007/01/default.htm, September 2007.

Fleisig, Heywood (2006), *Indicators of Success in Secured Transactions Reform*, Washington, DC: Center for the Economic Analysis of Law, CEAL Issues Brief, June (rev. September 2007), available at www.ceal.org, September 2007.

Fleisig, Heywood and Nuria de la Peña (2007), 'How weak property rights limit finance, and supervision and regulation', in Carolin Crabbe (ed), *Banking on Small Business*, Washington, DC: Inter-American Development Bank.

Fleisig, Heywood, Mehnaz Safavian and Nuria de la Peña (2006), *Reforming Collateral Laws to Expand Access to Finance*, Washington, DC: World Bank, available at http://rru.worldbank.org/Toolkits/Collateral/.

Group of Ten (1997), 'Financial stability in emerging market economies; A strategy for the formulation, adoption and implementation of sound principles and practices to strengthen financial systems', April, available at www.bis.org/publ/gten02.htm. See p. 3, but also pp. 15, 25, 27, 37, 66 and 74.

Group of 22 (1998), *Report of the Working Group on International Financial Crises*, October, available at www.imf.org/external/np/g 22/#crises.

Group of 22 (1998), Working Group on Strengthening Financial Systems, *Report of the Working Group on Strengthening Financial Systems*, October, p. 42, available at www.imf.org/external/np/g 22/sfsrep.pdf.

International Monetary Fund (2006), Independent Evaluation Office, *Report on the Evaluation of the Financial Sector Assessment Program*, Washington, DC: International Monetary Fund, 5 January.

International Monetary Fund (2007), World Economic and Financial Surveys, 'World economic outlook database', April, available at www.imf.org/external/pubs/ft/weo/2007/01/data/index.aspx, September 2007.

Joint BIS-IMF-OECD-WB External Debt Hub, 2007, available at http://devdata.worldbank.org/sdmx/jedh/jedh_dbase.html, September 2007.

Organization for Economic Cooperation and Development, Development Co-operation Directorate (DCD-DAC) DAC Reference Statistical Tables, 'FINAL ODA 2005', available at www.oecd.org/department/0,3355,en_2649_34447_1_1_1_1_1,00.html, September 2007.

US Department of Commerce, Bureau of Economic Analysis, 'Gross Domestic Product (GDP) by state, 2006', Table 1. 'Real GDP by state, 2003–2006', available at www.bea.gov/newsreleases/regional/gdp_state/2007/pdf/gsp 0607. pdf, September 2007.

US Department of Commerce, Bureau of Economic Analysis, National Economic Accounts, 'National income and product accounts tables', Table 5.5.5. 'Private fixed investment in equipment and software by type', available at www.bea.gov/national/nipaweb/SelectTable.asp?Selected=N#S5, September 2007.

US Department of Commerce, Bureau of Economic Analysis, National Economic Accounts, 'Fixed asset table', Table 2.1. 'Current-cost net stock of private fixed assets, equipment and software, and structures by type', available at www.bea.gov/national/FA2004/TableView.asp?SelectedTable=18&FirstYear=2001&LastYear=2006&Freq=Year, September 2007.

US Department of Commerce, Bureau of Economic Analysis, National Economic Accounts, 'National income and product accounts table', Table 5.7.5B. 'Private inventories and domestic final sales by industry', available at www.bea.gov/national/nipaweb/TableView.asp#Mid, September 2007.

4. Firm-level evidence on collateral and access to finance

Mehnaz S. Safavian

4.1 INTRODUCTION

Collateral requirements for loan contracts are an important part of financial sector contracts: most loan contracts require some type of security or collateral. This is true across the globe, irrespective of a country's income, growth or financial sector development. And yet collateral requirements often preclude businesses from participating in credit contracts: businesses without 'sufficient' collateral will not be able to access bank finance for many types of investment loans, and even for short-term working capital lines of credit.[1]

Conventional wisdom would suggest that these firms are excluded from financial sector contracts because they are asset-poor. But this is not true: most businesses have a wide array of assets at their disposal, assets that in many countries would be considered excellent sources of collateral. In certain countries it is only because the legal framework governing movable property precludes these assets from being used productively in loan contracts: in other words these assets are 'dead capital'.[2]

The main objective of the chapter is to build a greater understanding of the role of firms' assets in accessing formal financial markets. I use data collected on firms from across the world, and highlight their experience with access to financial contracts. I relate these experiences to the level and type of assets these firms hold. Additionally, I look at the varying impact of

---

[1] In this chapter, I examine only the role of collateral in credit contracts for enterprises, for the purpose of either working capital or investment requirements. However, many of the points made in this chapter would largely apply to consumer/retail loans as well. Similarly, the analysis is limited to bank credit because we only have data on collateral requirements for bank loans. The importance of non-bank lenders, however, is not underestimated.

[2] Hernando de Soto's famous characterization, set out in De Soto, Hernando (2003), *The Mystery of Capital: Why Capitalism Triumphs in the West and Fails Everywhere Else*, New York: Basic Books.

collateral across different constituencies of firms. In particular, I examine how collateral requirements affect small and medium-sized firms (SMEs) and firms located in low-income countries.

The analysis suggests that firms do have valuable property, but in countries where laws on secured transactions (that is, the law governing the use of movable property as collateral) remain unreformed, these assets are unable to be exploited productively to secure formal finance. Additionally, I find that it is the small and medium-sized firms that are most affected, since SMEs hold the bulk of their capital in movable property rather than immovable property, which is what banks prefer and what unreformed legal framework often only permits to use as collateral.

4.2   WHAT THE DATA TELL US

The evidence provided in this chapter comes from the Enterprise Surveys database. The Enterprise Survey is a series of firm level surveys collected globally by the World Bank. The data-set used for this analysis covers five regions, 60 countries and approximately 53 000 firms. In addition to the five regions, the Survey also covers four OECD countries: Germany, Greece, Ireland and Spain. The Survey covers only registered firms, primarily from the manufacturing industry.[3]

The data show that firms located in most countries sampled perceive themselves as financially constrained. In fact, up to half of firms in the sample identify both access and cost of finance as a major or severe constraint for their firm (see Figure 4.1). However, enterprises located in low-income countries with poor financial systems are much more likely to complain about access than firms in higher income countries (see Figure 4.2). Furthermore, these figures likely underestimate the level of financial exclusion. This is because the firms sampled in the Enterprise Survey are registered and therefore part of the formal sector. Financial exclusion is likely to be considerably higher for unregistered or semi-formal firms.

In many low-income countries, bank credit is not widely used for either working capital or for investment purposes. Approximately 43 percent of firms have an overdraft facility or a line of credit, but this number is considerably lower for micro and small firms (see Figure 4.3) (for further developments on microfinance, see Engelhardt and Regitz, Chapter 6 and Holtmann, Chapter 7, this volume). In fact, on average, only 14 percent of

---

[3]   Additional information on the data-set, sampling methodology, and other firm characteristics can be found at www.enterprisesurveys.com.

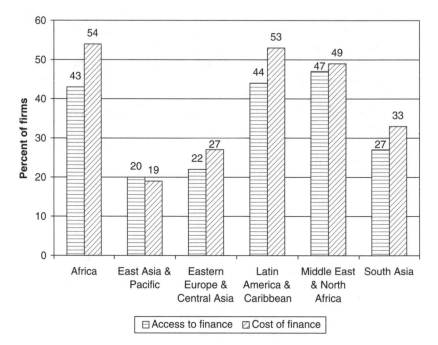

Figure 4.1   Finance is a major or very severe obstacle, by region

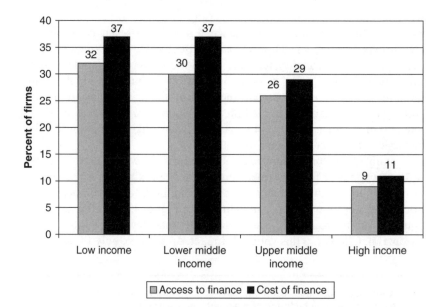

Figure 4.2   Finance is a major or very severe obstacle, by country income

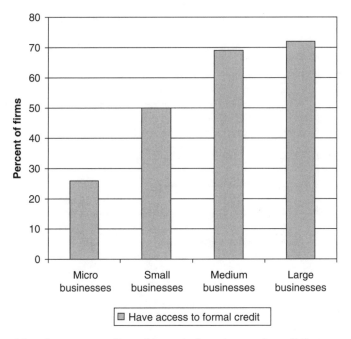

Figure 4.3   Access to credit problematic for micro and small firms

working capital finance comes from banks and 17 percent of investment finance is through commercial banks; the remainder comes from informal sources, retained earnings or non-bank lenders. Figure 4.4 highlights how firms are likely, instead, to finance both working capital and investment projects from retained earnings, informal sources (such as family, friends or moneylenders), or other non-bank creditors (such as trade creditors). Furthermore, it is micro and small firms which are the least likely to use bank credit.

4.3   ROLE OF COLLATERAL IN FINANCIAL CONTRACTS

Collateral plays an important role in financial contracts in countries around the world, and may explain, in part, some of the findings discussed above. The first point to note is that collateral is an integral part of most financial contracting. On average, close to 70 percent of loans require some form of collateral, depending on the region (see Figure 4.5). Furthermore, this number is increasing as country income declines. This is also true in

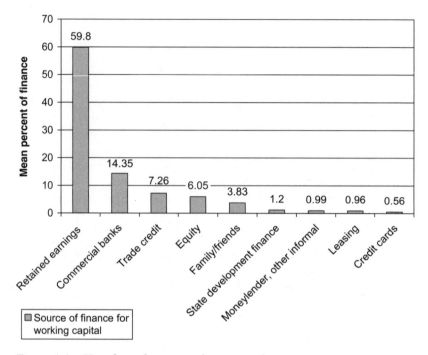

Figure 4.4   How firms finance working capital

countries with poorer legal systems: in these countries, only 20 percent of loans are offered as unsecured on average, while in countries with strong legal systems, 31 percent of loans are unsecured.[4]

Collateral requirements can also be high, relative to the size of the loan. In practice, this means that the value of collateral used to secure a loan contract can range up to 160 percent of the value of the loan (see Figure 4.5). While data on loan sizes is not available, collateral/loan size ratios for small firms are larger than for large firms (see Figure 4.6).

Furthermore, lack of collateral is an important factor in financial exclusion. Figures 4.7 and 4.8 illustrate this. Many firms do not have bank loans because their credit application was denied. In a large number of cases, credit applications were rejected by banks, and the main reason cited was

---

[4]   Countries with strong legal systems are defined as those countries in which firms consistently report having trust in the legal system to uphold and enforce property rights. Countries with weak legal systems are those countries in which most firms report lacking confidence in the court system to uphold property rights.

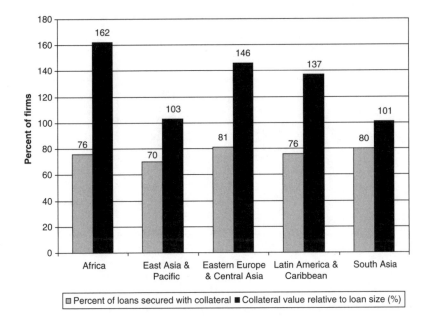

Figure 4.5   Role of collateral in financial contracts

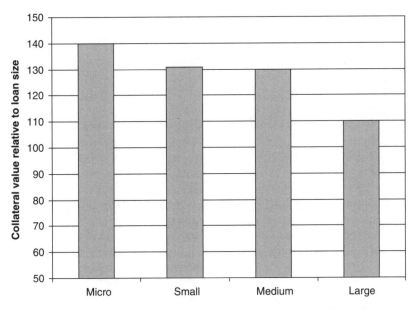

Figure 4.6   Micro and small firms pledge relatively more collateral

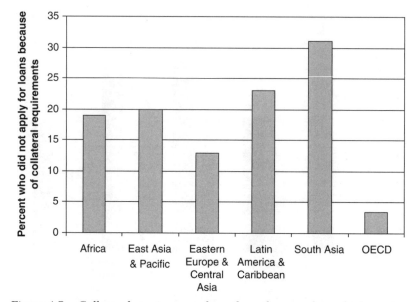

Figure 4.7   Collateral requirements keep firms from applying for loans in most countries

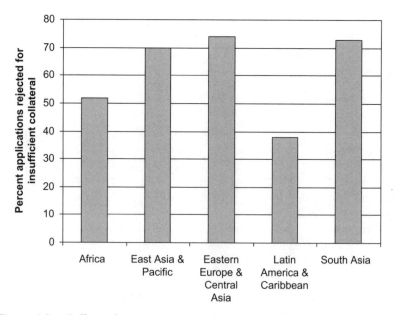

Figure 4.8   Collateral requirements are key reason why credit applications are rejected

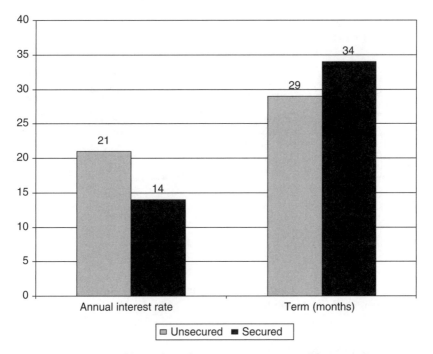

Figure 4.9   Secured loans have lower interest rates and longer terms

because firms have insufficient collateral to secure the loan. However, many firms never even apply for loans. A key deterrent is the collateral requirement to obtain loans. Across the globe, collateral keeps firms from entering the credit market, and thus accessing financial sources that could be used to increase investment or used productively as operating capital.

However, when firms do use collateral, they have better terms and conditions for their loan contracts.[5] Figure 4.9 illustrates this. When firms pledge collateral, they have access to loans with longer terms and with lower interest rates. On average, firms who secure loans with collateral receive a 33 percent lower interest rate (14 versus 21 percent). Additionally, firms with secured loans receive terms that are 18 percent longer (35 months versus 29 months). The upshot? Enterprises that are unable to secure credit

[5]   See Fleisig et al. for a discussion of bank loan terms and conditions for secured versus unsecured loans: Fleisig, Heywood, Mehnaz Safavian and Nuria de la Peña (2006), *Reforming Collateral Laws to Expand Access to Finance*, Washington, DC: copublication of the World Bank and International Finance Corporation.

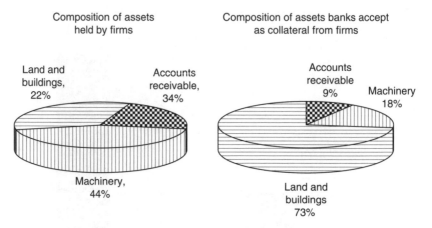

Figure 4.10   Assets held by firm / accepted by banks

lines and loans with collateral face higher costs and shorter loans than those firms that can secure loans.

4.4   DEAD CAPITAL

An important question regarding access to finance for firms is whether or not enterprises face financial exclusion because they do not have sufficient assets to secure loans. An analysis of firms' portfolio of assets points to a different story, however. The problem of financial exclusion is not a function of firms having insufficient assets. Rather the problem is that most banks do not accept the type of assets that firms hold. Figure 4.10 illustrates this mismatch between the type of assets firms hold, and the type of assets banks accept to secure a loan or a credit line. Firms in developing countries largely hold assets that are movable: on average 44 percent of their assets are in machinery and another 34 percent are in accounts receivable. On average, only 22 percent of total firm assets are in immovable property such as land and buildings.

This is in remarkable contrast to what banks accept as collateral. Over 70 percent of financial contracts are secured by immovable property, while less than 20 percent of loans are secured with various forms of movable property such as machinery and accounts receivable. On average, close to 80 percent of enterprise assets and property cannot be used to secure a loan or a line of credit. So, while most financial contracts do rely on collateral, the range of assets accepted as collateral is generally narrow. Most financial contracts require that collateral be immovable. Banks generally rely on land and buildings, either those belonging to the firm, or those that are the personal assets of the owner or manager. A much smaller percentage of loans are secured with machinery or intangible assets. This is a phenomenon I refer to as 'dead capital' – capital which cannot be used to leverage additional capital and resources for the firm.

4.5   IMPORTANCE OF REFORM

In countries where the legal system governing the use of collateral is unreformed, most of the assets that firms hold, especially movable property, cannot be used to secure loans. This is because many legal systems place unnecessary restrictions on creating collateral, leaving lenders unsure whether a loan agreement will be enforced by the courts. Where such restrictions mean that only agreements involving certain types of collateral (for example real estate or automobiles) will be enforced, only these assets can effectively serve as collateral for bank loans. Other property, such as machinery, equipment, livestock, accounts receivable, is worthless for this purpose.

But experience in countries that have undertaken reform shows how favorable the effects can be on the financial system. Reforming systems governing movable property transforms dead capital into productive capital. Reforming collateral systems creates a more stable financial sector environment. And, most importantly, reforming collateral systems not only increases access to finance for the private sector but can have a particularly strong effect on underserved segments of the private sector: micro, small and medium-size firms.

For example, in Albania reform happened in 2001, after a new law governing the use of movable property was passed and a pledge registry was set up. After the reform, the risk premium on lending fell by half, the interest rate spread by 43 percent, and the interest rate on lending by 5 percent. The pledge registry receives approximately 40 pledges per day on average, and the World Bank's Doing Business reports[6] ranks Albania fourth (among 154 countries) on the strength of the legal rights for borrowers and lenders.

Romania had a similar experience after it reformed its secured transactions law in 2000: the interest rate spread dropped by 6 percent and the interest rate on lending by 20 percent, while the number of borrowers

---

[6]   See www.doingbusiness.org.

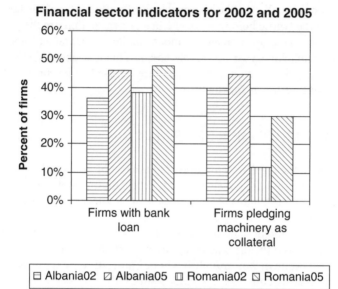

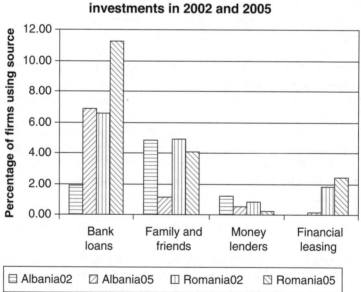

*Figure 4.11   Financial sector indicators and sources of finance for new
              investments in 2002, 2005*

increased by 30 percent.[7] A 2003 survey suggests that the Romanian registry system is in high demand, with at least 190 000 pledges registered annually (see also Lupulescu, Chapter 10, this volume).[8]

The situation for firms in Albania and Romania continued to improve between 2002 and 2005. More firms were able to borrow from banks, and the use of movable property as collateral continued to grow (see Figure 4.11). How firms financed investments also changed for the better. Firms relied increasingly on commercial sources of finance, such as bank loans and financial leases, and less on informal sources, such as family, friends or moneylenders.

4.6   CONCLUSION

Reforms to improve collateral regimes can be an important part of improving access to finance for the private sector. Businesses are not rationed out of credit markets because they lack enough assets to meet high collateral requirements of banks and other lenders. Instead, they are rationed out because the legal framework for collateral prevents them from using their assets to secure loans. Experience in Albania and Romania shows how reforms of collateral laws can improve firms' ability to finance their operations and investments, helping to generate economic growth and employment.

---

[7]   Chaves, Rodrigo, Nuria de la Peña and Heywood Fleisig (2004), *Secured Transactions Reform: Early Evidence from Romania*, CEAL Issues Brief, Washington, DC: *Center for the Economic Analysis of Law*.

[8]   European Bank for Reconstruction and Development survey of registries in the Balkans at www.ebrd.com/country/sector/law/st/core/pledge/core.htm.

5. Legal efficiency of secured transactions reform: bridging the gap between economic analysis and legal reasoning

Frederique Dahan and John Simpson

5.1 INTRODUCTION

The case for the importance of law and institutions to boost investment and access to credit does not have to be made. Other chapters in this volume have unambiguously demonstrated that secured transactions and creditors' rights are among the most influential measures. This need was acknowledged by the countries of Central and Eastern Europe and the former Soviet Union from the very beginning of the transition process. Since 1990 a huge effort has been made to transform their legal regimes. From the moment communism had collapsed it was urgent to introduce the changes that were necessary to develop modern market economies. The laws and institutions relating to commercial transactions (such as the laws of contracts, companies, property and insolvency) were hopelessly inadequate and economic reform had to be accompanied by major programmes for legal reform. Never before did so many legal systems have to change so much and in such a short period of time.

The European Bank for Reconstruction and Development (EBRD or the Bank) has engaged in many aspects of legal reform in the region. Its involvement in secured transactions reform began in 1992 and has continued every since. The objective of the Bank is to encourage countries to modernise their secured transactions laws[1] and it offers assistance at all stages of the reform process to achieve an effective legal framework for

---

[1] In this chapter we use the term 'secured transactions' to embrace all transactions such as pledge and mortgage where the principal aim is to give security over property, not in the more limited sense (as given in the US under Article 9 of the Uniform Commercial Code) of relating only to security over movables.

secured transactions, building a consensus for those reforms and then assisting in the preparation of necessary legislation and the implementation of the law. To a large extent, this call has been heard in Central and Eastern Europe. When the EBRD Secured Transactions Regional Survey was published in 1999[2] most countries in the region had undertaken reform on this part of their legal framework. By 2004, all of the countries had done so. Yet, the assessment of their regimes is not consistently positive. In fact, in some cases, despite what seem to have been considerable efforts, users are still denouncing restrictions or problems in the legal and institutional framework for secured transactions. Why?

In this chapter we look at two questions that constantly arise, and that we have been able to observe while engaged in this reform work:

1. How do you define the precise objectives of a law reform proposal and ensure that they are adhered to throughout the reform process?
2. How do you assess whether a law reform is successful?

To address the first question we will draw in particular on our experiences of what happens in the transition countries of Central and Eastern Europe when a secured transactions law is proposed. We do not have the space for detailed case studies and we seek rather to give a broad overview of how the reform process works (or fails to work) (but see Mathernová, Chapter 9 and Ancel, Chapter 12, this volume). Every reform project has its own list of successes and failures, and there is always scope for presenting critical analyses of specific cases. However, when one takes the time to look back at what has been achieved it is more constructive to do so in a sense of learning and building on past experience. Our intention is not to draw attention to past failings and mistakes but to look at the lessons that can be learnt from the experiences of the past 15 years. On the second question, surprisingly little has been done to develop methods for assessing whether a law reform is successful – or, to use other words, what makes a secured transactions system 'legally efficient'. We will describe the concept of 'legal efficiency' and explain how we use that as the basis both for establishing the objectives of reform and for evaluating the result.

Of course, both questions are linked. During the first part of this chapter we will often refer to 'efficient' laws, and in the second part we will put forward the criteria that may be used to determine what makes a law 'efficient'. The primary reason for introducing a secured transactions law is

---

[2] See in particular EBRD (2000), *Law in Transition* (Autumn), 'Special focus on secured transactions', available at www.ebrd.com/pubs/legal/lit002.htm.

economic. Secured transactions are encouraged because of the economic benefits that can be derived from them and the law is needed first and foremost to enable those economic benefits to be maximised. In spite of all the progress in collateral reform in recent years there has been a failure to create a coherent and constructive connection between the economic and the legal fundamentals, and it is this issue that we will try to address.

5.2   PROCESS OF LAW REFORM

The typical law reform can be divided into four stages:

1.   consultation and decision to reform;
2.   designing and passing of legislation;
3.   establishing the necessary institutions and implementing mechanisms;
4.   bringing the law into force.

Although these stages are interdependent, it is our experience that as the process develops the focus tends to become hazy, with the objectives somehow becoming lost and the gap between the economic and the legal analysis widening, sometimes alarmingly.

5.2.1   Decision to Reform

There has to be agreement at a political level that a new law is needed.[3] In the case of secured transactions this is likely to be based on a belief that a modern legal framework will boost the availability of credit and investment. The decision to reform should be taken because of the perceived benefits to the economy. If a Finance Ministry agrees to include a secured transactions law in the legislative programme mainly in order to placate a persistent international financial institution or other external influential organisation, the reform will be off to a bad start. There is a need for a broad consensus on the reasons for introducing the reform and what it is aiming to achieve (see Fleisig, Chapter 3, this volume). The breadth and depth of the decision-making process will often be critical for the reform's subsequent phases.

---

[3]   This does not exclude that the reform initiative may have come initially from the users and other stakeholders before being relayed to the executive (typically the government) or the legislative (Parliament).

Usually one ministry or other agency (for example central bank) will assume the task of developing the reform proposal. The approach at this stage can vary greatly. Sometimes it is limited to taking the necessary steps to obtain a government decision to adopt the proposal in principle and to put the requisite legislation on the parliamentary agenda. But much more can be done to put the reform on the right track and to increase the chances of a successful outcome. As with any project, early preparation and management is likely to be well rewarded. An understanding is required of the issues involved in the reform, the options that will be faced and the possible broader implications of what is proposed. Providing information to and seeking support from other ministries and organisations who may be involved is more than just part of the normal political process: it greatly facilitates subsequent work on transforming the proposal into reality.

The Ministry of Justice and other sectors of the legal community may merit special attention. Legal conservatism and a protectionist attitude towards 'legal traditions' can, if not appropriately managed, become major obstacles to successful reform (see Mathernová, Chapter 9 and Ancel, Chapter 12, this volume). Also, at this stage, external support and technical assistance may be sought but it is essential to understand that this assistance is precisely only technical: it cannot substitute for what is primarily a policy and political decision.

The most important outcome of this stage should be a broad consensus on what is to be achieved and the reasons for wanting to do so. Our experience is that a spineless reform project is unlikely to get strengthened at a later stage. A strong consensus at the outset on all of the key aspects of the reform will provide a powerful force for subsequently surmounting the many difficulties that will inevitably arise as the reform proposal proceeds.

5.2.2   Designing and Passing Legislation

Law reform is not just about writing and adopting laws – the other stages are equally important. But the process of preparing the necessary legal texts and steering them through the adoption process is often a lengthy and complex task, and if it is badly managed the whole reform may be jeopardised. The outcome of this stage should be a law or legal provisions that enable the desired reform to be implemented efficiently. We look later at how 'efficiency' can be gauged, but here it is appropriate to look at some of the factors that may impede this stage of the law reform process.

Losing sight of the objective
The lead players for preparing the legislation will most often be lawyers because drafting laws is essentially a legal role. If the decision-making

process has been well prepared, the economic objectives of the future law should be well analysed and presented. However that may not be enough to ensure that the legal drafting team fully understand the economic objectives and actively assess the draft they produce against economic criteria. The Ministry of Finance or Economic Affairs or the central bank, or any other 'champion' of the reform, needs not only to remain involved but continually to monitor the drafts that are produced against the economic rationale for the reform. Players from the financial markets can usefully be consulted (but see comments under market resistance below). Secured transactions may not be rocket science, but there are a number of details which, if not properly understood, could steer the reform off track. Without good management of the drafting process, the law presented is likely to fare badly when assessed against the legal efficiency criteria that we discuss below.

Legal conservatism

The drafting of legislation is a difficult skill to acquire which is not given to just any lawyer who is practised in drafting the legal documents required by his clients. It requires a deep understanding of the purpose of the law, an ability to visualise the effect that the draft law may have on the existing body of laws and, most importantly, a capacity to relate the law proposed to existing and future market practice. It is this capacity to perceive the way in which the law will support (or fail to support) market transactions that is especially important, and also quite rare. It should be possible to develop the requisite qualities within the drafting team, but the same cannot necessarily be expected for other lawyers who are consulted or who express views on the draft. Lawyers from their very training are likely to view with suspicion any departure from existing legal rules. The protection of legal tradition and the integrity of the legal system are to be encouraged but they have to be balanced against the need of markets to move forward. Regrettably it happens all too frequently that the lawyers who contribute to the legislative debate make little attempt to achieve that balance, and indeed often have little understanding of the economic objectives of the law.

Market resistance

It sometimes comes as a surprise that resistance to the introduction of an efficient secured transactions law comes from the persons who could be expected to derive the most benefit from it. Banks, lenders and other creditors who give input at the drafting stage will not always be favourably disposed to the reform, or to some of the features that are precisely designed to make it efficient. They may require some persuading that from their perspective the proposed changes will be preferable to the existing market practice. The lure of increased credit activity may be tempered by fears of increased competition and lower margins. The problem may be compounded if the persons giving input are not the managers who are capable of understanding the broad economic picture, but representatives from the legal department who are more concerned at how to document a transaction than its justification in a wider context. Even bankers may not understand all the reasons underpinning the reform. In one country recently, provisions in the draft pledge law designed to facilitate taking security for syndicated loans were struck out because of opposition from bankers who did not understand what a syndicated loan was, or assumed that it was undesirable or unnecessary in the local market.

The solution, however, is not to restrict consultation, rather to adapt the way in which it is carried out. If economists, bankers and investors, especially those who have been exposed to modern market practices, are not given a guardian role in the reform at the drafting stage it will be all the more difficult to keep the implementation on track later on. The fact that the banking sector in Central and Eastern Europe has seen a large strategic participation of foreign investors should facilitate the introduction of modern market practices. Paradoxically, because the domestic markets in many Western European countries have been protected from external influences and thus slow to introduce modern techniques (see Ancel, Chapter 12, this volume), resistance can sometimes come from those foreign dominated banks who do not understand why the transition country should need a 'modern' secured transactions law and prefer to see replicated the system they are used to in their home country.

Incompatibility of technical assistance and foreign input

In transition countries considerable technical support has been given for secured transactions law reform from national and supra-national providers of technical assistance (of which EBRD is one). Although much of that assistance has been efficient and has contributed to the success of reform, it has also to be admitted that the nature of the assistance and the way it is provided sometimes falls short of what could be expected. The role of the technical assistance provider is a delicate one. It is there to provide expertise, practical advice and guidance using experience of reforms elsewhere, and to ensure that the original objectives of the reform decision drive the process. It can also bring additional resources that would not otherwise be available. Its role is to assist, not to dictate or impose.

We put forward a few guidelines for assistance providers:

1. The drafting should be done by local lawyers. The law will have to fit
    into the existing legal framework and someone who is not from the
    jurisdiction, however knowledgeable, is ill-placed to draft it. It is also
    desirable that local lawyers acquire a full understanding of all the
    issues and accept responsibility for the draft. A home-grown product,
    as opposed to a foreign implant, will engender a sense of achievement
    and with that should come a greater commitment to defend it and to
    see it properly implemented over time. A very good example of this is
    found in Bulgaria, where the 1998 Pledge Law was developed by
    Bulgarian lawyers, who understood very well the objectives of the
    reform and are still actively following up on how the system is faring.
2. The temptation to import foreign law concepts should be resisted. In a
    civil law country you cannot, for example, introduce a trust by sleight
    of hand. It may take longer but the drafters have to understand fully
    each aspect of the result desired from the reform, and then work out
    how they can be achieved in the context of their own legal tradition and
    institutions. Foreign examples will certainly be a source of inspiration
    but will also be a source of confusion and inefficiency if imported
    without adaptation and reconstruction in order to fit to the local envi-
    ronment. Perhaps the worst sin is when assistance providers produce a
    draft in their own language substantially based on their own law and
    then present a translation of that draft as the law to be adopted. This
    caricature of technical assistance has for the most part now disap-
    peared in Central and Eastern Europe but unfortunately the negative
    effects can still be felt. In fairness to technical assistance providers, the
    fault does not always lie with them. In some instances, a ready made
    product is what the developing country will request and expect to be
    given.
3. Some understanding of the local legal tradition is essential. Ideally the
    assistance provider will mobilise experts who speak the local language
    and be well versed in the local law and practice. In practice that will not
    often be feasible but the assitance provider needs as a minimum to
    acquire a basic understanding of the approach of the local law and
    practice. Without that he will operate under a severe handicap.
4. The approach should be dispassionate and impartial. Once again the
    underlying philosophy is to encourage and support the local ownership
    of the project. The assistance provider is there to help develop a con-
    sensus on the reform objectives which is compatible with the original
    rationale and then to ensure that those objectives are translated into
    the legal system with maximum efficiency. The issues need to be pre-
    sented in a manner which is balanced and conducive to rational deci-
    sion. One of the more difficult aspects of the international expert's

work is to detach himself from his legal roots and to present legal issues objectively. Every lawyer is conditioned by his legal training and may tend sub-consciously to believe that his own law is superior, but that has to be resisted. It is sad to witness how often well-meaning lawyers working on law reform in transition countries press for solutions based on their own law, when with a little objective analysis it can be seen that the solution proposed is not appropriate for the local context or that other routes may just be as valid.[4]

Once finalised the draft law will pass through the parliamentary process. At this stage the drafting team needs to be vigilant to ensure that the draft does not fall victim to the uncertainties and excesses of the political process. (see de la Peña, Chapter 11, this volume). One of the greatest dangers is amendments made at this stage by politicians who have their own agenda which may have little to do with the issues covered by the law. However, if the draft has been well prepared, objectives are clear, consultation process wide, and the presentation is persuasive, the chances are that political battles will not interfere with the adoption of the law.

5.2.3 Establishing the Necessary Institutions

Institutions will be established to enable the new law to operate. In the case of a secured transactions law a registration or 'notice filing' system is needed (see Lupulescu, Chapter 10, this volume) and viable and efficient procedures have to be established to enable the security to be enforced. Often at this stage the people involved will change. Drafting a law is high profile, even more so if it involves amending the Civil Code, and may attract considerable high level interest. Setting up a pledge register is definitely not sexy work and may be left to administrators and IT experts. If they do not have a proper grasp of why the register is being established and the implications its use will have on market practice, there is a risk that inefficiencies will be introduced through superfluous or inappropriate requirements. The instinctive approach of a registrar towards pledge registration may be quite

---

4   When the secured transactions project was set up at EBRD in 1992 a policy was introduced that there should always be in the team at least one lawyer from a common law background and one from a civil law background. The transition countries are civil law based but much of modern financial practice is inspired by common law solutions. That policy has been conscientiously pursued ever since and it has had a certainly had a considerable influence on all EBRD's work in this field. If you have to discuss and agree issues across legal boundaries in-house, you are that much better prepared to adopt an open-minded approach when working in a local jurisdiction.

different to that intended by the law. If he is not properly briefed on the purpose and aims of the law he may, for example, build a title registration system modelled on a land register, which would definitely not be an efficient way of publicising pledges.

Similarly, enforcement procedures often lose sight of the fundamental objective in the context of secured transactions, which is of achieving a rapid sale of the assets given as security at a high price. There are many opportunities for creating overly bureaucratic public auction and other procedures, which provide 'protections' which are of little benefit to the debtor or creditor who are party to the enforcement. The gap between the economic analysis which underlay the original reform decision and the mindset of those developing the register or the enforcement procedures is sometimes alarmingly wide, especially when those responsible for the initial reform initiative have moved on to other things and fail to ensure effective follow through.

5.2.4 Bringing the Law into Force

Once the new law enters into force the task of making the new regime work in practice is entrusted to market players, institutional administrators and, in the final count, judges. How it works will be determined, to a large extent, by how the new regime is explained, and the support and guidance that is given to those to whom it is entrusted. Lawyers and bankers may be happier with the old system they were familiar with and slow to realise, or fearful of, the scope the reform gives for new deals. As with any new product, the way it is introduced into the market may be just as important as the quality of the product itself. But often those active in the reform process will have moved on to the next task and there are few resources available to analyse whether all the effort bears fruit. A common problem is the lack of a good understanding of the new law by those who will apply it at the moment when it is most needed: the courts. Unfortunately, it is rare for the judiciary to be closely involved in developing the reform from the outset. The danger is that the courts may then not grasp the effect (or intended effect) of the law and interpret it in a narrow or limitative way.

Much can be done to assist at this stage: education and awareness programmes, dissemination of promotional and explanatory material, training programmes, pioneer transactions sponsored by IFIs, and monitoring of the way the law is working (or not working) in practice against what was intended. The idea that the reform will be perfectly applied first time is a myth, especially in the fragile and fast-changing environment of a transition country. Reform is a continuing and gradual process and after any major step is taken, such as the introduction of a new law, careful monitoring is necessary to identify problems and find solutions. Inevitably the legal implementation of a law will not always correspond to the underlying economic rationale. If discrepancies are addressed rapidly solutions can most often be found relatively simply. If they are left to develop there is a danger that they can eventually jeopardise the success of the reform. In Poland the Pledge Law when introduced in 1996 was a good example of a modern pledge law but, in contrast to neighbouring countries that introduced similar laws, it has failed to deliver the expected benefits precisely because of the way it has been implemented.[5]

But, in order to be effective, the nature and purpose of the monitoring and evaluating task has to be clearly understood. It is not a policing task aimed at disciplining those that do not behave as intended, nor is it a kind of audit to enable the external assistance provider to verify the success of the project. It is more in the nature of an active after-sales service designed to ensure that the new product works, that its users derive maximum benefit from it, and that the economic benefits that were assumed from the reform indeed materialise. It requires encouragement and support from the reform's champion since it can only be successful when it is underwritten by a commitment to carry it through effectively. It also requires sound methodology and benchmarking, and this leads us to the second part of this chapter: the question on how a reform's success can be assessed.

5.3 ASSESSING THE SUCCESS OF REFORM: THE CONCEPT OF LEGAL EFFICIENCY

The process of reform is not an easy one. It is hampered in particular by an often inadequate analysis of what the reform is aiming to achieve, and a lack of clear directions to guide the work as it progresses. Government proposes a secured transactions law in order to facilitate access to credit. A team of local and foreign experts help the government prepare the necessary legislation, which is duly passed. A different set of government employees and external contractors establish a register or notice filing system and a public auction procedure. Everyone has done their job, the reform is complete, and yet the result in terms of facilitating access to credit may fall well short of what was intended. Or, as is most often the case, nobody has a clear idea of what the result of the reform actually is. What is missing are the constant and well-defined goals which determine the direction of the process and ensure that it leads to the desired result.

---

[5] See the EBRD Report (2005), *The Impact of the Legal Framework on the Secured Credit Market in Poland*, July, available at www.ebrd.com/st.

A lawyer who is drafting a pledge law or an administrator who is setting up a pledge registration system needs to be given a clear picture of the end objective, not just as a technical description of the law or register but also by way of indication of the ways in which it should actually facilitate access to credit. In this way he gains an understanding of the broader issues involved, including the economic function of the law, and will realise that the outside world will be judging the law or register with these in mind. In practice, surprisingly often that is not the case.

In order to address this gap we use the concept of legal efficiency. What do we mean by 'legal efficiency'? We use it as indicating the extent to which a law and the way it is used provide the benefits that it was intended to achieve. We look at the concept against the background of secured transactions law because we prefer to link it to our direct experience in transition countries, but we believe it is capable of much wider application.

As mentioned before, the prime purpose of a law regulating pledge or mortgage is economic, since the secured credit market has essentially an economic function (whilst recognising that it may also have important social functions and consequences); and it is essentially facilitative since a secured credit market is not a necessity, it being possible for any jurisdiction to function without it. We work on the premise that the basic legal framework should be *conducive* to a flexible market for secured credit. There are also social issues, for example relating to consumer credit and housing, but the driving force behind the introduction of a law on secured transactions is the benefits that it is expected to bring to the economy.

A relatively simple indicator of the success of a secured transactions law reform (or primary motive for undertaking the secured transactions law reform) would be the subsequent increase in the *volume* of secured lending. But that is a crude and narrow indicator, inadequate by itself. The intended function of the secured credit market may be more than just to boost the amount of credit granted against security. It may also include, for example, opening up credit to new sectors of society, encouraging new housing construction, or allowing privately funded infrastructure projects.

The intended function of a law has to be looked at within the context in which it is to operate. Its ramifications have to be considered not just in economic terms but in social and cultural terms as well. An appropriate balance has to be found between fulfilling the law's economic purpose and ensuring that the effects of the law are acceptable in context. The purpose of the reform needs to be carefully analysed and agreed at the outset, failing which the potential achievements of the law in terms of legal efficiency may be curtailed. It sometimes happens that the goals of the reform are not clearly defined, or that they are not perceived in the same way by all persons involved. That can be fatal to the subsequent implementation. Without

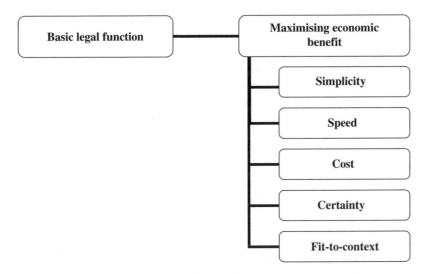

Figure 5.1   Criteria for legal efficiency of secured transactions law

well-defined and accepted goals there ceases to be unambiguous criteria against which the reform can be assessed. The boat is sailing with no sense of direction and it is unlikely it will reach port safely.

5.3.1   Legal Efficiency Criteria

We analyse legal efficiency by looking at the degree to which the legal framework enables secured transactions:

a. to achieve their basic legal function; and
b. to operate in a way which maximises economic benefit.

As shown in Figure 5.1, we break the second criterion into five separate headings: simplicity, speed, cost, certainty and fit-to-context.

Basic legal function
The basic legal function of a secured transactions law is to allow the creation of a security right over assets which, in the case of non-payment of a debt, entitles the creditor to have the assets realised and to have the proceeds applied towards satisfaction of his claim prior to claims of other creditors. If a secured transactions law only gives the creditor a personal right but no right in the assets, or if there is no right to enforcement, or no priority vis-à-vis other creditors, the law fails to achieve its basic legal function. An absolute priority for taxes and other state claims ahead of the secured

creditor, or the right in insolvency of ordinary creditors to share in a portion of the proceeds, are more than inefficiencies in the secured transactions law, they are defects which prevent it from fully achieving its basic function. They may be intentional (a superpriority of the state usually is) but they reflect a compromise between two laws with conflicting purposes. Any such compromise inevitably inhibits the effective operation of the secured transactions law and introduces uncertainty into the minds of lenders.

If the legal framework for secured transactions is to operate in a way which *maximises economic benefit*, the system for creation and enforcement of pledge or mortgage should be simple, fast and inexpensive, there should be certainty as to what the law is and how it is applied, and it should function in a manner which fits to the local context.

Simplicity

Simple does not mean simplistic: it is necessary to strike a balance between simplicity and the sophistication required by the market. In many countries complexities have developed and become entrenched over time as laws have been adapted to new circumstances, not because of the sophistication of these circumstances but rather from inherent limitations of the legal system. There exists in transition countries a huge opportunity to reduce down to the essential elements and to introduce laws which are directly adapted to modern market requirements. Part of simplicity comes from the lack of restrictions and barriers. If the law is to facilitate the use of secured credit it needs to provide a base which offers the necessary flexibility to adapt with the trends of the market.

Speed

For most aspects of the legal process, the less time it takes the more efficient it is. There are exceptions: a notice period or a cooling off period has to be of appropriate length, but for registration of a pledge or mortgage, for example, there can only be benefits if it takes only a few minutes rather than a month, and a lender who knows that enforcement of the pledge or mortgage is likely to take several years will derive less comfort from his security.

Cost

Legal costs almost inevitably have an adverse impact on the economic benefit of a transaction. Delay, complexity and uncertainty all tend to add to costs so there is a close relationship with the other aspects of legal efficiency. Some costs are, at least to an extent, within the control of the parties. Before taking legal advice on structuring a transaction the parties can assess the value of doing so. The cost of legal advice on a complicated transaction may be outweighed by the benefits, but the cost of legal advice incurred because of defects in the legal framework always reduces efficiency, as do fixed costs (for example registration, notary or court fees).

One does not have to be an economist to understand that if the legal procedures for creating and enforcing a pledge or mortgage are slow, expensive and complex the cost of secured credit will be higher and the economic benefit of using pledge or mortgage reduced. There are however two other elements that need to be taken into account when assessing legal efficiency. They are sometimes overlooked by economists because they are more difficult to translate into quantifiable indicators but they are critical to the success of a legal system.

Certainty

Certainty is a critical element of any sound legal system. A grain of uncertainty in the legal position can have a pervasive and disproportionate effect. Once a banker hears that there is some doubt in the legal robustness of a transaction, he will fast become hesitant. The difficulty is one of measurement. If the legal uncertainty relating to a pledge or mortgage could be stated, for example, as a 5 per cent chance of proceeds on enforcement being reduced, with the amount of the reduction being on average 20 per cent, the risk would be quantified and it would become easier to manage as there would be relative certainty. But in reality legal opinions cannot be expressed in that way. And the natural reaction to unquantifiable uncertainty is extreme caution. Transparency can often strengthen certainty: for instance easy access for all to information in the land register allows potential mortgage lenders to find out about the property and any other mortgages that may be claimed.

Fit-to-context

The 'fit-to-context' criterion is the most elusive but nonetheless important since it covers a number of facets. Simplicity, cost, speed and certainty are all concepts which are relatively easy to understand and to relate to economic benefit. The 'fit-to-context' concept however merits more explanation. It is not enough to adopt a law which establishes clearly and unambiguously a simple, fast and inexpensive regime for pledge or mortgage security. The efficient functioning of the law will also depend on whether it is adapted to the economic, social and legal context within which it is to operate. It needs, for example:

a.   to respond to the economic need: markets are constantly changing, and the law has to be able to adapt to new products, as for example when loans are proposed with flexible interest rates;

b.   to fit to the broader financial context within which the law operates; for example the rules applicable to transfers and pledges of secured loans should not hamper the use of mortgage-backed securities and covered bonds and the secured transactions law should take into account the way in which pledge is used for securitisation transactions involving unsecured loans and other assets;

c.   to fit with existing market practice: whereas much can be learned from other markets, a law has to be compatible with existing market and legal practice and to give confidence to those who rely on it;

d.   to achieve an appropriate balance between fulfilling the economic purpose and ensuring that the effects of the reform are acceptable in context; the rights of consumers and occupiers of property to appropriate protection cannot be eliminated to suit the economic needs of the secured transactions law, rather they have to be framed in a way which enables borrowers and lenders to derive the benefits afforded by a flourishing secured credit market, while at the same time ensuring the necessary protections to persons in a vulnerable position;

e.   to achieve particular objectives of the law; for example, the law may aim to extend secured lending to a wide range of banks as opposed to creating a lending cartel, or to reduce constraints on the types of pledge and mortgage product that can be offered.

5.3.2   Legal Efficiency and the Functional Approach

An issue which can be used to illustrate the importance of the fit to context criterion is the functional approach to security interests over movable property. This was originally introduced under Article 9 of the Uniform Commercial Code in the US. During the first half of the twentieth century there had developed a vast range of different rules and practices in the US that were applied for securing claims using movable property. In an attempt to introduce some order into what had become a somewhat chaotic and highly complex field of law, Article 9 provided for a unique set of rules, governing creation, notice filing, priority and enforcement, for *all transactions* whose function was to create a security interest in movable assets. Those rules apply irrespective of the form of the agreement between the parties if the substance of the transaction is to create a security interest. For example, an agreement between a buyer and seller of goods for title in the goods only to pass to the buyer upon full payment for the goods would not be effective as such, but would create a security interest over the goods with title passing to the buyer and the seller having a pledge in the goods.

In the context of the US in the 1950s the functional approach under Article 9 no doubt met the fit-to-context criterion. It was a key to providing a cure to the defects of the system that had prevailed until then and the sophisticated American market was able to understand it and apply it. But in the very different context of transition countries the functional approach may be assessed otherwise. They have a lack, rather than a surfeit, of devices and practices for taking security. The introduction of a sophisticated concept of definition by reference to substance not form, and the recharacterisation of transactions that can result, does not fit easily with a civil law system and brings with it unnecessary complexity and uncertainty. Western European countries do not have a functional approach: England has recently rejected the proposal that such system would be of benefit. Retention of title and financial leasing, fixed and floating charges, for example, are used extensively. A country from Central or Eastern Europe thus needs to reflect carefully before adopting an approach which would bring considerable complexity and would touch on fundamental elements of its legal system such as freedom of contract[6] and ownership rights,[7] whilst being diametrically different from the approach in operation of its neighbours.

A few transition countries have adopted a functional approach (for example Albania, Kosovo and Montenegro). No clear assessment has been made of the effect but anecdotal evidence suggests that the meaning of the relevant provisions has not been understood and that they are largely ignored in practice.

5.3.3   Measuring Legal Efficiency

Legal efficiency is thus relevant both when defining the general and detailed objectives for the reform and when subsequently measuring what has been achieved. A basic assessment whether a law maximises economic benefit may appear relatively simple. If the law enables a pledge or mortgage to be taken, and if necessary enforced, simply, quickly and cheaply the cost of security by way of pledge or mortgage is minimised and the benefit of the security is maximised. But as we showed above, there are broader aspects that also have to be taken into account. Legal inefficiency may not merely reduce the economic benefit that might otherwise result from the law (for example a lower interest rate for a secured loan compared to that of an

---

[6]   A contract for a financial lease or a credit sale or retention of title would be recharacterised as a pledge.

[7]   An agreement with purports to govern transfer of ownership would have the same effect of creating a pledge.

unsecured loan), it may also have a dissuasive effect. This is particularly pertinent to factors where the economic impact is difficult to measure. If the legal process is complex or takes a long time, or if there is uncertainty, potential players may never pass the decision threshold, and not proceed with the transaction at all. And if a few people take that line the impact may be multiplied as their conduct influences others.

Measuring legal efficiency is clearly challenging and any attempt to develop an accurate scientific basis is unlikely to be convincing. However, a close examination of a legal system against the legal efficiency criteria listed above can provide indicators of how efficient the system is. EBRD has done this for mortgage law in transition countries and it gives an interesting comparative insight into the strengths and weaknesses of existing legal regimes.

5.4   CONCLUSION

In most transition countries the basic reforms of the legal regimes for pledge and mortgage are well advanced, but there remains much work to do to assess those regimes and to fine-tune them to ensure that secured credit markets are supported by laws that are appropriate and conducive to the operation of the market for the mutual benefit of lenders and borrowers. We believe that the failure to define the general and detailed objectives of a reform and subsequently to measure what has been achieved against those objectives often prevents emerging markets from realising the advantages they should derive from legal reform programmes. The use of legal efficiency criteria provides a basis for bridging the gap between economic analysis and legal reasoning.

---

[8]   See Simpson and Dahan, Chapter 8, this volume and EBRD Publication *Mortgages in Transition Economies* (2007), available at www.ebrd.com/pubs/legal/mit.htm.

PART 3

Taking security in practice: microfinance and mortgage

6. The state of nature and lending in an unreformed environment: experience from early transition countries

Thomas Engelhardt and Benjamin Regitz

If a covenant be made, wherein neither of the parties perform presently, but trust one another; in the condition of mere nature, which is a condition of war of every man against every man, upon any reasonable suspicion, it is void: but if there be a common power set over them both, with right and force sufficient to compel performance, it is not void. For he that performeth first, has no assurance the other will perform after; because the bonds of words are too weak to bridle men's ambition, avarice, anger, and other passions, without fear of some coercive power; which in the condition of mere nature, where all men are equal, and judges of the justness of their own fears, cannot possibly be supposed. And therefore he which performeth first, does but betray himself to his enemy; contrary to the right, he can never abandon, of defending his life, and means of living.

Thomas Hobbes, *Leviathan*[1]

6.1 INTRODUCTION

This chapter analyses the conditions for lending in an 'unreformed' environment. If, as the evidence provided in other parts of this book suggests, the legal regime matters for the efficiency of financial sectors, what are the choices for someone doing business in a less-than-perfect regime?

Our contribution is based on practical experience from operating the Micro Finance Bank of Azerbaijan (MFBA).[2] After laying out a theoretical

---

[1] Hobbes, T. ([1651] 1955), *Leviathan*, M. Oakeshott (ed), Oxford: Basil Blackwell.
[2] MFBA was set up in 2002 as the country's first commercial bank focusing on microfinance, and has since become the leading provider of financial services for micro and small businesses in Azerbaijan. MFBA is owned by a group of IFIs and its strategic partner Access Microfinance Holding AG, and is managed by LFS Financial Systems. For information see www.mfba.az.

framework provided in Anthony T. Kronman's article 'Contract law and the state of nature'[3] and its interpretation of Thomas Hobbes' ideas, we will discuss important specifics of the microfinance target group and derive key implications and principles for lending in such a setting. Against this background, we will detail a practical enforcement mechanism for lending purposes within Kronman's theoretical concept for reducing transactional insecurity in the 'state of nature'.

We highlight the importance of understanding the fundamentals of borrowers' businesses, the significance of transaction costs, the necessity of intertwined enforcement incentives and the relevance of demonstration effects.

6.2   HOBBES, KRONMAN AND THE STATE OF NATURE

Kronman calls the state 'an enforcement machine'. The state's coercive powers establish the law of contracts as a valuable and important institution for contracting parties. The absence of this 'enforcement machine', in turn, can be referred to as a 'state of nature', scrutinized not only by philosophers like Hobbes but also by economists and lawyers.

In our understanding, the 'state of nature' does not necessarily presume nonexistence of government but can also describe an inadequate 'enforcement machine'. A state, such as the transition country Azerbaijan, may not be an efficient, fully functioning machine guaranteeing proper contract enforcement. What are the consequences for a lender who faces such a 'defect'?

Kronman follows Hobbes' differentiation between 'vulnerability of possession' and 'transactional insecurity'. While the former highlights that possession may be subject to expropriation, the latter refers to the danger that one party may breach an agreed exchange after the other party already delivered. Kronman more narrowly defines the 'state of nature' solely as 'transactional insecurity' because (a) 'transactional insecurity' is more difficult to overcome than 'vulnerability of possession' and (b) 'transactional insecurity' is more practically relevant in the context of a loan. Kronman's definition of the 'state of nature' is very useful because it allows isolating the transactional difficulties of extending credit in an unreformed transition environment.

---

[3]   Kronman, Anthony T. (1985), 'Contract law and the state of nature', *Journal of Law, Economics, and Organization*, **1** (1), 5–32.

But why does transactional insecurity exist? Two phenomena have been widely discussed both scientifically and from a practitioner's stance: adverse selection and moral hazard (see Fleisig, Chapter 3, this volume). Adverse selection has been most prominently studied in Akerlof's 'Market for lemons'.[4] In short: sellers of defective used cars, that is, the lemons, will drive sellers of good used cars, the cherries, out of business. For buyers, lemons and cherries look alike; but they will pay only the lower price for a lemon unless an inspection is done. Similarly, a lender would price loans for lemons, that is, bad risks, and lose the cherries, the good risks, for unfavourable loan conditions unless information deficiencies can be overcome. Further, if a transaction takes place, it is still subject to moral hazard. Even if one party made a promise under perfect information, it would deviate from the promise as incentives may change once the other party completed its part of a transaction.

While in this chapter we usually speak from the perspective of the lender, in particular a hopefully good and reliable microfinance bank, the borrower in a transition economy faces uncertainty about the lender in many regards as well, for example bribes, appropriation of collateral, bank failure, etc. As a result, many businessmen are extremely reluctant to work with a bank. This holds true not only for depositing own funds, but also for taking out a loan. Consequently, a lender does not only need to protect its interests against those of the borrower, it must also and foremost convince the borrower that taking a loan will be beneficial.

6.3   MEANING OF UNREFORMED ENVIRONMENT

Kronman's article was written with a view to a developed economy where a failure of the 'enforcement machine' may be the exception rather than the rule. But what are the specific characteristics of an unreformed environment in a transition country like Azerbaijan? Is it just that everything is a bit worse, that people and banks are a bit more inclined to cheat each other? Or are there specific regulative problems or other circumstances which make lending difficult?

---

4   Akerlof, George A. (1970), 'The market for "lemons": quality uncertainty and the market mechanism', *Quarterly Journal of Economics*, **84** (3), 488–500.

6.3.1   Vulnerability of Possession

To find an answer, we have to go back to Hobbes and the 'vulnerability of possession'. Contrary to the condition in a developed market, in a transition economy like Azerbaijan it may well be that possession is not safe, especially not safe over time. Examples of this vulnerability are arbitrary state decisions and unfair competition. In many businesses and sectors, one has to be aware that the state may introduce new adverse regulations or makes decisions against individual businesses. Such acts cannot always be explained by ambition for common welfare, but are rather due to particular interests of state representatives. In Azerbaijan, protection of such interests is very widespread. Often competition is suppressed, be it through arbitrary tax and customs practises or use of government and state enterprise spending, that is, using state power to give unfair advantages to own or related businesses. Furthermore, 'problems' for competitors can be deliberately created by using state authority to produce unfair disadvantages for competitors. Such discrete state influence is a major problem for the development of domestic industries, aggravated by classical Dutch disease symptoms caused by the Azerbaijani oil wealth.[5]

This description should not be understood as a one-sided accusation of the state and its representatives as being tyrannical and corrupt. Reality is much more complicated. In many cases, privatization and accumulation of wealth has been achieved through bending rules or by benefiting from a regulatory and administrative vacuum, especially in the early years of transition. Obviously, these fortunes are vulnerable to expropriation.[6] For example, buildings or businesses are not or only incompletely registered. It is understandable that the state wants to arrange and document rights in an orderly fashion, while at the same time one can understand the businessman who complains about having to bribe the official not to interfere.

The risk of 'loss of possession' in such an environment is thus much higher than in a more orderly one, say a developed economy. Accordingly,

---

[5]   First used with regard to the economy of the Netherlands in the 1970s, the term Dutch disease refers to the problems of an economy rich in natural resources, where the booming of one economic sector (here: the oil sector) leads to a general increase in profit margins and interest rates, which in turn negatively affects other economic sectors which have to produce at similar margins. For a country like Azerbaijan an additional side-effect of the oil-related influx of foreign exchange is that it reduces reform pressures.

[6]   The events and worldwide discussions around some of the Russian 'oligarchs' are prominent examples of assets accumulated in such ways.

we deal not just with the transactional insecurity of adverse selection and moral hazard but also with a higher 'real' business risk.

This risk is further aggravated by the general volatility of a transition economy. Most businesses are just a few years old. Political, macroeconomic and sectoral stability is relative at best, even without any of the 'unfair' intervention described.

The result of all the above is higher risk. And as we know, higher risk translates into higher margins, or, more severely, in transactions not taking place.

6.3.2 Occurrences of the 'State of Nature'

A second characteristic of an 'unreformed' environment is the wider scene of the 'state of nature'. The state is not able to be an 'enforcement machine'; occurrences of the 'state of nature' dominate. This inability can take various forms: lack, inadequacy or abundance of regulation.

Absence of adequate collateral regulations

In economic and political transition, many laws are not yet adequate to the needs of modern banking, which we will illustrate with a few examples. One of the most striking problems in Azerbaijan is the absence of regulations for pledging unfinished buildings (see Simpson and Dahan, Chapter 8, this volume). Ownership documents for real estate are only issued after the completion of construction work. As a result, traditional construction financing is impossible. In spite of a construction boom in the Azerbaijani capital of Baku, banks can only provide financing and participate in this sector if the borrower provides other collateral not connected to the construction object. In this situation, transactions do not take place although, in principle, they would be profitable for both lender and borrower.

Secondly, registration of finished buildings is generally very expensive. This is true for official charges but more severely for unofficial 'side costs'. Many individuals do not fully register homes or other real estate. Accordingly, they cannot mortgage such property to a bank, unless they complete registration first. As potential borrowers perceive there is little other benefit from registering real estate, registration is seen as a cost of borrowing and can be prohibitive in many cases.

A third example: collateral regulation in Azerbaijan lacks the legal instrument of the land charge (see Simpson and Dahan, Chapter 8, this volume), a mortgage not connected to a specific claim or loan. As a result, borrowers have to repeat cumbersome registration procedures for each single loan given by a bank. Costs in terms of time and money are substantial.

Finally, a central register for mortgage over nonresidential real estate is not kept. While some official procedures exist in this regard, a bank cannot completely be sure that the property of concern is not already mortgaged to another bank. Consequently, the bank will be more reluctant to accept such collateral.

High transaction costs

Apart from outright absence of regulations, a 'state of nature' occurs when the procedures prescribed by the state are too expensive, lengthy or lack transparency. This refers to collateral registration as much as to contract enforcement in case of default.

Long procedures and widespread corruption make registration of security over real estate and vehicles time-consuming and costly. Although state fees have been reduced from 6 per cent of the evaluation price in 1998 to much lower levels today, state organs as well as notaries still levy informal extra charges. For small loan amounts, registration fees are prohibitive in most cases. By failing to control its own agents and employees, the state fails to provide the means to contract security at an acceptable price.

Post-contractual security is best provided by clear and swift state enforcement rules. But again, a combination of long and complicated procedures, especially for court decision enforcement under corrupt court officials, bailiffs, and auctioneers, make enforcement a very lengthy and possibly endless process, if the borrower does not co-operate.

Informality of business

The Azeri economic 'state of nature' is most obviously observed in its informality. The country's economy is characterized by an extremely high share of unrecorded transactions. Hardly any small business reports more than 5 per cent of its real business assets and activities in financial statements. Many businesses, especially those that operate on large bazaars, are not registered at all, mostly for tax evasion reasons. Quite often, the real business owner uses a nominee as a front man for running the business. Motives range from profiting by using a member of a tax-privileged group, such as a war veteran, refugee or disabled, to simply avoiding visibility of the real owner, possibly a state official who is not formally allowed to run a business.

These circumstances do not only worsen moral hazard problems (or increase loan analysis costs, seen from the lender's perspective) they also pose a risk of their own. If most businesses constantly violate state regulations in one area or another, they are quite vulnerable for adverse changes in their business environment, be it through improved state control or due to pressure from state officials seeking private gains.

BOX 6.1 IMPORTANT CHARACTERISTICS OF AN UNREFORMED ENVIRONMENT

- Collateral regulations are inadequate. The collateral law lacks provisions for important ways to create, register and enforce a pledge.
- Fees, bribes and lengthy procedures considerably increase transaction costs.
- Almost all businesses operate informally and violate state regulations.

Finally, the nature of micro and small businesses, the core target clients of a microfinance bank, raises a specific problem. Most businesses are only partly registered, and practically none of them have meaningful financial statements. It becomes a severe problem of its own right to identify what the prospective borrower actually possesses. Obviously this in turn enhances the problems of both adverse selection and moral hazard. We will come back to the importance of business analysis further below.

6.3.3 Target Group Specifics for Microfinance Banks

There are a few specific features of the target group of a microfinance bank or programme which make lending even more difficult. The strategic client focus of a microfinance bank is on micro and small businesses.[7] Accordingly, the following refers to this client group, even though mature institutions will also serve medium-sized and even corporate enterprises as clients grow.

Small transaction size
The first target group characteristic to name is the small size of each individual transaction, which makes transaction costs for both sides the

---

[7] While exact definitions of micro, small, medium and corporate businesses in terms of size in assets, turnover and staff vary among countries and stakeholders, we refer to the intertwined structure of business and owner household for differentiation purposes, which is a common reality in transition and developing economies. Generally, all micro and most small businesses are strongly characterized by such an interdependent structure while medium businesses rarely and corporates never show this attribute in our understanding.

decisive factor: in the Micro Finance Bank of Azerbaijan, 96 per cent of all disbursed loans are for amounts below US$10 000; 90 per cent are below US$5000; and 34 per cent are even below US$1000.[8] The median loan amount is around US$1200. At a monthly interest rate of 3 per cent and a 1 per cent disbursement fee, the total gross income of the bank for a US$1000 loan with a maturity of six months and annuity repayments is around US$118. Obviously, the bank has to be quite efficient in analysing and administering this loan in order to be profitable.

From the borrower's point of view, US$118 is the financial cost for the loan. It is obvious how crucial it is whether or not he or she will have to pay an extra US$50 upfront for a notary, to spend US$10 for documented confirmation of his or her place of living, and – not least – whether or not it will be necessary to close the business for half a day to queue in the bank or in some registration office.

Absence of collateral

Another obstacle for many borrowers is the lack of traditional collateral. This is not only true for micro borrowers but also for owners of a small or medium-sized business in comparison to more developed economies. The main reasons are the relatively short period of capital accumulation since the change of economic system, and the lack of formal registration of real estate, as described above, and even cars. Vehicles are usually sold on the basis of a power of attorney, rather than by a formal change of ownership.

Balance of power

A positive aspect of the small size of client businesses is the relatively strong position of the bank in times of stress. Large businesses tend to be very well informed about legal tricks to prevent or delay loan enforcement and may even be able to influence court decisions by virtue of informal connections or payments. This is much less the case for micro borrowers, which gives an important advantage to a bank that deals with a large number of similar cases.

6.3.4   Key Implications and Principles

Asymmetrical distribution of information is the key problem

As can be easily seen, the asymmetrical distribution of information between the borrower and the lender is the key problem. While an efficient and proper state 'enforcement machine' may render informational security

---

8   Information as of 31 December 2007.

less crucial, the opposite is true in an unreformed environment (see Beck, Chapter 2, this volume). The central consequence for the lender is to place the highest priority on loan analysis and the appraisal of a client's business fundamentals. If the essential assumptions about capacity and willingness of the borrower to repay are not correct, no covenant in the loan agreement will do the trick.

In absence of registration documents and reliable financial statements, repayment capacity must be assessed by first-hand on-site gathering of data. That means the loan officer extensively works outside the bank, conducts a site visit to the borrower's business and place of living, counts, asks, compares and investigates. As a result, the loan officer compiles a simple balance sheet and cash flow account for the loan applicant. Especially in a country like Azerbaijan, such an assessment includes a detailed and obviously not easy analysis of the real ownership of the business. Put differently, the micro banker examines the economic and social dependencies of the borrower. All acquired information is reviewed from a risk point of view, evaluating the likelihood of changes and potential negative effects on the borrower's economic position.

After this exercise, the bank is reasonably sure of what is really going on in the business of concern. The maximum monthly instalment for the loan is then set as a percentage of the borrower's free cash flow after indispensable business and family expenses. The bank can assess the probability of a borrower's ability to repay this amount with a very high certainty. This is the advantage of dealing with great numbers of relatively simple and similar businesses.

In addition to and mostly in conjunction with the financial analysis, the loan officer performs a character check to assess the willingness to repay of a potential client. Analysis includes the honesty and openness in providing information to the bank as well as checking payment habits and general reliability with suppliers, customers and neighbours of the applicant. Obviously for repeat customers, credit history plays a central role in client reputation appraisal.

In summary, the bank's analysis must ensure that the disbursed loan is actually good for the borrower. It is in the bank's own interest that each client benefits from a loan, that he or she can and wants to repay under anticipated circumstances, that is, that the borrower understands and seeks the benefit of the loan and, therefore, sticks with the conditions of the loan contract.

The described loan appraisal approach considerably reduces asymmetrical information and avoids adverse selection in terms of repayment ability. Both the client and the bank usually get a cherry, not a lemon. Further, by anticipating willingness to repay, risks of moral hazard can now also be

---

**BOX 6.2   KEY PRINCIPLES FOR LENDING IN AN
                 UNREFORMED ENVIRONMENT**

- Reduce the information asymmetry between borrower and lender. Analyse all business fundamentals including ownership and cash flow first-hand.
- Minimize transaction costs for the borrower. Avoid useless paper requirements.
- Spend on demonstration effects to educate borrowers about expected behaviour. Be strict.

---

managed. But defining the future client relation including an enforcement mechanism is still important to prevent moral hazard. We will come back to this in section 6.4.

Transaction costs are the key 'battleground'
For small loan amounts, as has been illustrated above, transaction costs play a larger role than financial costs. The bank faces two central challenges in this area: it must make borrowing profitable for the borrower, and it must make lending profitable for the bank. Apart from efficient internal organization, which is not the subject of this chapter, there is one key answer to both tasks: the bank needs to minimize the borrower's cost, and especially that part of the cost which is not paid to the bank but to third parties or incurred as opportunity costs. In other words, the bank must very carefully weigh the additional informational security provided by an extra document against the cost for the borrower. We will provide only a few examples.

- Does the borrower have to fill out a long application form and provide a written business plan? Probably, the borrower will seek professional help to produce these papers, which then have little to do with reality. Would a borrower note in the business plan that his or her landlord is a minister and charges unfair rent? In consequence, such papers would cost the borrower around US$50, that is, more than 40 per cent of the financial cost of the example loan, and provide little additional information to the bank. Do not require a business plan!
- Does the borrower have to provide a recent proof of residency, issued by the local police officer? This document will cost about US$10, but give some security to the bank. Requiring a recent proof of residency depends on alternative methods to cross-check residency.

- Do pledges on movable assets need to be notarized? This will cost the borrower something in the range of US$20 and may give very little security to the bank. Such notarization is rather unnecessary, so unless legally required, it is preferable not to opt for notarization.
- Does a borrower need to insure a car pledged as collateral? The insurance premium is usually around 3 per cent of the insured value per annum. Yes, such a cover provides additional security to the bank. But if the bank knows from experience that only a very low percentage of clients actually get into an accident losing the car during the lifetime of the loan and, moreover, that in most cases such a loss does not lead to default, a car insurance contract may not be required.

The list could be extensively continued. What becomes obvious for the design of loan conditions and procedures is: the bank needs to see the loan deal with the eyes of the borrower. Each dollar stripped off the borrower's transaction cost makes a loan more attractive for more potential clients. And each dollar spent less on the loan makes a repeat loan more attractive and, hence, is an incentive to repay on time.

From the bank's point of view, reducing cost appropriated by third parties through fees and bribes and reducing costs that are simply lost, that is, the time spent for obtaining the loan, also means that the bank can charge a higher price. A relatively high interest rate is needed to cover the bank's administrative costs.

Let us return to the US$1000 sample loan once more: the difference between a 2 per cent and a 3 per cent monthly interest amounts to about US$36, unsurprisingly one-third of total financial costs. For the borrower, just dropping the requirement of a business plan will more than outweigh this interest step. Obviously the bank would much rather earn one-third more than have the borrower pay this amount to a business plan writing agency.

Demonstration effects are the bank's key advantage
Besides the proper design of the loan product, the bank has to use all advantages from the high number of similar transactions. This refers foremost to the efficiency of internal organization, which is not discussed here. But furthermore, the bank can determine the meaning of 'normal behaviour'. Why does one see thriving microfinance programmes with less than 1 per cent portfolio at risk side-by-side with corrupted, often state- or donor-financed programmes that have 60 per cent default rates? Is it because they choose different clients? To a large extent not: most people are not good or bad per se but behave according to the situation and incentives.

Designing the right product and preventing corruption is one aspect of good practice. But equally important is a prompt and strict reaction in case of default. Loan portfolio information is checked on a daily basis. If a borrower fails to meet his or her payment terms, the loan officer visits the client the very same evening. Loan officers will be quite insistent in finding out the reasons for default and in demanding remedy. We will go into further detail on monitoring in section 6.4.

Looking at this one transaction only, the bank seems very irrational. Why spend so much money only to run after a US$185 loan instalment that will most probably be paid in a few days anyway? The answer is the demonstration effect on the thousands of other clients who will most definitely get to know about this procedure. Accordingly, the bank can educate clients (or inform them if you want) on expected behaviour, on the rules of the game. The high number of transactions will allow the bank to make great efforts and incur large costs for one small case. This also refers to a real defaulter who is taken to court with the bank applying its entire machinery of lawyers to get the remaining US$200 of a US$1000 loan back. Is this sensible to do? Looking at an isolated case it is not; but for the overall business it is as this strictness demonstrates to each borrower that compliance is cheaper than default.

Word of mouth is the most important means of communication and the most trusted one in a country like Azerbaijan. If you succeed in implementing an image of 'these strange Germans: you don't need to know anyone in the bank and don't even have to pay a bribe and still you get a loan in one day; but if you are just one day late with a payment they go crazy', then your chances of building up a good and large micro loan portfolio are quite good.

6.4   ENFORCEMENT MECHANISMS

Let us turn to Kronman's article again. Assuming a 'state of nature', he characterizes four mechanisms or techniques which contract partners can use to reduce moral hazard. They involve (1) 'use of hostages'; (2) 'use of collateral'; (3) self-enforcing 'hands-tying'; and (4) encouraging a 'union'. We will use this very useful distinction to show the importance of intertwined enforcement mechanisms (see Figure 6.1).[9]

---

[9]   One will note that Kronman uses these four mechanisms to show how contractual partners overcome a 'state of nature' in absence of an enforcing authority. Earlier in this chapter, we have implicitly modified his definition by examining the state's role in guaranteeing the efficiency of these instruments; for example citing

Union with the bank

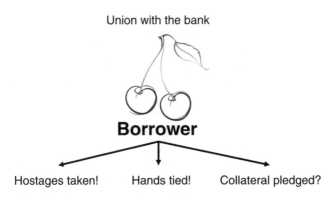

Borrower

Hostages taken!   Hands tied!   Collateral pledged?

Monitored by loan officer

Figure 6.1   Intertwined enforcement mechanisms

6.4.1   Taking Hostages

Kronman writes: 'I may insist that you give me a hostage to hold until your performance is completed. The hostage can be anything (or anyone) of value to you; knowing that I can destroy the hostage if you fail to perform, you have an incentive to keep your end of the bargain and I, knowing this, am made more secure'.

In lending, hostages play a very important role to us. As we have seen, for most borrowers, providing real collateral which the bank may be able to sell in case of default is not an option. Either clients do not have any and/or transaction costs are prohibitive. Microfinance banks, therefore, usually take a pledge on trading stock and on home equipment, such as furniture, TV sets, refrigerators, etc. They are quite strict in confiscating these items in case of default and put great effort into identifying ways to do so without going through legal procedures beforehand. This mechanism does clearly not aim at selling the items. Indeed, they rarely cover the cost of the loan. Most importantly, the borrower does not want to lose these items. The loss and the unpleasant circumstances in which confiscation takes place will be less acceptable than having to repay the loan, usually even in times of liquidity shortage. In this context, the importance of the cash flow analysis becomes obvious once more. Only if the bank is reasonably sure that the

lack of registration possibilities for certain types of collateral as an occurrence of the 'state of nature' in its own right. While there may be some definitional inaccuracy here, we believe the point is clear enough anyway.

borrower can repay if he/she wants it 'hard enough', it can apply the necessary pressure without losing the moral authority to do so. This is a big difference to reckless moneylenders who extend loans not based on the repayment capacity. Losing the moral authority would be disastrous because of the (deterring) demonstration effect it has on other borrowers.

As has been mentioned above, loan contracts and pledge contracts are usually prepared by a notary in Azerbaijan. This is, however, no legal requirement. For real estate and vehicles it is, and also has clear advantages for the bank. In MFBA we decided, against the general environment and strong reservations of our own lawyers, not to register contracts for hostage-type collateral with a notary. This choice saves each client an estimated US$10–20 and two hours per loan. It has not had any negative consequences for default rates and not even for obtaining court decisions in case of default. With 4500 loans disbursed every month, this means that a simple decision now saves our clients US$45–90 000 and around 1000 working days per month – truly substantial figures that explain how a microfinance bank can be competitive in spite of charging interest rates at the top-end of the market.

6.4.2   Use of Collateral

The term collateral, used throughout this chapter in a rather general meaning, Kronman also broadly defines as 'something that has direct exchange value'. In this case, the lender's interest is in the value of the pledged item. In spite of the registration difficulties described above, having a flat in central Baku which is mortgaged for a loan is of course a nice thing to have for a bank. This is the case especially because the borrower will usually place an additional 'hostage' value on top of the flat's market price. In practice, such collateral is not required for micro loans below US$10 000 thousand.[10] For larger loans disbursed to small and medium enterprises, the disadvantages, although still present, are less severe. First, such borrowers usually have gone through some period of wealth accumulation, that is, they are able to provide some collateral. Secondly, transaction costs tend to grow less than proportionally with loan size and, thus, become relatively less important than financial cost. Thirdly, if the borrower does possess the collateral and pledging costs are bearable, not demanding the collateral would send the wrong signal about the importance of the loan. Finally, we have identified a way to reduce

---

[10]   With increasing experience in the market and more and more repeat borrowers, such limits will increase.

effective cost and at the same time enhance borrower loyalty: instead of registering a mortgage on a specific loan, the collateral is registered under a multi-year credit line contract. For this contract, tranches are individually approved and disbursed, while a new registration of collateral is not necessary. This way, we are able to achieve the same results as when using a land charge (see above at 6.3.2).

6.4.3   Hands-tying

The third mechanism for reducing the insecurity of transactions Kronman 'calls "hands-tying"' – actions that make a promise more credible by putting it out of the promisor's power to breach without incurring costs he could otherwise have avoided'. In contrast to hostage-giving, which is a similar technique making breaching more costly to the promisor, hands-tying schemes make punishment self-executing.

An example of using a hands-tying scheme in lending is the requirement of one or more guarantors for obtaining a loan. In case a borrower defaults, not only his or her reputation is at risk but also the reputation of his or her guarantors. By knowingly agreeing to the bank's actions in case of default, the borrower is aware that non-compliance will be expensive in financial and social terms. The guarantor tied with the borrower in the loan agreement should from the bank's perspective always have an influence on the borrower, for example the father-in-law. The guarantor's financial position is of secondary concern. The reputational interests of such a guarantor are very likely to produce a 'home-made' enforcement mechanism as the guarantor will put active pressure on the borrower to repay.

Additionally, side-effects of a possible confiscation of hostage items are a hands-tying scheme to some degree in their own. Family members may be involved when the loan officer repossesses home equipment (and children usually dislike the idea of the TV set being taken away during their favourite show); neighbours will watch. Business partners will usually get to know that trading stock was confiscated. All unpleasant consequences from a loan agreement breach serve hands-tying ends and reduce moral hazard over the maturity of the transaction.

6.4.4   Encouraging a Union

Kronman's last but for our business most important mechanism is encouraging and creating a 'union'. 'The parties to an exchange . . . can reduce the risk of opportunism by taking steps to increase the likelihood that each will see his own self-interest as being internally connected to the welfare of the other'.

Here, the contract parties create common long-term interests that let them prefer compliance over default. In a broader sense, the entire lending technology, from analysis over collateral to monitoring, can be seen as an attempt to create 'union'. Everything is designed to make compliance cheaper or more profitable than default.

In a narrower sense, we use the term 'union' only for the positive incentives given. The key aspect is an implicit long-term relationship between bank and customer. Although micro loans are usually short-term, both parties know that the entrepreneur will have a constant need for financial services, especially loans. With each follow-up loan, the informational asymmetry is reduced and, accordingly, information and risk costs are smaller. This benefit is shared between bank and borrower by applying a graduation principle: borrowers with excellent repayment records are eligible for better loan conditions. Graduation advantages include longer maturities, higher loan amounts, quicker procedures and ultimately lower interest. The bank should strive to apply conditions which are better for both sides, that is, reduced transaction costs and lower risk, before including price reductions, as this obviously has a downside.

For the Micro Finance Bank of Azerbaijan, we have been very successful in this regard. More than 85 per cent of all first-time borrowers were granted a follow-up loan later. As eligibility criteria are quite strict, with a single repayment delay of a few days often being reason enough for declining a second loan, they demonstrate the importance of creating common interests beyond a single loan. In many cases, it seems that the credible promise of long-term partnership is one of the key market advantages of a microfinance bank, especially in a non-transparent environment where longer-term planning is often impossible.[11]

Creating a 'union' between the bank and its customers, especially through the application of graduation scheme, reduces the risk of moral hazard for most first loans that exists from the very beginning of a client relationship. Credible promises also help realize future business opportunities.

---

[11]   We believe that insider lending that dominated the Azeri banking system at least until a few years ago is the reverse side of the same effect: if banks do not believe in the effectiveness of contracts and the legal system and, further, lack the possibility to apply a credit technology as described here, they will limit lending to cases in which loyalty is produced by factors outside the loan contract: family ties, friendship and other business relationships. The downsides are obvious: related risks, lack of transparency and lack of scalability.

6.4.5 Monitoring

The importance of tight monitoring has been repeatedly addressed in this chapter. Having performed its part of the loan contract, the bank becomes subject to moral hazard at the moment of disbursement. However, it can still influence the borrower's behaviour afterwards. Effects on clients include positive contacts, such as offering further products or talking about future business, as well as early warnings. Most important in this context is a strict scheme of monitoring in case of default. Each loan officer has the personal and financial responsibility for each loan in his or her portfolio. He or she checks repayments on a daily basis and is obliged to contact the client on the very same day a default has occurred, usually in person or at least by phone.

While such monitoring procedures may seem overly strict and costly at first sight, the benefit is substantial. First, most of such defaults happen by negligence. The immediate contact leads to repayment on the following day. Very short arrears periods are not only important for the bank from a provisioning cost point of view, they also relieve the loan officer of more follow-up work since the number of 'uncritical' short-term overdue loans has a direct impact on the productivity of the loan officer. Secondly, by applying immediate pressure, the bank shows its seriousness and commitment about the case, which often prompts the borrower to pay. Thirdly, for cases of more severe and prolonged repayment problems, the early contact provides the bank with more time to prepare and take action. If the default persists beyond the next day, clearly defined procedures guide the loan officer, his or her superiors and ultimately the bank's management as well as the legal department through further steps.

This monitoring system is supported by relatively heavy penalty payments for overdue loan instalments and by quality-oriented performance salaries for the loan officers and higher-rank lending staff.

Altogether, the high frequency of repayments that are usually monthly but sometimes biweekly or even weekly, combined with strong reaction in case of default allows the bank to reduce regular monitoring of non-defaulting micro loans to a minimum. This is very important for loan officer productivity and, thus, transaction costs.

6.5 CONCLUSION

In summary, lending is possible in a difficult environment and even to a difficult target group like informal micro and small businesses. To ensure scalable, profitable and sustainable lending, the lender has to take specific circumstances into account and adhere to certain principles. Loan assessment needs to disclose a borrower's business fundamentals; low transaction costs are crucial; and demonstrated enforcement incentives bring long-term success.

In MFBA at the moment, around 4500 small-scale entrepreneurs receive a loan every month. The portfolio has increased to over US$140 million and 55 000 outstanding loans. More than 90 per cent of the borrowers had no prior experience of borrowing from the formal banking sector. The annual growth rate is close to 150 per cent.

At the same time, the default risk is controllable. In its five and a half years of operation, MFBA has disbursed more than US$350 million in loans and lost less than US$400 000. This is about 0.1 per cent of the disbursed amount – much less than most banks in developed markets would be prepared to lose. Return on equity for the bank reached 37 per cent in 2007.

But is then everything just fine? Are all the described obstacles and difficulties mere local specifics that need to be taken into account when lending in an unreformed environment, just like differences between the legal systems of France and Germany? Unfortunately, the answer is 'no'. Even though lending is possible, it is not necessarily efficient. Risk is only controlled by heavy investment into analysis, monitoring and internal control. Accordingly, costs are high; and so must be interest rates. Not surprisingly, according to EBRD data[12] domestic credit to the private sector in Azerbaijan was just 9.5 per cent of GDP in 2005, compared to also 9.5 per cent in Georgia, 26.7 per cent in Kazakhstan and 85.8 per cent in the European Union. While there is certainly not just one basic cause for these differences, we do believe that a suitable legal system and an according legal reality play an important role for financial systems. An economy pays a high price for affording legal defects and inefficiencies: high costs, high margins and, most important of all, fewer loans, fewer borrowers and fewer lenders, in short, lost opportunities.

---

[12]   European Bank for Reconstruction and Development (2006), *Transition report 2006*, London: EBRD, p. 46.

7. Use of security in challenging environments: the microfinance perspective

Martin Holtmann*

7.1 INTRODUCTION

Microfinance has come of age. The top league of the microfinance industry currently consists of approximately 940 organizations with combined assets of US$26 billion.[1] Around the world, microfinance institutions (MFIs)[2] are serving tens of millions of customers. Most of them provide access to credit, but many MFIs also offer deposits and a range of other financial services such as insurance, housing finance, leasing, etc. In fact, it is fair to argue that microfinance is increasingly becoming integrated in the mainstream financial system.[3]

MFIs operate in difficult environments such as developing and transition economies, post-conflict countries, and remote rural areas. MFIs were the first providers of finance in post-conflict Kosovo and the Democratic Republic of Congo. A microfinance NGO, BRAC, is the leading mass lender in Afghanistan.[4] In such kinds of environments, collateral and secured lending present huge challenges. The main goal of this short chapter is to investigate whether the microcredit experience holds any lessons for the future development of the secured lending and collateral reform agendas.

* The author would like to thank Christoph Freytag (IPC Frankfurt), Julia Abakaeva (CGAP, Washington, DC), Alexander Yeriomin (Trast Bank, Kiev) and Richard Nalela (ES Global, Kampala) for their valuable contributions and many helpful discussions.
[1] The Microfinance Information Exchange (MIX) is the most comprehensive and up-to-date source of data and information on microfinance organizations. See www.mixmarket.org.
[2] It is common (bad) practice to use the term 'microfinance institution' rather than the more appropriate 'microfinance organization'.
[3] See Helms (2006), ch. 3.
[4] See www.misfa.org.af.

After a brief overview of some major institutional and operational advances on the access to finance frontier, I then will look at the role of collateral and secured lending instruments in microfinance. Throughout, I will take the point of view of a practitioner (which I can credibly claim to be) and not that of a legal expert (which would be a gross misrepresentation).

7.2   INSTITUTIONAL INNOVATIONS IN MICROFINANCE

Since the late 1980s there has been a growing consensus that institutions are at the core of financial market development.[5] Relevant institutions include, first and foremost, solid financial intermediaries, but also financial markets as well as the establishment and enforcement of property rights. It is not an exaggeration to argue that the expansion of microfinance is fundamentally rooted in the highly successful institution building that has been occurring at the retail level. There are several major types of microfinance institutions: non-governmental organizations (NGOs), 'greenfield' banks, as well as other types of 'alternative' financial institutions such as savings banks, cooperatives and (state-owned) postal banks.[6] The large Bangladeshi MFIs such as the Grameen Bank and BRAC all began as NGOs, and the NGO model is important in all major regions. The 'greenfielding' approach is exemplified by the Procredit group as well as KMB Bank in Russia, in which the EBRD was a founding shareholder. These are microfinance banks 'from scratch'; in other words, they were specifically designed as newly established banking institutions with a specific focus on microfinance and small business finance. It is important to point out that not all microfinance is delivered by 'specialized' or 'alternative' financial institutions: many commercial banks have begun to offer microfinance as a new business line. This approach, which is sometimes called 'downscaling', has been particularly successfully applied by the EBRD in Central Eastern Europe, Russia and Central Asia. At least in the regional domain of the EBRD, greenfield banks and 'downscaled' commercial banks have been experiencing the highest growth rates in terms of lending operations.[7] It is also useful to keep in mind that the Unit Desa microfinance arm of Bank Rakyat Indonesia (BRI), a state-owned commercial bank, is one of the largest microfinance providers in the world.[8]

---

[5]   See Krahnen and Schmidt (1991) pp. 22–5.
[6]   See Christen et al. (2004).
[7]   See Pytkowska (2006) pp. 3–9.
[8]   BRI is undergoing (partial) privatization. The UD system currently serves approximately 3.5 million borrowers and 31 million savers.

7.3 ADVANCES ON THE ACCESS TO FINANCE FRONTIER

So what are the main elements of the 'microfinance revolution'? While there are a multitude of factors that account for the success of microfinance, the following stand out from a practitioner's point of view:

a. customer-focused products that are adapted to the specific needs and environments that clients live in;
b. focus on institutional sustainability, which includes professional management, solid governance, decentralization of decision-making to the branches, and a willingness to charge prices that as a minimum allow the organization to cover its costs;
c. design and provision of appropriate incentives, both at the client level and also for staff members engaged in retail operations;
d. adequate information and control systems to deal with thousands (or millions) of customers and transactions;
e. relentless focus on quality and productivity, especially in lending operations.

Let us look in more detail at the constituents of successful lending technologies in microfinance, before we move on to the specific challenges of lending in developing and transition economies:

1. Microlenders typically look at the whole socio-economic unit of the prospective customer; in other words, to analyse a business loan they will take into account the prospective client's total income and expenses, from all sources.
2. Good microlenders ensure immediate follow-up when clients experience repayment problems. Good information systems flag the problem the moment they occur, and delinquent clients are typically contacted within a day or so. Adequate staff incentive schemes can play an important role in delinquency management.[9]
3. Perhaps most importantly, successful microlending has entailed a move away from the traditional focus on assets to a focus on cash flows.[10] MFIs typically focus on the cash flows of their clients in order to analyse their capacity to repay.

---

[9] See Holtmann, and Grammling (2005).
[10] For general background, see Von Pischke (1991) pp. 252–62.

4. Given the dearth of assets and traditional collateral, MFIs have developed a large number of collateral substitutes, including the solidarity group mechanism.[11]
5. MFIs provide 'dynamic incentives' to their clients. [12] Increases in loan size and other 'bonuses' are dependent on repayment behavior. Client education includes a focus on the long-term benefits of the relationship with the microfinance institution and a realization that the credit relationship is a 'repeated game'. An attempt is made to generate large cohorts of regular customers who regard the MFI as 'their' banking institution.

7.3.1 Lending and Use of Collateral: Developing Country Context

Since the early 1990s, the author has had the chance to work with a number of microfinance institutions and commercial banks in East Africa and Latin America. As a general characterization, the lending environment was (and still is) extremely adverse. Much lending had been done without the use of any security or collateral, and without the use of collateral substitutes. Furthermore, even where collateral had been offered, loans had become delinquent and the lending organization had found it practically impossible to seize and liquidate the pledged collateral items. As a consequence, commercial banks either had ghastly portfolio-at-risk rates[13] or refrained from retail lending and rather invested in treasury bills.

So far, there has been little relief in those countries from secured lending or collateral reforms such as the ones promoted by the World Bank Group and the EBRD. Dedicated microfinance institutions and some commercial banks in the region have thus established and expanded their microlending operations on the basis of a number of alternative mechanisms.

Focus on cash flows
MFIs strictly adhere to the analysis of cash flows as the basis for the determination of the customer's ability to pay. Trainee loan officers are taught that a focus on collateral is detrimental for the lending decision, not only since most collateral is useless in the event of default but also because it reduces the lender's willingness to thoroughly investigate the underlying economics of the client's (business) activities.

---

[11] See Hartarska and Holtmann (2006) pp. 149–51.
[12] Morduch, and Armendáriz de Aghion (2005) pp. 122–6.
[13] PAR measures the percentage of the outstanding principal that is affected by customer arrears. If there is only one loan outstanding and the customer has missed one payment, PAR would be 100%.

Use non-conventional collateral and collateral substitutes

Faced with a lack of enforceable and cost-effective collateral regimes, many MFIs accept non-conventional collateral. For example, some MFIs in Uganda use so-called Kibanja-mortgages, 'traditional' land titles signed by the local council that certify that the borrower has customary rights to use a piece of communal land. Also in Uganda, some lenders have been using post-dated checks as security: borrowers are asked to sign a check which the lender promises to post (so that it would 'bounce') if an installment has been missed. Since the penal code punishes this offence with immediate imprisonment, the practice has turned out to be very effective. Lenders have also developed the practice to take security over items belonging to the borrower and that can be used by the lender in case of default. These items are typically comprised of simple household goods, whose market value is dubious at best. The point is not to generate any liquidation value but rather to build a 'pressure point' in case the client falls in arrears. Other lenders post photographs of delinquent borrowers outside the branch building or advertise in the local newspaper with warnings 'not to engage in business with this person'. The common attribute of these kinds of instruments is that they build up alternative enforcement mechanisms where conventional collateral does not exist or is too costly to use.

Invest in lender's reputation

MFIs make significant investments in order to build up a reputation as serious lenders who will demand their money back. Typically, one of the first vehicles delivered to a new branch (apart for the ubiquitous motorcycles that loan officers use to reach their clients) is a pick-up truck that is occasionally used to haul items from the business or house of a defaulting borrower back to the branch where they are put on display. The point here is that such events are typically well advertised in order to generate the maximum possible effect in terms of building the lender's reputation. For the same reason, good microlenders relentlessly (and immediately) follow up on client delinquency. In some environments affected by corruption, lenders are even known to have threatened defaulters who were touting their good connections to the magistrate that they would double any bribe that the defaulter would offer to the court in order to prevail. Efforts are also made to use local 'multipliers' such as community leaders and church people to help build the reputation.

Reform the credit culture

The leading lenders in developing countries have successfully engineered a fundamental change in the credit culture in their communities. They have established a reputation as trustworthy and agile providers of financial services who *will* demand their money back, regardless of the status of the borrower and regardless of the underlying collateral. If the examples sketched above may appear somewhat drastic, the fact of the matter is that these actions have been used extremely rarely, if at all. The point that matters is that the lender is able to exercise a credible threat (namely to recover the loan regardless of the cost) that is taken seriously by the potential defaulter – and, perhaps more importantly, by potential future borrowers.

Despite the dearth of secured lending and modern collateral regimes MFIs have been able to establish thriving business lines of micro and small business lending. The leading MFIs boast returns on equity and assets that are significantly above those of the mainstream commercial and corporate lender. And, as already mentioned, the portfolio quality of MFIs is generally excellent.

It should be pointed out that there is some evidence linking land titling efforts in developing countries to increased access to credit from the banking system,[14] as postulated by de Soto.[15] But more recent research on the basis of a natural experiment in Argentina does not support the notion that land titling improves the flow of credit from the established banking system.[16] In any case, the main point that I wish to make here is that in the vast majority of developing countries the absence of secured lending mechanisms is only one of the many uncertainties that economic agents need to cope with. And it appears that the private sector, as is so often the case, has been able to develop appropriate and sufficiently flexible 'coping' mechanisms.

7.3.2 Lending and Use of Collateral: Transition Economy Context

Microfinance in the transition economies of Eastern Europe and the Newly Independent States has in many ways been as challenging as in the 'traditional' developing countries. Not only did microcredit represent a completely new asset class that was not on the 'radar screen' of commercial bankers and regulators, but it took considerable time and effort to change the legacy credit culture (credit as a mandated transfer from surplus to deficit units) and to work against the new culture of connected lending. As is still the case in many developing countries, the regulations concerning the use of collateral and secured lending prevailing in the early 1990s did not make lending any easier. Here are a few anecdotes illustrating this point.

---

[14] See Feder, and Onchan (1987) and Feder and Nishio (1999).
[15] See De Soto (2000), p. 64.
[16] See Galiani and Schargrodsky (2005).

1. One of the early types of collateral in use in the region were vehicle registrations. When the EBRD Russia Small Business Fund (RSBF) established operations in Novosibirsk, the highway police department was opened for two hours a week for the registration of liens on vehicles. This amounted to a capacity of five registrations per week. The RSBF had to lobby with the regional assembly in order to secure an extension of the opening hours.
2. One summer, the real estate registration office in the city of St Petersburg closed down completely since the only person working in that office went on vacation. Dozens of mortgages could not be processed.
3. Real estate could not be sold in the market by the lender as long as anybody possessed a 'propiska', the right of residence, in the dwelling. The owner had the right to grant propiska to people even if the real estate had already been mortgaged to a lender.
4. At least initially, processing times and costs were exorbitant. In Russia, all relevant documents had to be notarized at significant cost. Sometimes, the process turned into such a maze that it became reminiscent of a Kafka novel.

As is still the case in developing countries, lenders reverted to a number of alternative mechanisms. At the most basic level, some banks established pawn lending departments that granted tiny loans to customers who handed over jewelry (or sometimes fur coats) for safekeeping (for instance in Siberia and Georgia). Thus, clients were able to build up a credit history. Some banks repossessed items that clients had pledged when those clients had defaulted. This practice was illegal at the time; however, it helped the banks to establish a firm reputation as serious lenders.

Like their peers in the rest of the world, MFIs and commercial banks engaged in microfinance successfully re-engineered the credit culture by focusing on cash flows, using the probation and graduation principle, and by ensuring prompt follow-up in case of irregular payment and delinquency.

Through a variety of mechanisms and cash-flow-based lending practices the microfinance industry in this part of the world has achieved portfolio quality that is excellent even by international standards. Collateral and other types of securities have not played any significant role in this. For example, almost 100 per cent of the micro loans that the Procredit Group disburses in the region are in effect unsecured. In most cases, clients are asked to provide up to two personal guarantees, which are rarely, if ever, enforced. Otherwise the banks have been able to maintain their formidable repayment record and asset quality at the micro level without having to use formal collateral.

Not least because of the support from the EBRD and the World Bank Group, collateral reform has made significant progress in Eastern Europe. And the lending environment has indeed improved. Appendix Table A7.1 includes an overview of the current situation in Russia, Romania and Ukraine. In each case the situation has improved significantly during the past five to ten years. This is especially relevant since Eastern Europe has developed dynamically to produce significantly more lending to small and medium-sized enterprises than other regions. Once loan sizes go above the equivalent of US$50 000, even banks of the Procredit group routinely ask for formal collateral. This can take several forms: real estate, machinery and equipment, and vehicles. Clearly, the improvements in collateral regimes across the region have a positive effect on lending (and borrowing) arrangements and costs. Positive examples are the central pledge registry in Bulgaria as well as the use of promissory notes in Serbia.

7.4 SECURED LENDING AND COLLATERAL REFORM: SOME GENERAL COMMENTS

Around the world, lenders have to overcome the problem of an asymmetric distribution of information. While the borrower knows his or her repayment capacity as well as his or her willingness to repay, the lender is faced with the difficult task of establishing an appropriate incentive structure that compensates for his own lack of information. The value of collateral is that it can help to overcome this information asymmetry by enabling the borrower to make a credible pledge confirming her commitment to repay the loan (in the sense of posting a bond). Lenders attempt to develop mechanisms to counteract ex ante opportunism (see Fleisig, Chapter 3, this volume).[17]

As the examples quoted above set out to demonstrate, MFIs around the world have been able to develop such mechanisms and have established excellent lending operations despite the lack of secured lending. Despite operating in very challenging environments MFIs boast extremely high portfolio quality.[18]

There are a number of reasons to believe that, at least as far as traditional microfinance is concerned, this situation is not likely to change very quickly:

---

[17]   See Milgrom and Roberts (1992) pp. 141–7.
[18]   Average PAR for the 940 banks and MFIs reporting to the MIX is 5%.

1. Many microfinance clients operate in the informal sector and under the radar screen of the authorities. They might not be interested in using 'reformed' collateral even if it was available, if this meant coming out in the light.

2. Despite all the efforts at titling and creating mortgage systems, the vast majority of traditional microfinance clients really do not possess much that could be used as conventional collateral. Collateral reform is not likely to change that situation. In fact, it is the willingness of alternative financial institutions to look at cash flows rather than assets that has made a decisive difference in terms of access to credit.

3. On the practical level, one would suspect that collateral reform, for instance in the area of land and real estate, is an extremely complex undertaking.[19] There are many mutually dependent elements such as titling, mortgaging and foreclosure. Also, it would appear that collateral reform without bankruptcy reform would not make much sense.

4. Financial system development depends on institutions and is path dependent. One could suspect that in some cases the 'path' of microfinance is sufficiently well-trodden so that it might bypass secured lending reform.

7.5 SUMMARY AND PREDICTIONS FOR THE FUTURE

The purpose of this chapter was to argue that the availability of secured lending instruments is not one of the most burning issues for the global microfinance industry. There are several other bottlenecks in microfinance that are probably more relevant. Institutional capacity remains a big challenge. Operating costs are stubbornly high, and much more innovation will be needed in order to reach the many rural areas where there is currently no access to finance. Indeed, a new focus on secured lending and collateral might actually provide a disservice to the industry in that it would focus undue attention on an issue that the pioneer microfinance organizations and practitioners have worked very hard to reduce to a 'lower status'.[20]

Microfinance is but a small part of the bigger financial system. If one takes the system perspective, there can be no doubt that secured lending

---

[19]   See Dam (2006) ch. 7.
[20]   This has for instance been the case in a large commercial bank in Kazakhstan where the recent real estate boom has convinced management and lending staff that all that is needed to approve business loans is the mortgage of some good real estate.

and collateral reforms will generally help to boost access to credit. The statistical evidence compiled by some of the promoters of secured lending is convincing.[21] It is entirely plausible that the financial sector work of the multilateral development banks should entail a good dose of secured lending reform.

The impact of these reforms would appear especially significant for the provision of finance to small and medium-sized firms. Once lenders actually use collateral in order to better gauge the client's willingness to repay (which is routinely the case for small and medium-sized enterprises) faster and less costly collateral regimes will be a great help.

REFERENCES

Christen, Robert P., Richard Rosenberg and Veena Jayadeva (2004), 'Financial institutions with a "double bottom line": implications for the future of microfinance', Occasional Paper No. 8, Washington, DC: CGAP.

Churchill, Craig (1999), *Client-Focused Lending: the Art of Individual Lending*, Toronto: Calmeadow.

Dam, Kenneth W. (2006), *The Law-Growth Nexus: the Rule of Law and Economic Development*, Washington, DC: Brookings Institution Press.

De Soto, Hernando (2000), *The Mystery of Capital*, London: Bantam Press.

Dixit, Avinash K. (2004), *Lawlessness and Economics: Alternative Modes of Governance*, Princeton, NJ: Princeton University Press.

Feder, Gershon and Akihiko Nishio (1999), 'The benefits of land registration and titling: economic and social perspectives', *Land Use Policy*, **15** (1), 25–43.

Feder, Gershon and Tongroj Onchan (1987), 'Land ownership security and farm investment in Thailand', *American Journal of Agricultural Economics*, **69** (2), 311–20.

Fleisig, Heywood, Mehnaz Safavian and Nuria de la Peña (2006), *Reforming Collateral Laws to Expand Access to Finance*, Washington, DC: World Bank.

Galiani Sebastian and Ernesto Schargrodsky (2005), 'Property rights for the poor: effects of land titling', working paper, Universidad de San Andres, Argentina.

Hartarska, Valentina and Martin Holtmann (2006), 'An overview of recent developments in the microfinance literature', *Agricultural Finance Review*, **66** (2), 147–65.

Helms, Brigit (2006), *Access for All: Building Inclusive Financial Systems*, Washington, DC: World Bank, Consultative Group to Assist the Poor.

Holtmann, Martin and Mattias Grammling (2005), *A Toolkit for the Designing and Implementing Staff Incentive Schemes*, Nairobi: MicroSave.

Krahnen, Jan-Pieter and Reinhardt H. Schmidt (1991), *Development Finance as Institution Building*, Boulder, CO: Westview Press.

Milgrom, Paul and John Roberts (1992), *Economics, Organization, and Management*, Upper Saddle River, NJ: Prentice Hall.

---

[21] See Fleisig et al. (2006) ch. 1.

Morduch, Jonathan and Beatriz Armendáriz de Aghion (2005), *The Economics of Microfinance*, Cambridge, MA: MIT Press.

Pytkowska, Justyna (2006), *2005 State of Microfinance Eastern Europe and Central Asia*, Warsaw: Microfinance Centre for Eastern Europe and the Newly Independent States.

Von Pischke, J.D. (1991), *Finance at the Frontier: Debt Capacity and the Role of Credit in the Private Economy*, Washington, DC: World Bank.

APPENDIX

Table A7.1 Lending parameters in Russia, Romania and the Ukraine

	Russia	Romania	Ukraine
General market characteristics	High competition in banking sector, credit boom	Political stability, economic growth, growing competition in all sectors due to EU accession	Political instability
Lending without collateral	Most of the Russian banks do not require any collateral for loans up to US$20 000–30 000	For loans up to EURO 100 000	Loans up to US$10 000
Typical collateral for business loans	Equipment, vehicles, real-estate, goods in stock	Land, real estate	Real estate, equipment and goods in stock
Average time and cost associated with registration of collateral	1–2 weeks	2–5 days, legal and closing fees average EURO 600	1–2 weeks, notary fees 1% of the loan amount in case of real estate as collateral
Typical collateral for consumer loans	Proof of income (optional, the bank will charge the higher interest rate if the client does not provide any proof of income) Guarantor (optional) Vehicle and full coverage insurance (in case of car loans)	None Vehicle and full coverage insurance (in case of car loans)	Proof of income Guarantor Vehicle and other personal assets

	Restrictions: age of the borrower (between 21 and 50)	Corruption of authorities dealing with property titles causes delays in title registration
Problems	(1) Property rights: difficult to prove that the assets (except land and real estate) offered as collateral belong to the potential borrower (2) Second rank pledge: impossible to check whether the proposed collateral has not been already pledged to another creditor (3) Limited market and long procedures to sell the second-hand goods	
	Very flexible approach to collateral. More professional approach to lending based on client's risk assessment. Young professionals care about their future careers; thus more resistant to corruption	Electronic registry of collateral is available for everyone for a symbolic fee. Growing competition between banks for the SME clients forces banks to ease or even waive collateral requirements
General comments	Bubble of consumer lending, especially of car loans. Credit bureau is still an idea. Legal procedure against a debtor is long but once the bank has the court decision in its favor it can arrest the debtor's assets and even restrict the debtor traveling abroad.	

171

8. Mortgages in transition economies

John Simpson and Frederique Dahan

8.1 INTRODUCTION

In the transition countries of Central and Eastern Europe, South Eastern Europe and Central Asia, access to private home ownership is a relatively recent phenomenon, principally as a result of the privatisation policies of governments moving from a communist to a capitalist system. With a rate of private home ownership now exceeding 80 per cent in a number of transition countries,[1] it is evident that there is a huge capital stock which can be mobilised as collateral to secure loans for financing not only property acquisition, but also improvements, business activities or personal consumption. It is also widely seen as one of the keys to fostering economic prosperity, political stability and wider equality.[2] In the business sector a significant proportion of the assets of many companies is in the form of real property and can be used as a means of facilitating access to finance.

In the early 1990s, the legal problems surrounding ownership of real estate were numerous in transition countries. The lack of reliable cadastral and title registration combined with uncertainty over restitution rights restrained the scope for using real estate as security for credit. Although mortgage over real property was often the most favoured security for credit for all the classic reasons, the security was generally tainted by lack of certainty of the mortgagor's title and the threat of competing claims to the mortgaged property. The development since then of land registration systems across much of the region and the resolution of restitution claims have made mortgage a much

---

[1] See European Mortgage Federation (2006), *Hypostat 2005, A Review of Europe's Mortgage and Housing Market*, which indicates that this is the case in Bulgaria, Croatia, Estonia, Hungary, Latvia, Lithuania, Romania, Serbia and Slovenia.

[2] See for example International Monetary Fund (2006), *Global Financial Stability Report*, ch. II on 'Household credit growth in emerging market countries', p. 69: 'the healthy development of household credit is likely to generate important benefits for borrowers, lenders, the financial system, and the economy. It can also alleviate some of the current global imbalances. The resulting welfare gains could be substantial. Therefore, there is a need to encourage the sound development of this still-nascent market in Emerging Markets and developing countries'.

more viable form of security and have opened up new possibilities of mortgage financing. The considerable efforts that have been made to stabilise and modernise the financial sectors in transition economies also expanded the scope and nature of new products that can be developed.

But mortgage markets are not only growing, they are changing fast with more and more new mortgage products. On the legal front the challenge facing transition countries is not just to ensure a suitable legal environment for established forms of mortgages but also to have in place the rules and institutions that are sufficiently adapted to the latest techniques of the market, and further will be able to adapt to the new techniques of tomorrow. Are they ready for the challenge?

During 2006 and 2007 the European Bank for Reconstruction and Development (EBRD) carried out a detailed study of mortgage law as it is currently used in transition countries against the background of global developments in mortgage finance markets.[3] In this chapter we examine some of the results of that work: first, the analysis of the legal basics of mortgage law in an economic context and the opportunity that exists for transition countries; secondly, the results of a survey in which we examine against the criteria of legal efficiency whether these legal basics are being met in some 17 selected transition countries; and finally, certain specific issues that stand out as particularly important when one looks at mortgage law in transition countries against the criteria of legal efficiency. The meaning of legal efficiency and its importance for law reform have been developed elsewhere in this book (see Dahan and Simpson, Chapter 5, this volume).

8.2 LEGAL BASICS OF MORTGAGE LOOKED AT IN AN ECONOMIC CONTEXT

8.2.1 Economic Context

The current volume of residential mortgage lending in advanced economies is impressive and there is every indication that, notwithstanding the current sub-prime saga, there remains scope for further growth. In the transition countries, current volumes are lower, but the rate of growth is faster and the potential for future growth correspondingly greater. Figure 8.1 shows the ratio of residential mortgage debt to GDP in 2005 in 14 transition economies, the average being 7.5 per cent, against the average in the former EU-15 Member States of 50 per cent. Figure 8.2 shows the

---

[3] See (2007), *Mortgages in Transition Economies – the Legal Framework for Mortgages and Mortgage Securities*, available at www.ebrd.com/pubs/legal/mit.htm.

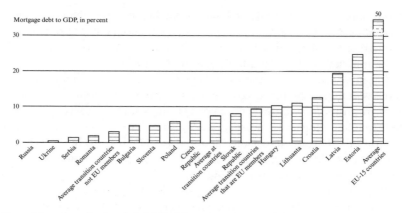

Note: The volume for Russia is 0.01%. Figures on other transition countries are not available. Average are highlighted for ease of reference.

Source: European Mortgage Foundation

Figure 8.1   Volume of residential mortgage debt to GDP in 2005

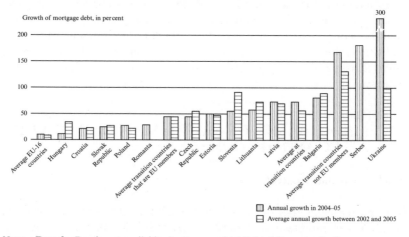

Note: Data for Russia not available. Averages are highlighted for ease of reference.

Source: European Mortgage Foundation

Figure 8.2   Growth of mortgage debt between 2002 and 2005

growth of residential mortgage debt between 2002 and 2005 where the average for the transition economies was 56 per cent against an average for the EU-15 of 9 per cent. Figures on commercial (non-residential) mortgages are not available but indications are that the sector is growing too.

Naturally, countries of Central and Eastern Europe are keen to understand the factors that determine the market growth for mortgage credit in advanced economies, and consequently what may be needed to encourage and maintain growth in their own markets. In this respect the way mortgage loans are funded is critical and has recently been changing fundamentally. In many countries mortgage credit has mostly been funded in ways which create no legal links between the mortgage loans and the source of the funding. The lender obtained funding from traditional sources (for example customer deposits, inter-bank borrowing or issue of bonds) and the fund provider had no direct right or interest in the mortgage loans for which the funds were used. However, two models have been used which facilitate funding by creating such a link.

In the US model, banks originated mortgage loans, but they were not kept on the banks' balance sheets; instead they were packaged and sold to specialist government sponsored entities (such as Fannie Mae, Freddie Mac and Ginnie Mae). These entities in turn financed their portfolios through the issue of securities which were given a high credit rating, not only because of the underlying mortgage loan portfolio, but also based on either an implicit or an explicit government guarantee. By contrast, under the German model of *Pfandbriefe*, mortgage loans were retained on the balance sheet of the lending bank but used as security for bonds issued by the bank to finance its mortgage lending business. These models use very different techniques but the common point is precisely the link created between the mortgage loans and their funding. This has in turn put strong emphasis on the quality of mortgage loans.

Behind the many permutations that may be offered to borrowers, the basic mortgage product tends to remain, in legal terms, essentially the same. It involves a contract for credit secured by mortgage over real property. Historically the specific features of domestic mortgage markets influenced the shape of the mortgage product; however the global trend towards more open and more competitive markets both for customer lending and for bank borrowing has led to huge change. Frontiers have blurred and an increasingly broad array of different mortgage products is now offered to potential borrowers. There is a move away from the inflexible standard mortgage, the one-product-fits-all approach, towards the adaptable product which can be tailored to the needs of the market and of the transaction. For transition countries this represents both a challenge and a huge opportunity.

Every opportunity for facilitating and accelerating the transition process needs to be used to the full and one of the ways in which this can be achieved is through adapting the legal framework to support the legitimate and justified needs of the market. Laws and the way they are implemented have to be 'efficient' (see Dahan and Simpson, Chapter 5, this volume).[4] The process of modernising laws through reform can be fraught with problems, and the pragmatic solution often is to adopt ad hoc laws which are limited in scope, or for lawyers to devise somtimes complex structures within the existing legal rules. But in transition economies there is the option of carrying out a dispassionate review of the legal framework against economic and market prerequisites in order to propose comprehensive reforms which aim at maximising the economic advantage that can be derived from the use of mortgage credit.

8.2.2 Legal Basics for a Mortgage Law

At the outset it is necessary to emphasise two important features of a law regulating mortgage: first, its prime purpose is economic, since the mortgage market has essentially an economic function (whilst recognising that the housing market which mortgages finance has an important social function); and second, it is essentially facilitative since a mortgage market is not a necessity, it being possible for any economy to function without it. We consistently work on the premise that the basic legal framework should be conducive to a flexible market for mortgage credit. There may be local political considerations which determine how far a country wants to allow its mortgage market to develop and what restraints or conditions it wants to impose on its operation, but they do not change the economic arguments that underpin the need for a legal framework for mortgage to be flexible and efficient.

For a transition country which is seeking to revamp its legal and institutional system for mortgage in order to encourage growth in mortgage finance, the obvious starting point is to look at how the law works in advanced Western economies. That exercise reveals a variety of different systems, mostly shaped in a different era, which have been more or less adapted over the years to accommodate market changes. Some aspects are highly efficient and show how long-standing laws and practices can be moulded to follow the needs of subsequent generations. Others are restrictive and preclude (or unduly complicate) techniques commonly used in modern financing.

Copying advanced Western economies ignores the fact that a transition economy may start with a deficient legal framework and limited market

---

[4]   While ensuring that the legal framework is capable of meeting market needs each jurisdiction has to strike a balance between protection of debtors and encouragement of creditors. Debtors need some degree of protection, but over-protection inevitably leads to a reduction in availability of credit. We do not attempt to address where the balance should be struck but start from the proposition that greater availability of credit will lead to economic benefits. It is important to analyse different debtor protection measures so that their likely impact on credit availability can be assessed.

practice, but wants to move in a short space of time to being able to compete with developed economies. One of the opportunities that the transition country may have is precisely the ability to avoid the kind of obsolete elements in the law which often hinder development in advanced economies. What therefore should be the benchmarks for a modern, efficient mortgage law?

For a number of years, the EBRD Core Principles for a secured transactions law have been widely used in the countries of Central and Eastern Europe as a starting point for reform of laws on security. They are very basic and simple but they contain the essential requirements that the legal framework has to meet, leaving it to each country to decide on the best way to achieve them in the context of its own jurisdiction. They apply to mortgage as much as to any other proprietary security such as pledge. The principles are set out in Box 8.1.[5]

The first principle is overriding:

> If the legal framework for mortgage does not lead to a reduction in the risk of giving credit and an increased availability of credit on improved terms, then there is no point in the law providing for mortgage at all.

And every element of the legal framework should be analysed against this basic principle.

This brings home a very important point, which is often overlooked: economically speaking, there is no distinction between a pledge and a mortgage. As a transaction in immovable assets the legal regime for mortgage may be found within the law of real property but this is only for convenience. Many countries in fact do not make a distinct legal classification between the two institutions and the generic term 'the law of secured transactions' is used more and more often.[6] Whatever legal classification may be used and wherever the legal provisions may be included in the statute book, the regime for mortgage should be similar to that for security over any other asset. Some special rules specific to the particular nature of real property are needed, but having different rules apply to common issues (such as the description of the secured debt and the method of enforcement)

---

[5] The language has been adapted to refer specifically to mortgage (for example, the person granting the security is referred to as the 'mortgagor' and the person receiving the benefit of the security as the 'mortgage creditor') but the substance remains unchanged.

[6] In the US the term is often used in the context of security over movables only (as in Article 9 of the uniform Commercial Code, Secured Transactions), but in a global context it increasingly embraces all security transactions.

BOX 8.1   EBRD CORE PRINCIPLES FOR A MORTGAGE LAW

1. A mortgage should reduce the risk of giving credit, leading to an increased availability of credit on improved terms.
2. The law should enable the quick, cheap and simple creation of a proprietary security right without depriving the person giving the mortgage of the use of his property.
3. If the secured debt is not paid the mortgage creditor should be able to have the mortgaged property realised and to have the proceeds applied towards satisfaction of his claim prior to other creditors.
4. Enforcement procedures should enable prompt realisation at market value of the mortgaged property.
5. The mortgage should continue to be effective and enforceable after the bankruptcy or insolvency of the person who has given it.
6. The costs of taking, maintaining and enforcing a mortgage should be low.
7. Mortgage should be available (a) over all types of immovable assets (b) to secure all types of debts and (c) between all types of person.
8. There should be an effective means of publicising the existence of a mortgage.
9. The law should establish rules governing competing rights of persons holding mortgages and other persons claiming rights in the mortgaged property.
10. As far as possible the parties should be able to adapt a mortgage to the needs of their particular transaction.

---

depending on whether the asset is movable or immovable does not make sense. The inefficiency of such an approach becomes all the more apparent in the context of securitisation of mortgage loans and issues of covered bonds,[7] when security is often given both in the form of mortgage and of pledge.

The EBRD approach has always been to treat mortgages as an integral part of secured transactions and to apply the same legal principles (whilst

---

[7] Bonds issued by a mortgage lender and secured by a pool of mortgage loans.

recognising that, in some respects, the mechanics may vary). The context for pledge law reform has been different, yet, economically speaking, pledge and mortgage fulfil the same purpose and it is illogical that the reform of the legal framework for each should be conducted in isolation. Such a unified approach has been adopted for example in Hungary and Slovakia, where the same legal provisions apply to both pledges and mortgages.

Core Principles 2 to 10 are more prosaic and are relatively self-explanatory. We look in more detail below at how these principles apply and what they involve in the context first of creation of mortgage (including registration), and then of enforcement. The trio of simplicity, speed and cheapness, as emphasised in the second, fourth and sixth principles, is fundamental and ties in directly with the concept of legal efficiency (Dahan and Simpson, Chapter 5, the volume). Every cost, irrespective of who bears it, that is involved in the creation of mortgage or its enforcement detracts from the benefits that mortgage provides. Any delays or complexities translate into additional cost.

8.2.3   Creation of Mortgage

For the creation of a mortgage there are three basic steps:

1. proof by the mortgagor that he owns (or will own) the property to be mortgaged;
2. agreement for the mortgage between mortgagor and mortgage creditor;
3. publicity of the mortgage through registration.

The creation of a mortgage is sometimes mystified as a result of a complex and formal process. In fact, it should be very simple as long as there is a clear understanding on these three basic steps, and in particular (a) what preliminary checks need to be made, (b) what matters the agreement should address, and (c) the process and purpose of registration. Later in this chapter we examine certain specific legal issues which arise, and which can make what could be a simple process unduly complex or inefficient, but here we summarize the essential elements of each step.

Proof of ownership
This covers:

- certainty that the mortgagor has (or will have) a mortgageable right in the property. A mortgage is an ancillary proprietary right which can only be given by the person with a principal proprietary right over the immovable asset which is most often established through title registration;

- certainty as to the scope of the mortgagor's property. Any dispute as to the scope of the mortgaged property will adversely affect the role of the mortgage as a credit risk mitigant. Title registration is usually based on a cadastral definition which needs to be both accurate and reliable so that the risk of a subsequent dispute is minimised;
- certainty as to any qualifications on the mortgagor's proprietary right. Immovable property can be subject to a variety of rights of third parties: mortgages or encumbrances, servitudes, such as a right of passage, occupation rights, rights of expropriation. In many cases these will be recorded in the title (or other) register. Where they are not the law needs to define the extent and the nature of those rights.

Agreement for mortgage
This defines:

- the parties: (1) the mortgagor, that is, the person with a principal proprietary right over the property that is mortgaged; (2) the mortgage creditor to whom the mortgage is granted; (3) the debtor of the secured claim: in most cases this will be the mortgagor but sometimes one person will give a mortgage to secure the debt of someone else. In this chapter we generally assume that the debtor is the mortgagor;
- the mortgaged property. This will usually be defined by reference to the title register. The agreement may need to further define what is, and what is not, included in the mortgaged property: would, for example, the mortgage creditor be entitled to receive payment of rents? Does the mortgage creditor's right extend to all constructions on the land, equipment in the manufacturing plant?
- the secured debt. This will include the principal debt and any interest. It may also include accessories such as costs;
- other conditions relating to mortgage. It is usual to include rights and obligations of both the mortgagor and the mortgage creditor concerning the mortgaged property.

In many jurisdictions certain matters concerning the mortgage will be set out in the law and will not need to be expressly provided in the agreement.

Publicity of the mortgage
This:

- is achieved through registration against the property, but without needing the onerous requirements involved in title registration since the purpose is different;

- enables third parties, and especially those subsequently seeking to establish a claim, to discover that the mortgage creditor may have a prior opposable right in the mortgaged property;
- establishes the priority between competing mortgages (most often based on the chronological order of registration).

8.2.4 Mortgage Enforcement

What gives a mortgage its value, and therefore enables borrower and lender alike to derive benefit from it, is the confidence that it can be enforced, if necessary, to repay the lender's claim. That is obvious: the greater the doubts of the lender as to his ability to enforce, the less will be the influence of the mortgage when he decides whether to lend and on what terms. When difficulties arise the parties will usually undertake negotiations to try to resolve the situation in a way that is satisfactory for both sides. If the process that would apply on enforcement is unclear, uncertain or inefficient, the mortgagor will have scope for evading his obligations and the creditor may be forced to compromise in a manner contrary to the original agreement between the parties. Ironically this means that the better the system of enforcement, the less it is likely to be needed.

First and foremost, it should be kept in mind that the overall context of enforcement results from an *agreement* between borrower and lender, and is intended to provide the means of assuring the creditor that he will be repaid even in case of default. It is intended neither to enrich the creditor nor to penalise the mortgagor.

Enforcement of a mortgage can be broken down into three basic steps:

1. establishing the right to enforce;
2. realising the mortgaged property;
3. distribution of the proceeds.

Realisation is the most visible step, since it determines the ultimate value of the security that the mortgage creditor took at the outset, but inefficiencies at any one of these steps can reduce such value.

Establishing the right to enforce

The sale of a property on enforcement is a serious measure and should not be undertaken before a number of preliminary steps have been taken to establish that the right to enforce exists and that realisation can proceed. The precise nature of these steps varies considerably from one jurisdiction to the next, but broadly they involve establishing that:

- the mortgage creditor has a valid claim against the debtor;
- the claim is secured by a valid mortgage over the property to be realised;
- an event has occurred which entitles the mortgage creditor to enforce (and it has not been remedied);
- the mortgagor has been given notice of the intention to commence enforcement and has been given the opportunity to remedy;
- the mortgage creditor has fulfilled all other conditions (often in terms of timing, notice, procedural steps, etc.) for the realisation procedure to start.

Realisation of the mortgaged property

Realisation aims at generating money out of the mortgaged property which will be used towards repaying the claim secured by the mortgage. This usually entails the sale of the property to a third party acquirer, although in some cases the mortgage creditor may accept, at least initially, solely to derive revenue from the property. What is paramount is that the realisation is conducted in a fair manner and that the proceeds of the realisation are maximized. Fairness implies that the mortgagor has the right to challenge the procedure but not in a way which is intended to deprive the mortgage creditor of his legitimate rights.

Distribution of the proceeds

Where the mortgage creditor is the only creditor claiming a priority right in the money proceeds of the realisation, distribution should be straightforward, with any surplus returned to the mortgagor. Where there are other mortgage creditors or creditors with prior rights in the proceeds from the property, there must be an orderly process by which the ranking order is respected. Where the mortgagor is insolvent, the insolvency procedure should allow the proceeds due to the mortgage creditor to be distributed promptly upon receipt. The rights of competing privileged creditors and their respective rank should have been determined well before the proceeds become available and thus, even in a complex case, it should be possible for the proceeds to be distributed expeditiously.

For the transition country that wants to encourage a thriving market for mortgage credit and to ensure that the economy derives maximum benefit from it, there is the possibility to use reform to 'leap frog' older, more established markets. As will be seen from the next section many have come a long way but still display inefficiencies that could be removed relatively easily.

8.3 MORTGAGE REGIONAL SURVEY: A SNAPSHOT OF CONTEMPORARY MORTGAGE IN TRANSITION ECONOMIES

8.3.1 Survey Description

The Mortgage Regional Survey (MRS) was designed and compiled during 2006 and 2007, based on an analysis of the relevant legal texts, published information and experience of the EBRD, supplemented by information and advice received from practitioners in the relevant countries.[8] The survey is intended as a tool for anyone interested in the modernisation, improvement or reform of mortgage law. It presents basic information and a comparative assessment of the legal regime for mortgage in transition economies where the EBRD operates. In the 17 jurisdictions covered either there already exists an active mortgage finance market, or preparations for developing such a market are well advanced. The questions address simple practical issues which highlight the strengths and weaknesses of the mortgage regime in each country in a way which is useful to credit providers and their advisers when assessing the potential value of mortgage security.

The questions in the survey were inspired by market reality, not by legal theory. Based on the EBRD Core Principles for a Mortgage law (see Box 8.1 above), the survey covers four main areas of mortgage (creation, commercial effectiveness, effect on third parties and enforcement) and gives a reasonable indication of the extent to which these principles are upheld. For each of the 17 countries each question in the survey was given one of four possible gradings (ranging from a clear yes to a definite no). These gradings give an indication of the strengths and weaknesses of each country. The MRS is not specifically designed as a means of *measuring* legal efficiency, but the information contained in it is easily linked to the criteria of legal efficiency (see Chapter 5). In this section, when presenting the survey and what it reveals, we have therefore regrouped the questions according to the six legal efficiency criteria, that is: basic legal function of mortgage law and the five elements of maximising economic benefit which are simplicity, speed, cost, certainty and fit-to-context[9]. Figure 8.3 gives a composite summary of the survey findings.

---

[8] The MRS has been developed in a similar manner to the regional survey of security over movable and intangible property which was first published by EBRD in 2000. See www.ebrd.com/country/sector/law/st/facts/survey.htm.
[9] For explanation of these criteria, see Dahan and Simpson, Chapter 5, this volume.

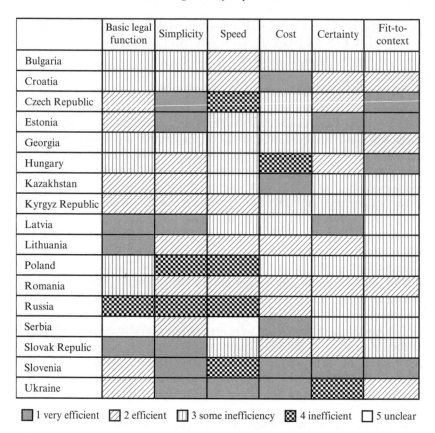

■ 1 very efficient   ◪ 2 efficient   ▥ 3 some inefficiency   ▩ 4 inefficient   ☐ 5 unclear

Figure 8.3   Legal efficiency indicators, composite table

8.3.2   Basic Legal Function

Before looking at whether a mortgage law maximises economic benefits it is necessary to assess whether it meets the fundamental criterion of fulfilling its basic legal function. This is addressed in five questions in the survey:

- Is the manner of creation of mortgage clearly established?
- Does mortgage give priority in mortgaged property?
- Does the mortgage creditor have priority in bankruptcy?
- Is the manner of enforcement of mortgage clearly established?
- Is realisation likely to be at market value?

It is encouraging to see that across all countries the basic rules for creating a mortgage are clear and in almost all there is established practice. However, the question only indicates the very basic position. Uncertainties arising out of the law are highlighted in other areas in the survey. In Georgia, for example, whereas the overall creation process is established, some provisions of the law, such as the time of creation of the mortgage, are unclear.

Similarly, at a basic level the manner of enforcement of mortgage is clearly established. Where enforcement has to be carried out through the courts (which is the case in approximately half the countries covered[10]) there may be uncertainties concerning court procedure and practice. Even where enforcement is usually out of court such uncertainties are damaging since they weaken the fall back position on which both mortgagor and mortgage creditor should be able to rely. In Russia the enforcement process is relatively clear but the courts have a discretionary power to decide whether or not enforcement can proceed depending on whether it is considered 'proportionate'. In Serbia there is as yet little practice of mortgage enforcement based on the 2005 legislation.

The answers to the priority questions show that there continue to exist some claims which take precedence over the right of a mortgage creditor outside the mortgagor's bankruptcy (regardless of their date of creation), even in some cases where such super privileges no longer apply in the case of bankruptcy (for example wages claims in Poland and Hungary). In practice it is not always clear how such claims would be enforced and to what extent they pose a significant risk to the mortgage creditor. In Russia, Croatia and Ukraine there is uncertainty as to whether tax claims may take precedence.

The priority position of the mortgage creditor on bankruptcy has greatly improved over recent years, especially in the case of legal entities, but wages and health and safety claims still have priority in some jurisdictions (for example in Russia and Kazakhstan). The system of giving priority only to a portion of the secured claim which used to apply in Czech Republic, Hungary and the Slovak Republic now continues only in Georgia (although the new insolvency law is expected to abolish this rule). Tax priority is now generally limited to unpaid taxes that directly relate to the mortgaged property (but Russia and Croatia are exceptions). It should be noted that personal bankruptcy (where the mortgagor is an individual) is barely developed in transition economies.

A country may have clear rules for creation, priority and enforcement of a mortgage but their usefulness is curtailed if the proceeds on realisation

---

[10] Bulgaria, Croatia, Georgia, Latvia, Lithuania, Poland, Romania, Russia and Slovenia.

are not expected to be at or near to market value of the property. Mortgage markets in the region are still far from fully developed and in most countries enforcement practice is still in its infancy, so results on this question have to be treated cautiously.[11] However, in four countries (Kazakhstan, Lithuania, the Slovak Republic and Ukraine), realisation is considered likely to be at market value. In Bulgaria, Croatia, Georgia, Hungary, Poland, Romania and Russia, it is expected to be only at somewhere between 50 and 80 per cent of market value. In some countries booming property markets may have ensured that where enforcement has occurred, it has often been relatively easy to achieve satisfactory realisation. The robustness of mortgage enforcement procedures will only be truly tested when a downturn in the market leads to borrower defaults in less favourable conditions.

8.3.3 Simplicity

Simplicity, speed and cost are each examined in questions in the survey evidencing two key moments of the mortgage process: creation and enforcement.

- Is creation of mortgage simple?
- Is enforcement procedure simple?

A priori creation of mortgage can be achieved by a simple agreement and a simple registration, but review shows quite a range of practices, some very simple and some complex. In Poland, a practice has developed for lenders to require the creation of two mortgages: one mortgage securing the principal debt and a separate mortgage securing interest and accessories.[12] This complexity is due to the rigid approach towards defining the secured debt and doubts on the correct interpretation of the law.[13] The registration process is often responsible for the downgrade on simplicity because of complex or formal procedures (as for example in Hungary, the Kyrgyz Republic, Poland and Russia) or onerous documentation requirements (as for example in Bulgaria, Kazakhstan, Lithuania and Russia). In Bulgaria, the Czech Republic and the Slovak Republic, multiple copies of the mortgage agreement have to be presented to complete registration. Although

---

[11]   Information was derived from local practitioners and is to a large extent impressionistic since hard statistics are not available.
[12]   *Hipoteka zwykla* and *hipoteka kaucyjna*.
[13]   See EBRD Report (2005), *The Impact of the Legal Framework on the Secured Credit Market in Poland*, available at www.ebrd.com/st.

not sufficient by itself to make registration complex, this is an example of an unnecessary administrative burden. Requiring a notarial deed is not per se an unacceptable complexity (for example Ukraine has established a simple process) as long as the benefits of such deed are clear to the parties. Generally the other aspects of creating a mortgage are quite straightforward. In Bulgaria there is a requirement to re-register a mortgage after 15 years and in Romania it seems there is a similar requirement after ten years, although opinions differ. Requiring renewal of registration after a given time has little justification. The onus and inconvenience of renewing outweighs any advantage of clearing redundant mortgages from the register, which should remain the responsibility of the parties.

Enforcement of a mortgage, by its nature, is a more sensitive process than creation, but the law and institutions should not provide a system which is inherently complex. The realisation procedure is shown as relatively simple in a surprising number of countries (14 out of 17). In the three countries (Georgia, Poland and Russia) where realisation procedures were not rated as simple, the proceeds on realisation were also shown to be well short of market value. In Poland, the procedures are formalistic and the operation of the bailiff system is reported to be highly inefficient, and that is also the case in Russia. In Georgia, court practices can cause uncertainty among parties as to the correct procedure and likely outcome. Complexity is often linked with the need to obtain a court judgment confirming the borrower's default and allowing for the enforcement of the mortgage. Countries where the realisation procedure is simple generally apply either a simplified court procedure for issuing an executory title (as in Bulgaria or the Czech Republic) or alternative out-of-court options such as a notarial stamp (as in Ukraine) or clauses in the mortgage agreement on the basis of which the mortgage creditor is granted a direct enforcement right in case of default (as in Estonia, Latvia and the Slovak Republic).

8.3.4   Speed

The criterion of speed was explored in the survey through two questions:

*   Is creation of mortgage rapid?
*   Is enforcement of mortgage rapid?

In practice taking a mortgage may take time because of negotiations or because it is linked to the acquisition of the property being mortgaged, but the creation of the mortgage itself should not be the element that causes delay. If property searches are available on line and registration becomes a notification procedure without authentification (see further below) it

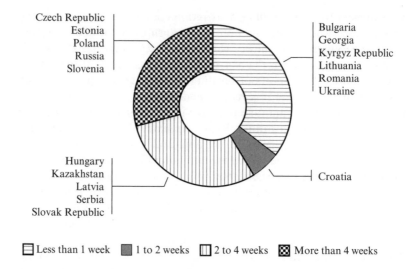

Czech Republic
Estonia
Poland
Russia
Slovenia

Bulgaria
Georgia
Kyrgyz Republic
Lithuania
Romania
Ukraine

Hungary
Kazakhstan
Latvia
Serbia
Slovak Republic

Croatia

▤ Less than 1 week   ■ 1 to 2 weeks   ▦ 2 to 4 weeks   ▨ More than 4 weeks

Figure 8.4　Average time taken to obtain mortgage registration

should be possible to carry out all formalities for creation within a day. The survey shows however that this has not yet become the reality. In more than half the countries creation takes on average over two weeks, and in most cases the principal cause of the delay is registration. Figure 8.4 shows the average time required for registration of a mortgage.

Other causes of delay exist as for instance in Estonia, where it is reported to take two weeks to obtain the requisite appointment with a notary, and in Kazakhstan, where title checks habitually take two to three weeks. In some countries it is frequent practice to advance a mortgage loan prior to completion of registration formalities (for example in the Czech Republic, Estonia, Hungary, Kazakhstan, Poland and Serbia). Where there are delays on registration but there is little doubt as to the outcome then early disbursement is an indication of the market finding a pragmatic solution to reduce the effect of slow or bureaucratic procedures. But where early disbursement is subject to the mortgagor providing insurance or additional security (as for example in Poland) it indicates a more deep-rooted inefficiency.

The speed of enforcement is not as bad as it is sometimes perceived, especially when compared with the average time required in advanced markets: in seven countries out of 16,[14] enforcement is on average completed within six months (these are: Estonia, Hungary, Kazakhstan, Latvia,

---

[14]　There is no data on Serbia, as the law is too recent for enforcement practice to have developed.

Lithuania, the Slovak Republic and Ukraine) and in another four (Bulgaria, Croatia, the Kyrgyz Republic, Romania), within one year. Unlike mortgage creation, realisation on enforcement cannot become a virtually instantaneous operation. There are certain built-in delays, such as a grace period to give the mortgagor the opportunity to remedy prior to realisation commencing, time for publicising the sale and time for the formalities of sale to be completed. Completing the process within six months is commendable; few Western European jurisdictions achieve that.[15] Of the five countries where enforcement is reported to habitually take over a year (the Czech Republic, Georgia, Poland, Russia and Slovenia) all except the Czech Republic require realisation to be via a court-led public auction, and all except Georgia also have a negative grading for the time for creation. Taking creation and enforcement together, more than half the countries have at least one negative rating.

8.3.5 Cost

The question address the issue of cost in the MRS:

* Is creation of mortgage inexpensive?
* Is enforcement of mortgage inexpensive?

In most countries the cost of creation is not a significant problem. Hungary is the only country which is given a negative grading for cost of creation as a result of the high notarial fees that generally apply. Notary costs are sometimes denounced as excessive but a closer examination shows that in some transition countries notary involvement does not always mean high costs. In Ukraine costs are low, despite the fact that a notarial deed is required. However in the two countries where creation is shown as the least expensive, the Czech Republic and Russia, notarisation is not required. In Russia costs have fallen following the bold recent decision to lower notary costs (which used to be relatively high) and to repeal compulsory notarisation for mortgage.

The position on cost of enforcement is not as good. Almost half the countries indicated that enforcement costs (excluding advisory fees) amounted to more than 5 per cent of the amount claimed or the mortgaged

---

[15] Based on EMF study, only in Denmark and Netherlands, enforcement process usually takes less than six months. Countries like Italy, France or Greece are reported to sometimes require years of procedure (respectively: 5–7 years, 10 months – 2 years; 3 months – 2 years). See further European Mortgage Federation (2007), *Study on the Efficiency of the Mortgage Collateral in the European Union.*

property's value.[16] Most often high costs are attributable to scale fees paid to bailiffs or public auctioneers.

8.3.6 Certainty

Certainty is relevant to all aspects of a mortgage law but five questions in the MRS are especially relevant:

- Can existing title to property be established with sufficient certainty?
- Is the mortgage creditor protected from subsequent claims which may adversely affect the mortgagor's title to the property?
- Can a third party determine whether property is mortgaged?
- Is the mortgage creditor protected against mortgagor obstruction?
- Is the purchaser in enforcement procedure protected?

Somewhat surprisingly, given the negative perception of land registers in the region, in eight countries, establishing title to property does not cause difficulty. At the other end of the spectrum, establishing title is a major problem in Bulgaria and Serbia, in both cases because of the unsatisfactory state of the land registration system. In general, countries have significantly reduced the amount of unregistered property but this is still a problem for several jurisdictions (Croatia, Poland, Romania, Russia and Serbia). The majority of countries have unified their property records and use one comprehensive public register for all immovable property rights.[17] Some countries (for example Kazakhstan, Serbia and Ukraine) have the relevant records registered in two or more registers which can hamper the process of establishing title. Although vast progress has been made in improving land registration across the region, the downgrades on this question mostly indicate reform that is not yet complete.

Subsequent claims adversely affecting title did not show up as a problem. There remains some risk of restitution claims on property, but only in Lithuania, Romania and Serbia was it considered that there is a significant risk that they could invalidate or restrict the value of the mortgage. In Ukraine lenders are concerned by a law designed to protect families with children, which makes eviction subject to approval from the Ministry of Youth Affairs. Mortgage loans are sometimes made conditional on receipt of such administrative approval, which can involve a lengthy procedure

---

[16]   In some countries costs are calculated as a percentage of the amount realised, in others as a percentage of the amount claimed.

[17]   In Lithuania the mortgage register is separate from the real estate register, but information entered in either is automatically fed to the other.

without predictable results, but this could not cover the case where children become occupants after the mortgage is created. This uncertainty is a deterrent to mortgage lending to young families.

Only four countries indicated difficulties with determining whether a property is mortgaged. In Kazakhstan and the Kyrgyz Republic there are limits on publicly available information; in Bulgaria the way the information is registered can make it hard to find; and in the Czech Republic tax liens created on the debtor's property may not be registered in the land register immediately whilst being immediately opposable to third parties. The progress being made towards transparency through on-line availability of land registry information should make it increasingly easy to find out about existing mortgages. Already in the Czech Republic, Estonia, Hungary, Latvia and Lithuania all basic information from the land register is publicly available via the Internet.

Debtor obstruction to enforcement is to some extent a problem in every jurisdiction. There are recalcitrant debtors everywhere who will use all available techniques to frustrate a creditor's attempts to enforce, so it is not surprising that only four countries (the three Baltic states and Slovenia) report that obstruction is not a significant problem in practice. The situation is shown to be worst in Georgia and Poland, followed by Russia and Ukraine. In Russia debtors often apply for postponement which can be granted by a court for a period of up to one year. A similar right to apply for postponement exists in Kazakhstan. In Georgia, the mortgagor and dependants are legally allowed after realisation to remain in the property as tenants of the property purchaser.

The purchaser in enforcement procedure is generally protected from subsequent challenge that could be brought against his title to the property. In only five countries (the Czech Republic, Hungary, Kazakhstan, the Kyrgyz Republic and Ukraine) can the mortgagor or a third party challenge the purchaser's title in the absence of fraud or exceptional circumstances. In the Czech Republic the challenge can be made only for certain defined reasons and in Hungary it can be made only if the sale was not conducted by a professional auctioneer or dealer.

8.3.7   Fit-to-context

The fit-to-context criterion is wide-ranging and seven questions in the survey are directly relevant:

- Can a mortgage be granted by any person?
- Can any person take a mortgage?
- Can the mortgage secure any type of debt?

- Can the mortgage cover all types of immovable asset?
- Can the secured debt be in any form?
- Does the mortgaged property include subsequent constructions and additions?
- Are subsequent mortgages permitted over the same property?

The first four questions together reflect much of the essence of EBRD core principle 7 (see Box 8.1 above): 'Security should be available (a) over all types of immovable assets (b) to secure all types of debts and (c) between all types of person'. The results on these questions are encouragingly positive. No country is given a negative grading on any of these questions; there are merely some reservations. In the Kyrgyz Republic and Ukraine there are restrictions on mortgaging agricultural land. In Romania mortgages under the Mortgage Lending Law can only secure debts used for investment in the mortgaged property (but this does not apply to mortgages which are regulated by the Civil Code). There are no restrictions on who can grant a mortgage, and only minor reservations (in Croatia and Romania) on the person who can take a mortgage.

However if one analyses more closely as to whether the secured debt can be in any form there is only an unqualified 'yes' (meaning that the regime is very efficient in this respect) for Estonia, Hungary, the Slovak Republic, Slovenia and Ukraine. In Croatia, Georgia, Kazakhstan, the Kyrgyz Republic and Romania, the regime is also flexible but some reservations apply. In the seven remaining countries, on the other hand, requirements for specific definition of the secured debt restrict the ability to use a mortgage to secure future or fluctuating debts. In Latvia registration requirements effectively place limitations on securing foreign currency claims. Although such claims can be secured by mortgage, the amount secured is the Lat amount shown in the Land Register. In Slovenia 'maximum amount' mortgages can be used to secure future and fluctuating debts and so the grading is an unqualified 'yes', but restrictions on their assignment limit their availability to secure funding of the mortgage provider. In some countries the rules for defining the secured debt are less flexible for mortgage than those applicable for pledge. For example, in Bulgaria, Lithuania and Poland, following reforms of the pledge law, the secured debt for pledge can be in any form, whereas they all receive a negative grading on this question for mortgage.

Also if one looks specifically at whether the mortgaged property includes subsequent constructions and additions, problems come to light in seven countries. Buildings can be mortgaged but the division of title between land and buildings can give rise to practical difficulties (see para 8.4.3 below). In the Czech Republic, Kazakhstan and the Slovak Republic subsequent constructions on mortgaged land can only be included by a further mortgage. In Bulgaria, the Kyrgyz Republic, Romania and Serbia the position is unclear.

In all countries subsequent mortgages are permitted although their use may often be limited by negative pledge clauses, particularly in Kazakhstan, Romania and Russia. In Ukraine consent of the prior mortgage creditor is necessary and in practice a prohibition to sell the property, opposable to all parties, is often registered.

8.3.8 Legal Efficiency Indicators

The purpose of the survey is to indicate strengths and weaknesses, not to show a comprehensive assessment of winners and losers. The assessment methods are inevitably in part subjective and each country has to be viewed in its own particular context. The information covered by the survey is *not* comprehensive enough to provide a full assessment (especially for measuring the fit-to-context criterion) and a number of questions are relevant to more than one criterion. However, the composite table (see Figure 8.3 above) gives a useful broad overview of the survey results, indicating what has been achieved in each country and pointing towards what needs to be improved.

Taking the grades on the five questions that relate to basic legal function together, nine countries out of 17 score positively (that is, answer 'yes', even qualified) on all questions. All of those that do not score positively fail on the value likely to be realised on enforcement. In addition Russia fails to give first rank priority to the mortgage creditor. Improving enforcement procedures is not always easily addressed and the gradings not only on the question of realisation return but on most of the issues related to enforcement seem to confirm that this area needs attention in many countries.

With the exception of Bulgaria and Serbia all the negative gradings under the certainty criterion relate to debtor obstruction or purchaser protection on enforcement. Figure 8.3 above shows that uncertainty, unlike the other criteria for legal inefficiency, is more prevalent further East, whereas Central European countries (except Poland) and Romania provide more certainty. The issue of certainty permeates most of the questions in the survey. Uncertainties have been noted elsewhere on, for example, registration process, preferential claims and enforcement procedures. Similarly the answers to the question regarding the form of debt are commented on under fit-to-context above, but for Bulgaria, Croatia, Georgia, the Kyrgyz Republic and Romania they showed uncertainty as to the requirements for describing the secured debt.

As mentioned above the fit-to-context questions cannot be expected to provide a comprehensive assessment. It is nonetheless interesting to see the composite picture for the questions covered. The only negative ratings were on the question regarding the form of debt and the question on subsequent constructions. Three countries (Estonia, Hungary and Slovenia) have top grading on all questions and most have one or two downgrades. The Kyrgyz Republic has three downgrades and despite four downgrades, Romania is still maintaining a positive rating on all questions.

8.4 SPECIFIC ISSUES AFFECTING MORTGAGES IN TRANSITION ECONOMIES

The legal efficiency criteria have helped to draw attention to certain legal issues that can cause inefficiencies in the mortgage market. In this section we look at four of them and suggest how they can be approached. The issues are:

1. mortgage registration;
2. definition of the secured debt;
3. inclusion of constructions;
4. enforcement process.

8.4.1 Mortgage Registration

It is essential that a system is in place to publicise mortgages. The value of a mortgage to a creditor lies in the confidence that the secured claim can be recovered out of the mortgaged property in priority to other creditors. Publicity of the mortgage ensures that any person subsequently acquiring a right in the mortgaged property is alerted to the existence of the mortgage. Likewise, when creating the mortgage the creditor can discover any pre-existing mortgages or other rights providing similar protection to the holder (for example tax liens for unpaid taxes) which have a prior claim. Without a reliable system for publicity a creditor is unlikely to have sufficient certainty in his rights in the mortgaged property.

In most countries mortgages are registered in the same register as the title to the property and this facilitates the search process. Title to the property is already registered and the simplest system is to have mortgages registered against the title so that any person searching the title can see immediately the mortgages that have been registered. However, registration of title and registration of a mortgage serve quite distinct purposes.

Title registration has the effect of authenticating the title, guaranteeing its validity, based on the principle that any person should be able to rely on the accuracy of information shown in the land register. In legal terms, registration (for example of a transfer of land) often results in the creation of the proprietary right over the property. Registration of a mortgage is often given the same effect, confirming to the world the validity of the mortgage. However, in the context of the contemporary use of mortgage this approach is singularly inefficient: it means that the registrar (or another person, for example a notary, who is not a party to the transaction and on whom the registrar relies) has to be satisfied that the mortgage is validly created and for that he has as a minimum to check the mortgage agreement and the powers of the parties. It is this checking process which delays the creation of mortgage and means that it usually takes a number of days or weeks to obtain registration (see Figure 8.4 above). The case for the land register providing the public with guaranteed information on ownership of land is unquestionable, but the position for mortgage is different. The desired effects of mortgage registration are:

1. to alert third parties that a mortgage exists, *or is claimed to exist*; and
2. to establish the precise time from which it would have priority.

The validity of the mortgage is a matter for the mortgage creditor. He can establish the mortgagor's title to the property from the title register; he should be able to establish the validity of the mortgage agreement (in a similar way that he can establish the validity of the loan agreement). If the mortgage is enforced (which will only apply to a small fraction of all mortgages) any question of its validity can be raised at that stage (in the same way as any question of validity of the loan agreement). Requiring the registrar or any other external party to examine and be satisfied as to the validity of every mortgage that is to be registered is creating a heavy and unnecessary burden, which delays mortgage creation and is of little or no value to the parties or the public.

The requirements should be limited to what is necessary to achieve the intended effect. If, as in most traditional systems, registration is intended to 'authenticate' the mortgage, the process will be more onerous because the registrar will have to be satisfied either by his own enquiry or by relying on notarisation that the mortgage has been validly created. If, as explained above, registration is merely intended to publicise the *claim* of the mortgagor that he has created a mortgage, then the registrar should only have to:

*   check that the mortgagor is registered as owner of the mortgaged property;
*   check that the person requesting registration is the mortgagor or a person duly authorised by him; and
*   ensure the information relating to the mortgage in the register accurately reflects the information given by the person who requested registration.

That process may only take a matter of minutes and now that most registers are becoming electronic the possibility of immediate registration is becoming real – not just the same day but 'while you wait'. Some countries (for example Estonia, Hungary, the Czech Republic, Slovenia) have registration systems which ensure that the order of priority is the order of application for registration, or that the order is preserved by an immediate note being made on the register of any pending application to register a mortgage. Useful as these procedures may be, they become unnecessary if registration is quasi-immediate.

The extent to which third parties are able to rely on the entry of the mortgage in the register also depends on the intended effect of registration. As explained above, if registration aims to 'authenticate' the mortgage, a third party will expect the entry to establish the right of the mortgage creditor under the mortgage, just as the register establishes the mortgagor's ownership. It has been seen that in practice this is not necessary. Leaving the onus of proving validity on the mortgage creditor who seeks to enforce simplifies the process for creating the mortgage and reduces time and cost. The mortgage creditor (and any person to whom the mortgage right is transferred) should be capable of ensuring that the mortgage is valid without having to rely on the registrar, and third parties only need to know whether a mortgage is *claimed* on the property. A person searching the register does, however, need to rely on the fact that no mortgage can be claimed on the property other than those shown in the register. Reliance on the 'negative information' given by the register is an essential element in establishing certainty of title and first priority ranking.

8.4.2 Definition of the Secured Debt

The Mortgage Regional Survey has shown that the nature of the debt that is secured and the way it is defined can be the source of many legal problems in transition countries. The pragmatic requirements of the market are simple enough:

- there should be certainty between the parties as to what they have agreed;
- the requirements for defining the debt should be simple;
- there should be sufficient flexibility to allow the debt to be defined in a way which corresponds to the transaction that the parties want to carry out.

Certainty between the parties is normally required as a general principle of contract. However requirements to specify and quantify the debt at the time of mortgage creation are unnecessary and can greatly reduce the simplicity and flexibility of mortgage as a means of security. Certainty can be achieved notwithstanding a general description of the debt. The core requirement is that the description enables the debt to be determined with certainty *at the moment of enforcement* of the mortgage.

There can be much legal discussion as to how to define a debt, as to where one debt ends and another begins, and as to what additional requirements are to be made when defining a debt for the purposes of security. Is each instalment under a loan a separate debt? Is interest part of the same debt as the principal? Should it be expressed as a money amount too? Likewise theories abound as to whether a secured debt can fluctuate (as in the case of a bank overdraft, or a credit line) and as to whether the secured debt can include future debts that arise after the mortgage is created.

These issues have already been well rehearsed, and often satisfactorily resolved, in the context of pledge laws (the securing of debt by movable property),[18] yet they continue to present problems for mortgage. Here it is sufficient to summarise the basic elements needed to achieve a simple and flexible definition of the secured debt:

1. The secured debt may include debts arising in the future, for example further advances that a bank may make under a loan agreement, or additional loans that may be agreed subsequently. It should suffice for the description of the debt to make clear what is covered.
2. The debt may also fluctuate, for example in an overdraft or revolving facility where repayments can be made and amounts redrawn subsequently.
3. A general description should be possible. Formalistic requirements for specifying and quantifying each debt, for example listing each advance made by a bank under a loan agreement, are not needed to achieve certainty. In most cases the specific principal amount of the debt will be stated (typically in the case of a residential mortgage loan) but this should not be a legal requirement. In the case of a loan facility it is only the maximum principal amount of the debt that can be specified. In commercial and financial market transactions the principal amount may for example be calculated under a formula which gives sufficient certainty but means that it is impossible to quantify the debt at the time the mortgage is given. Some countries allow a wide description of 'all monies due from the debtor to the creditor'; others require that the legal

---

[18] See EBRD Regional Survey for Secured Transactions, available at www.ebrd.com/st.

nature of the debt is also specified. Frequently a maximum amount of the principle debt has to be specified when a general description is used.

4. The debt may include not only interest, but also items as agreed by the parties (costs, commissions, etc.) and the costs of enforcement.
5. The debt may be expressed in local or foreign currency.

Accessority is often cited as a curb on flexibility for mortgage creation and as an obstacle to the transfer of mortgage. The problems, in fact, do not flow from the concept of accessority which is self-evident: a mortgage always depends on the existence of a debt secured by the property, and in the absence of a secured debt a mortgage creditor can exercise no rights under it. In that sense there is no such a thing as a 'non-accessory mortgage'. Whereas there is general agreement that the secured debt has to exist and be defined with adequate certainty for a mortgage to be *enforced*, requirements for the debt also to be in existence and/or specified *at the time of mortgage creation* vary considerably from one country to the next. Difficulties often arise from the way in which in some jurisdictions the so-called 'doctrine of accessority' is applied. The requirements which result from such doctrine can limit the kind of transactions that can be secured by mortgage and the way they can be structured.

Perhaps the easiest way to present the issues surrounding accessority is to illustrate the progression in terms of the debt that can be secured from what is sometimes called 'strong accessority' through 'weak accessority' to what is normally meant by 'non-accessory mortgage': see Figure 8.5.

The non-accessory mortgage is often put forward as a solution to the problems that can arise from strong accessority. One of the best known examples in practice is the *Grundschuld* (or 'land charge'), which is successfully used for mortgage lending in Germany. It seems that one of the reasons why the land charge was developed by the banking sector was to circumvent problems under mortgages (*Hypotek*) when the interest rate was variable (as opposed to fixed). The land charge was then used instead of a mortgage: since it is created as an abstract security right, it could be used to secure debts that the mortgagor and the lender would define separately (and freely) by contract.[19]

---

[19] There is not space here to analyse the *Grunschuld* as used in Germany. Although it has been made to work successfully in Germany and is the principal instrument used in one of the largest mortgage markets in the EU, it should be noted that the documentation required is more complex than in most jurisdictions where an accessory mortgage is used. See also Stöcker, O. (2005), 'The Eurohypothec: Accessoriness as legal dogma?' in A. Drewicz-Tulodziecka (ed.), *Basic Guidelines for a Eurohypothec*, Warsaw: Mortgage Credit Foundation.

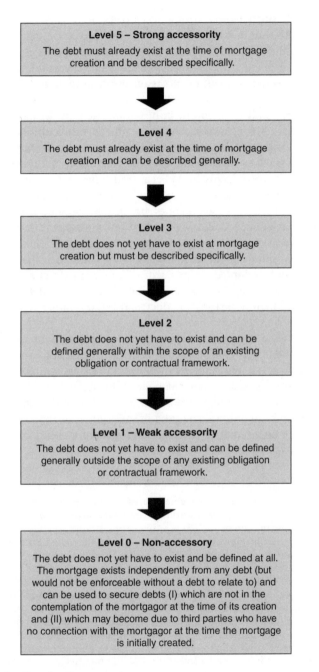

Figure 8.5   Levels of accessority

The distinction between 'strong accessority' and 'weak accessority' is centred on the way in which the secured debt has to be defined and the moment at which it has to be specified. At one extreme, the debt has to exist and be fully specified at the moment the mortgage is created. At the other, it is sufficient at the moment of mortgage creation to describe the secured debt (whether present or future) with sufficient certainty to enable it to be identified specifically at the moment of enforcement of the mortgage.

As seen above 'strong' accessority poses practical difficulties in mortgage transactions because it can restrict the ability to secure debts described in general terms (such as variable interest rate) and to cover future debts. There are arguments rooted deeply in the legal traditions of some civil law jurisdictions to adhere to the strong accessority approach, for example that a right in rem like a mortgage cannot be created without the debt being defined with absolute specificity. However developments in recent years in the laws governing pledge in transition countries show that simple and legally efficient solutions can be found. Decisions have to be made as to how far the law can be adapted to the needs of modern market practice or, on the contrary, whether the market should be restrained by legal principles which are mainly justified by doctrinal theory, rather than economic rationale.[20]

Any discussion of accessority is made complicated by the different approaches and interpretations that apply from one jurisdiction to the next. And each lawyer will naturally tend to view the issues against the particular backdrop of his own system which inevitably leads to crossed wires. But when the issues surrounding accessority are looked at detached from any specific legal system and are analysed in the context of the practical effect they may have on a mortgage transaction it becomes clear that the advantages of non-accessority may be illusory.

---

[20] It has been suggested that the non-accessory mortgage be used as the basis for the Eurohypothec. This derives from the difficulty of reconciling widely diverse systems operating in each of the 27 countries of the European Union without harmonising the existing regimes (which would be beyond the remit of the project), and currently remains under discussion. When seeking a common form of mortgage to facilitate and encourage cross-border mortgage financing the non-accessory route may avoid some of the incompatibilities between existing national regimes, but the legal efficiency of such a solution needs to be examined as a separate issue (as has been pointed out by stakeholders in the public commentary procedure on the European Commission Green Paper on Mortgage Credit in the EU). The Green Paper focused on a number of issues mostly relating to the obstacles faced by lenders from one EU jurisdiction providing mortgage finance in another EU jurisdiction. The White Paper on the Integration of EU Mortgage Credit Markets was published in December 2007, see www.ec.europa.eu.

8.4.3 Inclusion of Constructions in the Mortgaged Property

It is essential for the parties to a mortgage to be certain as to what is included in the mortgaged property. However, this is a problem in some transition economies. Most often constructions are included as part of the same property as the land plot on which they are built and thus would automatically be included in a mortgage of the land. However in some jurisdictions (for example the Czech Republic, Kazakhstan, the Kyrgyz Republic and the Slovak Republic) buildings are treated for purposes of ownership and registration as separate from the land plot, and it is then necessary to ensure that the description of the mortgaged property identifies not only the land plot but also any relevant construction on it. Problems can arise with later constructions. If buildings are treated as separate a mortgage lender could find it has a mortgage over the borrower's land plot and house, but not over a garage built on the land subsequently. It is desirable that later constructions and improvements are automatically included in the mortgaged property unless otherwise agreed. This is of particular significance for builders and developers where a bank financing their projects will expect a mortgage not only over the building land but also over new constructions on the land as and when they come into existence.

Practical problems frequently arise for new constructions. Property developments are fuelling mortgage markets across Central and Eastern Europe and mortgage credit has a major role to play in encouraging construction of new housing. Viable means are needed for using the land and the future construction as security for financing developments. In practice the parties may want to commit to the sale and purchase before the construction is complete (or even before it has started). In this way the vendor (developer) reduces his risk and needs for finance, and the purchaser is assured that he will obtain the residence he has chosen (particularly needed in markets where there is a shortage of new housing).

Without mortgage credit the new housing market is effectively limited to cash buyers or those who can persuade the developer to accept payment after completion. In this case, banks would have their right of mortgage recognised only as from the moment when the borrower registers his property rights – in other words, when the construction is completed. If this option is not viable, and in many cases it is not, banks can try to resolve this problem by taking as collateral during the construction period the rights of the borrower under his agreement with the developer.[21] However, lending

---

[21]   In some jurisdictions a system of 'housing certificates' is provided, that is, a security offering the right to purchase a share in a building in construction, which can be traded and also pledged.

remains risky since these rights may have little value if the construction is delayed or if the developer fails to deliver. In Russia for example the interest rate charged by banks on such loans can be between 2 and 3.75 per cent higher until the mortgage can be properly registered.[22]

8.4.4   Enforcement Process

The principal aim of enforcement is to realise the mortgaged property promptly at market value. The mortgagor and the mortgage creditor should share a similar interest that the mortgaged property be realised at the best price. The prerequisites to enforcement and the process by which it is achieved, from the formalities of commencement to the distribution of proceeds, should be legally efficient. If they are not, costs arising through delay and complexity are likely to reduce the net proceeds and may give the mortgagor opportunities to obstruct the process. Recent reports indicate that many transition countries are relatively successful in this respect, but that may be due as much to favourable market conditions as to the strength of their system. Allowing the mortgage creditor choice as to the manner of realisation, and control over the realisation process (linked to a duty of diligent execution), is likely to be conducive to improving and sustaining enforcement results. Realisation of the debtor's property, and especially his home, to enable payment of his debts remains an extreme solution, only to be used when other possibilities have failed. If the system for enforcement is to work efficiently there has to be a series of checks and balances. The mortgage creditor is often in the stronger position and it is easy to paint the picture of the creditor who ruthlessly abuses his position of strength at the expense of the defenceless debtor. This overlooks the fact that the situation was born out of an agreement between the two parties, not by force or law. And the system that leans too far towards protecting the debtor may deprive the mortgage of much of its value, with consequent repercussions on the availability of mortgage credit.

Throughout the entire enforcement procedure there should be the possibility for either party to involve the court if the circumstances merit it. The role of the court is important, but as a safety net rather than a lead player. If the mortgage creditor leads enforcement either directly or through professional executors appointed by him, the court should be available to intervene at the request of either party if enforcement is not being implemented as agreed and intended. In particular the mortgagor should have the right to apply to the court to challenge the right of the creditor to enforce or in case of failure by the creditor to respect his legal or contractual obligations

---

[22]   See Merrill Lynch (2007), *Russian Mortgage Market*, p. 13.

on enforcement. The mortgage creditor should be able to apply to the court to challenge, or to obtain protection against, actions of the mortgagor which prevent or impede enforcement.

The court should be empowered to order appropriate remedies, for example to order a stay on enforcement, or to order the mortgagor to take necessary action to enable sale of the mortgaged property to take place, or to desist from obstructive actions. It should also be able to order either party to pay damages to compensate the other for the consequences of wrongful acts. The role for the court is to put back on track a procedure which has derailed or gone against the parties' contractual agreement, *not* to take over the proceedings. The ability of the court to react promptly and to order appropriate remedies can be a determinant factor in the efficiency of enforcement. This may sound a very challenging role in transition economies, where courts may have limited experience in arbitrating between parties in commercial matters and logistical difficulties in intervening swiftly. However, this is the objective to strive for.

There can be many reasons why sales on enforcement frequently realise low value. Some of them have to do with the formalities and inefficient procedures involved. But one reason is that the enforcing creditor may have little motivation to realise more than is necessary to pay off the secured debt. Requiring court supervision of realisation or imposing special auction procedures will not necessarily lead to a high price. On the contrary, we think that if the mortgage creditor has been given a special advantage of being able to lead the enforcement process and choose the method of realisation, part of the quid pro quo should be that he is under a duty to act diligently and to maximise the price obtained. Failure to do so should lead to liability to the mortgagor in damages. The way that duty is framed will depend on the local legal context but it needs to be meaningful, similar for example to the duty that would be owed by a professional person who is commissioned to make a sale. At the same time it should be clear what the duty involves and care should be taken to ensure that it does not encourage opportunistic litigation. Where the mortgage creditor is required (or chooses) to appoint professional persons to conduct the sale on his behalf, those persons should be under a similar duty.

It is not just the mortgage creditor who has duties on enforcement. Realisation will normally require some cooperation of the mortgagor. It should be in the interests of the mortgagor to cooperate in order to achieve the best financial outcome. However there need to be rapid and effective remedies where he fails to do so, for example where he acts in a way which could diminish the value of the property or prejudice the sale. The mortgagor who fails to cooperate or who actively obstructs the realisation process should also be liable to the mortgage creditor for the resulting loss or damage.

8.5 CONCLUSION

The Mortgage Regional Survey shows that many transition economies have made remarkable progress in providing the legal and institutional framework for a mortgage market. Contrary to some continuing negative prejudice, the overall picture is beyond doubt encouraging. However, there are still certain areas where improvements to the legal efficiency of the mortgage process could translate into significant benefits for the economy. One of the most telling findings of the research carried out by the EBRD is that all of the 17 selected jurisdictions have some features which are highly efficient, but this efficiency is too often offset by other features which bring with them complexity and costs or which may even undermine the very purpose of mortgage law. Thankfully, policymakers do not need to go very far to find inspiration. Their next-door neighbours may well have taken the steps needed to remedy such deficiencies.

Ultimately, transition countries have a choice: either they can structure their mortgage law on the basis of established legal doctrine and let the financial markets design mortgage transactions around the rigidity that comes with it (which in a practice leads to unnecessary costs and complexity); or they can analyse how mortgage can be used to maximize economic benefit (for borrower and lender alike) and design the law and its implementation around market needs, even if that requires some innovation and a departure from the traditional legal approach.

The stakes may be higher than many transition countries currently realise. The funding of mortgage markets relies increasingly on attracting investors into covered bonds or mortgage backed securities. Notwithstanding recent problems with sub-prime mortgages this will continue to be the case, but investors are likely to become more demanding as to the quality of the mortgages that underpin these debt securities. There need to be simple and certain means for transferring or pledging the mortgage loans in favour of investors, but investors also need to be assured that the mortgages attached to the loans will provide an efficient and reliable means of recovering amounts due in the case of default by the borrower. For this there has to be (a) certainty that the mortgage affords adequate security rights, and (b) confidence that the procedures for enforcement permit efficient execution of those rights. The secret power of mortgage securities lies precisely in the strength of the underlying rights in immovable property given by the mortgage. In other words, the success of the so-called secondary mortgage market, which so many countries are craving to develop, depends on the legal efficiency of the mortgage law.

PART 4

Stories of reform: lessons learned and remaining challenges

9. The Slovak secured transactions reform: ingredients of a successful reform and reflection on its achievements

Katarína Mathernová*

9.1 INTRODUCTION

The reform process is often a mysterious one: unless one has been part of it (an insider), the ingredients that made the reform succeed, or fail for that matter, have left few tangible traces. This applies also to law reform. The final product – a law, a decree, a register – cannot testify for what had taken place. What makes reforms succeed in one country while they fail in another? What ingredients are necessary to lead to the adoption and smooth implementation of reforms?[1] The ambition of this chapter is to revisit the content and context of the secured transactions reform that was successfully concluded in Slovakia. And since the reform has now been in operation for several years, the chapter also tries to draw some conclusions as to whether the reform reached its objectives.

The parliamentary elections in September 1998 marked a major breakthrough for Slovakia in its political and economic transition from communism. They were followed by a full parliamentary term of profound reforms and reorientation of the country away from its authoritarian governments of the mid-1990s. Slovakia's reform trend and path towards European

---

*   Between 1999 and 2002, Katarína Mathernová served as Special Advisor to Deputy Prime Minister for Economic Affairs Ivan Mikloš. Currently, she is Deputy Director General in the Directorate General for Regional Policy in the European Commission in Brussels. The views expressed in this chapter are those of the author and in no way represent any views, policies or positions of the European Commission.
[1]   For a fuller discussion of these and similar issues please refer to K. Mathernová and J. Renčko (2006), ' "Reformology": the case of Slovakia', *Orbis, A Journal of World Affairs*, **50** (4), p. 629.

integration was reconfirmed in the 2002 elections with the reappointment of Mikuláš Dzurinda as Prime Minister. Although Dzurinda's two election cycles were characterized by quite different reform atmospheres, with different combinations of ruling parties, both implemented a broad range of reforms. During the first term, the government focused on the first generation of reforms: macroeconomic stabilization (to avert a financial crisis in 1998–1999); enterprise restructuring and privatization; restructuring and privatization of the banking sector; regulation of the financial sector and of natural monopolies; and institutional and legal changes regarding bankruptcy, access to credit and corporate governance. The results of these reforms created the fiscal space necessary for the second generation of reforms. These were undertaken during the second Dzurinda government, following the 2002 surprise election victory of the reform parties. This next set of reforms was aimed at improving and consolidating public finances, and included such ambitious efforts as a complete overhaul of the tax system (addressing the revenue side) and social welfare, labor, pension and health-care reforms (addressing the expenditure side). These were complemented by broad fiscal decentralization and reform of the public administration.

This chapter looks at the secured transactions reform in Slovakia that was implemented during the first Dzurinda term and attempts to tell two stories, one addressing the *process* of reform; the other its *content*. The author was personally involved in the design, consensus building, adoption and implementation of this reform. She offers personal reflections on the factors that made the reforms possible, on the reform process itself, and on the management of the reforms, including stakeholder management.

The rest of this chapter has three distinct sections: section 9.2 attempts to analyse the key aspects that allowed the implementation of the reform; section 9.3 presents the key features of the reform and how it radically changed the means by which creditors and debtors secure their transactions using movable and immovable property. Section 9.4 concludes with a few remarks on the reform's achievements and limitations, as can be seen four years on.

9.2   WHAT WERE THE SPECIAL INGREDIENTS WHICH MADE THE PROCESS POSSIBLE?

Several different factors positively influenced the reform process. They can be classified in three categories:

1.   The secured transactions reform was part of a clear, comprehensive and well-sequenced programme of economic reforms run by the top

tier of the Cabinet, namely the Deputy Prime Minister for Economic Affairs. Also, the team approached the legal reform in a holistic way; the process was not only about drafting a piece of legislation, but rather about building a new framework for secured transactions: from organizing the necessary support and consensus, through drafting about 18 new laws and legislative amendments, through developing a new register, through making the reform take effect via various written commentaries and practical guides, to monitoring its implementation.

2. The reform was led by a very effective team that invested heavily in consensus building for the reform and effectively managed the diverse stakeholders, mobilizing supporters and neutralizing opponents of the reform.

3. The team managed to take full advantage of international support, both for offering expert advice and for promoting the necessary reforms. Close cooperation with the European Bank for Reconstruction and Development (EBRD) whose experts were part of the drafting team was key to the success of the collateral reform.

9.2.1 Reform Process Led by a Clear Program of Economic Reforms; Holistic Approach to Reform

When the first Dzurinda government took over in the Fall of 1998, Slovakia was on the verge of an acute economic crisis, notably a credit crunch marked by the suspension of any external financing to Slovak enterprises. This contributed to a total indebtedness of the economy amounting to almost 60 per cent of GDP. The crisis had its roots in a mix of controversial policies pursued by the 1994–1998 Mečiar governments. These included an unsustainable macroeconomic policy mix; a contentious privatization program; failure to address the problems of the deeply troubled banking sector; and neglect of legal and institutional reforms. The government's expansive fiscal policy, financing large infrastructure projects from public sources and extending state guarantees on bank loans for large state-owned companies such as power stations and railroads, generated unsustainably high current account deficits that were financed by external borrowing rather than by inflows of foreign direct investment. The commercial banking sector was plagued with inexperienced staff, outdated IT systems, inadequate risk assessment procedures, insufficient internal control and limited supervision on the part of the National Bank of Slovakia (NBS). This fostered an environment that allowed fraudulent activities on the part of certain bank employees, extending soft loans to allies in politics and business. Given the weak internal environment and inadequate banking supervision, such activities were difficult to identify and stop.

The lack of structural reforms in the enterprise and banking sectors between 1994 and 1998 was paralleled by a complete neglect of any institutional and legal reform. Firms not only lacked a functioning market exit mechanism via a bankruptcy system, they also did not have any effective means to secure credit based on modern market practices. In 2000, the Slovak Republic was one of the few countries in Central and Eastern Europe which was noted as 'unreformed' by the EBRD in its survey of secured transactions regimes in the region.[2]

The first Dzurinda government was elected in the Fall of 1998 with a strong reform mandate to overcome the legacy of the Mečiar years, restructure the economy and achieve international recognition through membership in international institutions, notably the European Union. The three pillars of the reforms – macroeconomic stabilization; structural reform in the banking and enterprise sectors; and legal and institutional changes – were designed and undertaken as a complete reform package, on the basis of a Cabinet approved reform blueprint. While the reforms were sequenced over two years, the Cabinet's initial political decision in mid-1999 sanctioned the entire gamut of the reforms. It was important to bind up front the entire wide left-right government coalition to the reforms, while political consensus was still present. In the absence of the early Cabinet blessing, it would have been difficult to keep the momentum or even get a go-ahead for some of the reforms at a later stage when political disagreements in the governing coalition appeared.

The legal and institutional pillar of the reform package had three main components: a functioning bankruptcy regime; better corporate governance rules; and a new framework for secured transactions. The new bankruptcy legislation, which took effect in July 2000, strengthened the rights of creditors and, importantly, allowed companies to continue in operation after bankruptcy had been filed. This saved jobs while preserving the value of company assets, thus avoiding unnecessary damage to creditors. Reforming the bankruptcy system proved to be one of the most politically

---

[2]   See D. Fairgrieve and M. Andenas (2000), 'Securing progress in collateral law reform: the EBRD's Regional Survey of secured transactions laws', *EBRD Law in Transition*, Autumn, pp. 28–35, especially map on p. 32. The 1994 initiative in Slovakia, led by the Ministry of Finance and the Supreme Court, to revise the Civil Code provisions related to secured transactions was brought to a standstill in 1996 under the Mečiar government and the reform momentum was lost. Even if successful, the initiative with its unitary security right and registration provisions would not have met the needs of lenders and borrowers.

controversial and difficult parts of the entire reform package.[3] Extensive 2002 amendments to the Commercial Code addressed corporate governance problems such as the stripping of corporate assets ('tunneling'), the protection of minority shareholders through greater disclosure rights, and liability of statutory representatives of enterprises (officers and directors). Overhauling the secured transactions framework then became an important tool for the newly revitalized banks and restructured firms for more efficient credit flows. In January 2001, the Cabinet approved the initial legislative proposal for the secured transactions reform.

The success of the reform of the secured transactions framework was also due to the holistic approach undertaken. The reform did not limit itself to legal drafting and registry building. It encompassed extensive consensus building prior to and throughout the drafting process, but also active promotion of the new legal framework and its financial benefits once adopted. The reform team, with the assistance of EBRD, produced a 'practical guide' informing market participants of the new opportunities; a legal commentary for the legal and judicial audience; and 'frequently asked questions' on the new registration and search procedures which are posted on the Chamber of Notaries website. The team also engaged in 'product development' with Slovak banks to encourage the availability of new credit products, and judicial training was also provided to all judges from commercial courts (via a USAID-sponsored program). The latter was very important since the application of new laws is often reported by businesses as a real problem. Several team members ran a training program in the country on the most important features of the new framework, especially the new enforcement provisions.

9.2.2 Consensus Building and Team Work

The reform process in Slovakia could not have taken place without four elements being present. One was the political courage and leadership of the

---

[3] Given the huge level of inter-enterprise arrears, many in government were hesitant to adopt a new bankruptcy law. They feared a 'domino effect', in which the liquidation of one enterprise would lead to the insolvency of a great number of other firms. Advocates of the reform argued that an efficient exit mechanism for uncompetitive firms was needed so that their assets could be used for productive purposes. It was especially important to amend the bankruptcy law as soon as bank restructuring had been completed, Slovenská konsolidačná (the state-owned agency that administers and sells non-performing loans) had been established, and privatization tenders had been initiated, so that potential investors in the banks, in assessing the local business environment, would be able to take the bankruptcy amendment into account.

reform advocates within the government (as seen above). Another was the promise of international integration and advice from international organizations (see below). The third and fourth were the existence of a small reform team capable of absorbing the lessons provided through international assistance and designing individual reform steps, and the energy, time and resources that went into the consensus building and stakeholder management prior to launching the reform and throughout the adoption and implementation of the reform.

From the start, the government had established a two-tier reform management structure. The reform-minded members of the Cabinet made up the top tier, providing overall guidance for the reforms and making the political decisions. The other tier, strategically placed in the offices of the Deputy Prime Minister for the Economy and the Minister of Finance, consisted of external experts, financed through non-governmental funds (including NGOs, the academic community and foreign institutions), who possessed the professional, linguistic and management skills to design and carry out complex projects. Often, ministry officials were ill-prepared to address the needs of a modern market economy. Sometimes they also had a vested interest in maintaining the institutional status quo.[4] It was thus necessary to form a team capable of quick and efficient management. While quickly absorbing foreign know-how and applying it to specific Slovak conditions, this team at the same time designed proposals that would meet the formal procedural requirements of the state administration, and addressed the concerns of various reform stakeholders. Importantly, the team had access to the top policymakers, and thus was able to intervene and support the decision-making process at key junctures. Apart from their professional skills, these individuals were not beholden to any particular interest groups, willing to take risks and experiment, and had the determination to push reforms through.

Under this umbrella reform structure, in September 2000, the reform team authored a governmental decree according to which the secured transaction reform was formally led by the Ministry of Justice, in conjunction with the Office of the Deputy Prime Minister. Such arrangement, while rather unusual in the country, was part of a global strategy for the management of the reform process. Since amendments to the Civil Code envisioned under the reform fell under the responsibility of the rather conservative Ministry of Justice, it was critical to get them on board early on. While the initiative and drive for the collateral reform was led by the Office of the Deputy Prime Minister, the Ministry of Justice became, over time,

---

4   K. Mathernová (2002), *Law in Transition*, London: EBRD.

fully supportive of the project. Despite coming from vastly different background and political culture, the individuals ended up working effectively together and creating excellent synergies.[5] The principal drafter of the secured transactions provisions was a legal scholar retained by the Office of the Deputy Prime Minister who later, under the second Dzurinda government, herself became the Minister of Justice.

The reform team put a lot of energy, especially at the beginning of the reform process, into consensus building. The team first found support among entrepreneurs, economic think tanks and banks, and later also in the legal community. The team worked very closely for example with the Banking Association, since the reform was going to directly benefit the banking sector. The envisioned secured transactions reform, introducing for the first time in Slovakia a non-possessory security interest in movable assets, represented a distinct departure from the local legal tradition. It was therefore critical to give academic credentials to the project. The reform process coincided with on-going revision on the Civil Code (which traditionally contains legal provisions on security interests in movable and immovable property). Since the Civil Code revision was inevitably going to be a long and tortuous process taking several years, it was necessary to receive a blessing from the Civil Code revision committee for separate amendments of the Code, for the purpose of implementing the secured transactions reform. With the initial Cabinet approval of the reform blueprint in September 2000 and, a year later, with two more endorsements by the Legislative Council of the government and again with the Cabinet's specific legislative 'intention' to reform, the secured transactions reform received the necessary support from the rather conservative legal milieu. Only then could the actual drafting start.

9.2.3   Reaping the Benefits of International Support

Slovakia's exclusion in the mid-1990s from the first wave of accession to the OECD and NATO, and its failure to join the first round of countries negotiating EU entry alongside its peers from the so-called Visegrad Four,[6] were the result of the Mečiar government's unsuccessful economic policies, compounded by frequent transgressions against democratic principles. The first Dzurinda government therefore had to prove it was capable of radical

---

[5]   The team published a commentary of the law to coincide with its entry into force. Katarína Mathernová, Katarína Valová, and Mária Hucíková (2003), 'Reforma záložného prava', *Ekonomický a Právny Poradca Podnikatela*, **6–7**, 62–97.

[6]   The four Visegrad countries include the Czech Republic, Hungary, Poland and Slovakia.

reforms to regain the country's credentials on the international scene. The promise of international integration became the most potent unifying factor that enabled the wide coalition to remain in power for its full term and implement far-reaching reforms.[7]

Re-engaging in an open policy dialogue with international institutions, notably absent during the Mečiar government, was one of the key features of the Dzurinda economic reform team. It was useful in several respects. First, since Slovakia was a latecomer to structural reforms, the design of these reforms could benefit from quality advice and experience gathered by international experts in other transition countries, such as Poland, Hungary and Slovenia, that had gone through similar processes. Second, the knowledge and understanding that the international experts acquired about the reform process and agenda in Slovakia allowed them to be vocal vis-à-vis Slovak policymakers and media, which proved invaluable for sustaining the reform momentum. Third, the push for sometimes difficult and controversial reforms by the World Bank, the EBRD, the European Union or the International Monetary Fund often helped the reformers in the government make the case for their necessity on the domestic scene. In several instances, for example, the reformers requested that recommendations from individual World Bank mission documents containing details of the reform package be used to convince reform opponents about the necessity of the reforms and their extent and timing. During the design, approval and implementation stages, international experience was extensively used. A unique country-specific system of cooperation among foreign donors and local experts was established. This enabled the integration of assistance provided by the World Bank, the European Commission, EBRD, USAID, and other institutions into a mutually coordinated assistance package. When dealing with international institutions, it was the high-quality technical advice and the international credibility that resulted from open dialogue with them that mattered in reform design, less so the financial assistance.

The secured transactions reform was a bit of a paradox. While for most other reforms in Slovakia the prospect of EU membership provided a rallying objective and an opportunity for fundamental changes, this was not the case on secured transactions. Most of private law in the European Union is national and secured transactions reform was not part of the EU

---

[7]   In the case of the second Dzurinda government, the desire to fully integrate Slovakia into the EU's monetary system and enable the country to catch up with the EU-15 in terms of per capita GDP were the driving forces behind the reforms. In fact, the reforms of the second Dzurinda government outpaced the reform policies of many of the EU-15 countries.

acquis per se. Even today, the only true piece of EU legislation in the area of secured transactions is the 2002 Financial Collateral Directive, which was implemented in Slovakia after the new secured transactions law had entered into force. The team, however, successfully made an argument that a new legal framework for taking security over assets was necessary for increasing private credit flows in newly restructured banking and enterprise sectors. Implementation of the reform became a conditional covenant in the World Bank's Enterprise and Financial Sector Adjustment Loan, on which the World Bank was regularly checking progress.

While the support and pressure of the World Bank in the secured transactions reform process was critical for pushing the reform through, the legislative and institutional content and direction of the reform was developed in close collaboration with the EBRD team, notably Frederique Dahan and John Simpson. EBRD experts provided indispensable guidance and expertise both in the development of the new law as well as in starting a brand new pledge register.

From the outset of the reform it was clear that a new secured transactions legal framework would require the development of a pledge register where the security rights over movable property would be recorded (security over immovable property (mortgages) would remain recorded in the Land Cadastre). The state budget, however, did not foresee such expenditure. Since the only way one could reach a consensus on the need for the reform was without any implication for the state budget, private financing for the register had to be found. Under the auspices of the Ministry of Justice, the reform team launched a competitive selection process for the development and financing of the register in exchange for an exclusive licence for running the register. Apart from the obligation to arrange private financing for its development and operation, the selection criteria included, for example, the need to establish and maintain access points to the register at least in every district in the country. It also contained strict conditions specifying the public interest in the searching and registration. The Slovak Chamber of Notaries won the bid. It did indeed pay for the entire cost of the project; no public resources or grant money (apart from EBRD technical advice) were spent. Winning was not all: the Chamber of Notaries also had to be brought on board and to fully internalize the rationale underlying the reform and thus the operation of the register. For a while, the Chamber wanted the new registration procedure characterized as a full notarial process which tends to be rather formalistic and costly in civil law countries. Such result would have run counter to the fundamentals of the reform – mainly ease and simplicity of formalities. Ultimately, through establishing trust and a good working relationship between the Chamber, the Office of the Deputy Prime Minister, the Ministry of Justice and the

EBRD, an agreement was reached that registration was going to be a simple administrative act where the function of the individual notaries processing the registration was simply that of a registrar.

9.3 SECURED TRANSACTIONS REFORM: KEY FEATURES

The 2003 revisions of the Civil Code, the establishment of the pledge register and a number of other laws adopted as part of the secured transactions reform dramatically changed the restrictions and uncertainties that had hindered the development of a market for secured credit in Slovakia.[8] Prior to the reform, creditors mostly relied on the fiduciary transfer of title (art. 553 of the 1964 Civil Code) to secure their obligations. This legal concept, popular in jurisdictions with a similar legal culture such as Austria and Germany, has some appealing features, especially the ease of enforcement since the title to the asset is transferred to the creditor for the life of the secured obligation. Among its main drawbacks, however, are its secrecy and the inability to create a charge over future assets or assets with a fluctuating value, such as inventory.

Under the new secured transactions framework, Slovakia has acquired one of the most advanced regimes for charges and secured credit of any country in Europe.[9] The reformed Civil Code provisions allow broad scope for creditors and debtors to agree to the terms on which security is given so that it fits with the circumstances of their particular transaction. To get credit, for the first time, borrowers in Slovakia could consent to a non-possessory security interest on their own assets. Granting such security interest allowed them to keep the pledged asset in their possession, for example a car or a piece of industrial equipment, and use it, or even sell it in the ordinary course of their business.

Under the new framework, any legal or physical person can give a charge over its assets in favor of any creditor, to secure his own or another person's debt. The charge can be taken over any right or asset that is capable of being transferred. This may include any movable assets, land and buildings

---

[8]   The secured transaction reform consisted of a major amendment to the Civil Code, a number of amendments to over a dozen other pieces of legislation, a brand new law on privately held public auctions, and an amendment to the Notarial Law establishing the collateral registry. All the necessary laws and amendments came into force on the same day, 1 January 2003.

[9]   See 'Why Slovakia has the world's best rules on collateral', *The Economist*, 25 January 2003, pp. 80–81.

(residential or non-residential), rights and receivables, or even a group of assets, which is constantly changing, such as inventory, trade receivables, stock of raw materials or an entire enterprise. It may also include assets to be acquired in the future. Based on the Slovak legal tradition, the main provisions of the Civil Code on charges cover *both* immovable and movable property. Hence the creation of a charge over a piece of equipment or a building is subject to the same conditions (agreement, definition of collateral and of secured debt). The enforcement of the charge is also governed by the same provisions, which are very flexible and open to contractual arrangements. Only perfection (registration) is subject to different rules: a mortgage is registered at the Land Cadastre, while charges over movables are registered in the pledge register operated by the Chamber of Notaries.

The assets may be identified by a general description, and not specifically identified at the time of the charge agreement, provided that it is possible at any given time to identify the collateral. All types of claims may be secured. The secured debt may be denominated in any currency, may be of fixed or varying amount and may include claims that will arise in the future, as long as the maximum principal amount of the claim is stated. As the law is not restricted to bank lending but covers credit given by any person, it can be used, for example, in trade or supplier financing.

9.3.1 Simple Formalities

The aim of the reform is to permit a simple and rapid creation of a security interest. The requirements are a written agreement and publicity of the charge by registration against the name of the chargor in the pledge register (or in an asset register, where title to the asset is registered, for example for land, trade marks, patents, ships, aircraft, shares and bonds). There is no requirement to notarise or otherwise certify the charge agreement, although parties may of course choose to do so. The charge agreement must specify the secured claim (including its amount or maximum principal amount) and the charged assets.

The Chamber of Notaries maintains the new pledge register in a single electronic database. Registration is made instantly via a terminal in a notary's office. Parties may choose any notary throughout the country to register their pledge. The information that needs to be supplied by the chargor is the identity of the parties and a description of the secured debt and the charged assets. The information in the register is public and can be consulted by anybody free of charge over the Internet. A charge over assets to be acquired in the future may be registered in advance (this will ensure the priority of the charge) and is created automatically when the chargor acquires ownership of the asset. Fees for the registration are defined by a decree of the Ministry of Justice: they vary according to the amount of the debt secured, and range between €30 and approx. €350. Since the register exists only electronically and all the notaries have direct connections to the database, it takes only a matter of minutes to register a charge.

9.3.2 Priority

An acquirer of the charged asset takes it subject to the charge unless (a) the charge agreement permits disposal free from the charge; or (b) the transfer is in the normal course of business within the scope of the chargor's business activities (this protects normal commercial trading but does not apply where the charge is registered in an asset register); or (c) the purchaser acting with due care was in good faith (if the charge is registered, there is a presumption against good faith acquisition, subject to proof to the contrary). All rights and obligations concerning enforcement of the chargor become effective against the acquirer. The chargor and the acquirer are jointly responsible for registering the change in the person of the chargor. Enforcement by another creditor of an execution decision against the collateral is only permitted if the secured creditor consents.

Since several charges may be created over the same asset, clear priority provisions are critical. The creditor has a first right in the assets taken as security, subject to any prior security given to other creditors. Other persons dealing with the chargor are able to ascertain whether assets are subject to security by consulting the pledge register or the relevant asset register. Priority between charges is determined by the order of their registration.[10] An agreement between secured creditors on a different order of priority is effective upon registration, but has no effect as against a secured creditor not participating in the agreement if it has a negative impact on the enforcement of his claim.

An important innovation brought about by this reform is the abolition of the preferential tax lien (super privilege) that for many years made the assessment of credit risk by lenders very difficult. Under the lien, in case of enforcement of a charge (outside of bankruptcy), the tax authority had the possibility to enforce tax arrears ahead of all other creditors, including secured creditors with pre-existing secured debt. This of course created a major uncertainty for secured creditors who, despite having taken security, at the time of enforcement could see tax offices enforcing their outstanding

---

[10]   This applies even in the case of possessory charges: a possessory charge which is not registered will lose priority to a subsequent registered charge.

claims on the assets which had served as collateral. This superpriority, in effect, defeated the very purpose of taking security.

As part of the reform, a dialogue was undertaken with the Ministry of Finance, which reluctantly accepted to repeal this privilege. An amendment of the Tax Administration Law[11] has given greater certainty to secured creditors by abolishing the preferential tax lien. Instead, the tax authority can register their tax claims in the pledge register and thus rank with other secured creditors for priority ranking.

9.3.3 Enforcement and Realization

The secured transactions enforcement provisions in the Civil Code, combined with the new Law on Auctions, are some of the most important features of the new framework. Since they apply to movable as well as immovable assets, they have had, arguably, the most far-reaching consequences in easing the enforcement and realisation of collateral. They led to a dramatic decrease for example in the time necessary to foreclose on mortgages, from 560 to 45 days.[12]

If the debtor fails to pay the secured debt when due, the secured creditor has the right to take possession and to sell the assets given as security and to use the proceeds to repay the debt. Sale of the charged assets may be (i) in the way specified in the charge agreement; (ii) by sale at public auction under the new law; or (iii) by execution through the courts.

The secured creditor must notify the chargor in writing of the commencement of enforcement and, if the charge is registered in the pledge register, he must register the notice there. The notice must specify the mode of realization. Following the notice, the chargor is not allowed to transfer the collateral without the consent of the secured creditor. To protect debtors who may be in less favorable position when the charge agreement is negotiated, any agreement entitling the charge holder to acquire ownership of the collateral directly is void if it is made before the secured claim becomes due.

The new Law on Auctions, adopted as part of the reform package, makes it possible to achieve a rapid and effective sale of collateral at a public auction. These auctions are voluntary as they are not court-led but privately organized. The law requires the chargor and any third party in possession of the collateral or relevant documents to cooperate in the enforcement of the charge, including by handing over the collateral and the documents.

---

[11] Law No. 551/1992 on Tax and Fees Administration.
[12] *Doing Business in 2005*, Washington, DC: World Bank, p. 47.

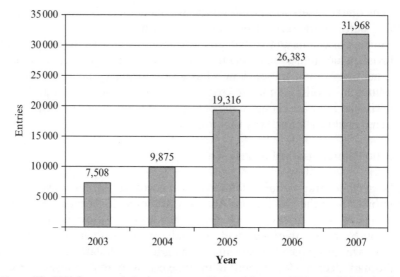

Note: The 2003 figures exclude charges created before 1 January 2003 and which had to be
registered to keep their original priority ranking.

Source: Register of Pledges, Slovak Chamber of Notaries

Figure 9.1   Number of entries in charges register

9.4   FOUR YEARS ON: HOW SUCCESSFUL?

The new secured transactions framework has been operational now for
over four years. It has successfully taken root in Slovakia. As Figure 9.1
shows, the number of new registration of charges in the collateral register
has consistently increased from year to year.

Three elements of the new framework have fundamentally increased the
legal security of all creditors. The reform dramatically expanded the scope
of assets that can be used as collateral; it eliminated the above-mentioned
preferential tax lien on tax arrears; and it gave creditors private enforcement rights, including the ability to repossess collateral and dispose of it
through private sale/auction. These changes, felt practically overnight, have
led to increased availability of credit. These changes importantly contributed to the assessment of Slovakia as the world's top reformer in the
World Bank's flagship publication *Doing Business in 2005*.[13]

---

[13]   Ibid.

The openness of the new provisions is now fully utilized in large structured transactions handled by international law firms and companies active in Slovakia. According to interviews with several law firms, for example the provisions on future and fluctuating debt are frequently used. Of course, the main litmus test for the success of the reform will come from the courts which will be called upon to uphold some of the innovative features in Slovak law.

There were also aspects of the reform process, however, which have been less successful. First, in the second half of 2003, the Banking Association petitioned the Ministry of Justice to amend the new provisions. This was rather disappointing, especially since the Association was an active supporter of the reform team and actively participated in the development of the reform concept. While *The Economist* called the system 'the best collateral law in the world' and the Slovak government was being praised in Washington at a World Bank-sponsored symposium, in Bratislava, the banks were expressing loudly their opposition: they resented the transparency provided by the register which they felt was in breach of bank secrecy.

The amendments were courageously resisted by the Ministry of Justice, which wisely considered that the new system needed some time to function before introducing any changes to it.

Second, once the reform was in place it has proven very difficult indeed to keep policymakers' focus on the issues of secured transactions reform. The Ministry of Justice had many demands on its limited resources and was working on many other fronts. Hence issues that still needed addressing were left aside. For example at the time of the adoption of the reform package, no decision had been taken as to whether fiduciary transfers of property (a technique that had developed as a way to circumvent the inability to take security over assets without having to transfer possession to the creditor, see above para. 9.3) would remain possible under Slovak law and whether it would require registration in the collateral register. It seems that other priorities, seen as more pressing, have prevented a discussion on this topic, which is regrettable since it leaves this aspect of the new law uncertain.

Third, while the collateral register functions generally well, it has several shortcomings that may reduce its efficiency. Reportedly, some required information is not always registered and some surplus information on the other hand is included. There was also initially a mismatch between the public application forms available on the Internet and the forms used by the notaries. These shortcoming are, however, not unusual during the initial period of a new system. It is important to pay attention and make adjustments and improvements as necessary. Since the adoption of the reform, the board of the Chamber of Notaries has completely changed and that could be one of the reasons contributing to the reported shortcomings.

9.5 CONCLUSION

There are a few conclusions that can be drawn from this reform experience.

Overall human capacity constraint can be a limiting factor: a group of well-placed advisors managing the reforms proved key to reform success. As stated earlier, the skills necessary to implement rapid and comprehensive reforms, to create the regulatory environment necessary for a modern market economy and to counter vested interests, were lacking in a state administration hamstrung by its own organizational structure, procedural rules and political ties.[14] The government's two-tiered reform management structure, combining members of the Cabinet with external experts placed strategically outside the bureaucratic hierarchy, provided both the political clout and the professional, linguistic and management skills to design and carry out complex reform projects, applying foreign know-how to Slovakia's specific conditions. With access to the top policymakers, and beholden to no particular interest groups, these external experts were extraordinarily effective in driving the reform process forward.

Interestingly, the capacity constraint applied conversely. The vested interest groups frequently lacked the capacity to mobilize forces and block changes (for example, enterprise and bankruptcy reform). This feature of a relatively young society and a country such as Slovakia is in stark contrast with established markets, such as Germany or France, but also in comparison with the neighbouring Czech Republic, where interest groups are well organized and entrenched, making any radical reforms politically more difficult and less likely.

Well-targeted international assistance can add value and credibility to domestic reform processes: targeted, high-quality international assistance was crucial in the Slovak case. The assistance was demand driven, rather than supply driven, with local staff able to shape the donors' agenda to meet the government's needs. Using the reform experiences of other countries was an important factor that facilitated the accelerated design of Slovakia's reform measures.

---

[14] Mathernová (2002), n. 5 above.

Once a reform is adopted, the reform momentum is likely to dissipate: even if the reform driver is still present, given other competing reform priorities, it is much harder to focus people's minds on issues of implementation and improvements to the already adopted reforms. However, especially in the case of legislative reforms, their adoption is just the beginning of an equally important, albeit admittedly less glamorous, process. Many reform efforts have not produced the results they could due to shortcomings in their implementation. It is also at this point when vested interests can more easily take over, once people's minds are focused elsewhere. It is therefore critical to design reforms well and invest heavily in the initial consensus building. This approach has paid off well in the case of Slovakia.

10. The Romanian Electronic Archive of Security Interests in Personal Property

Diana Lupulescu

10.1 HISTORIC CONSIDERATIONS

During 50 years of communism, until 1990, Romania had a highly centralized economy, imposed by the Romanian Communist Party. The rules that governed the economy and the relationships between Romanian economic organizations or commercial companies were not based on economic fundamentals. Almost all Romanian companies were state-owned and their relationships were decided by ministries and other centralized state organizations. Romania has had a legal system strongly influenced by French law; commercial matters were mostly governed by the Civil Code and Commercial Code.[1] However, although both Codes remained in force during the communist years, they were of very little practical use and therefore had not been developed or updated during the whole communist period.

At the beginning of the 1990s, the national consensus was that Romania would develop a market-oriented economy. Romania started a profound and global reform to update its legal system, institutions, commercial relationships and, most importantly, mentality and human behavior. The long and tricky road of transition had started! It was an obvious struggle, not always going in the right direction, a long and difficult journey, but essential to follow.

A modern market economy has credit at its core. It is thus crucial to have in place a legal framework that encourages the granting of credit by enabling creditors to get the loan repaid, including by selling the assets of the debtor whenever necessary.

---

[1] The Civil Code was adopted in 1864. The provisions regarding pledge were those from the 1804 Napoleonic Code. The Commercial Code provisions had been 'updated' in 1906.

The first years of the 1990s in Romania could be characterized, from an economic point of view, as 'wild capitalism'. Commercial and financial laws barely existed or were ignored. Those were the years when several very large banks[2] went bankrupt, the exchange rate between local currency and US dollar or Western currency was changing dramatically every day, or even several times a day. Banks were extremely cautious in their lending policies and the interest paid for the loan could surpass the principal amount lent.

Until the mid-1990s the Civil and Commercial Codes' approach to secured transactions was in the form of mortgages (security over immovable assets) and pledges (security over movable assets). Pledges required the transfer of possession of the collateral to the pledgee. Publicity of the pledges was made at the local courts of law and consisted in registration of the pledge contract in a paper registry. Mortgages were registered by notary public in land registries. The secured transactions provisions were cumbersome and impractical. Most of the banks preferred to secure their loans by mortgages.

Romania had been advised and 'supervised' in its struggle to a market economy by international institutions. The European Bank of Reconstruction and Development and the World Bank were, perhaps, the most influential and active organizations and played a most important role in the financial and economic reforms that started in the middle of 1990s and are still going on. Indeed, both organizations emphasized the need for secured transactions reform, among others, and the adoption of Title VI on Legal Treatment of Security Interests in Personal Property in May 1999 took place in the context of a larger World Bank project, which comprised many more aspects.[3] The Law[4] regulates the 'legal treatment of security interests in movables that aims at securing the fulfillment of a civil or commercial obligation arising from any contract concluded between natural or legal persons' (article 1 of the Law on Security Interests in Personal Property[5]). It introduced (article 29) the concept of an 'Electronic Archive

---

[2] Bankorex (Romanian Foreign Trade Bank), Bank of Religion, Dacia Felix Bank, Bankcoop, etc.
[3] Law Respecting Certain Measures for the Acceleration of the Economic Process.
[4] This refers to Title VI on Legal Treatment of Security Interests in Personal Property from the Law Respecting Certain Measures for the Acceleration of the Economic Process. In the interests of brevity, in this chapter 'Law', or 'Law on Legal Treatment of Security Interests in Personal Property' means Title VI from the Law respecting Certain Measures for the Acceleration of the Economic Process.
[5] The translation of terms from Romanian to English is taken from the original English version draft of the Law.

of Security Interests in Personal Property'[6] (the 'Archive'), a unique system of publicity for security interests over movable assets, which has deeply changed the way credit is offered in Romania.

The purpose of this chapter is to focus on the Archive as a system and an institution, and to describe how it was set up, its functions, organization and supervision, how it operates and the processes it runs. The reason behind the choice of the subject is clear when one looks at the statistics: the use of the Archive, from its very inception, has been remarkable and has grown over the years. All key players agree that the institution is a success. We believe there is therefore a lot to be learned from the Romanian experience for those countries who, once convinced that secured transactions reform matters for the economy, undertake the painful and long task of providing the tools for it.[7]

10.2　FUNCTIONS OF THE ELECTRONIC ARCHIVE OF SECURITY INTERESTS IN PERSONAL PROPERTY

The role of the Archive is to establish a sophisticated, yet easy to use, mechanism that supports businesses and individuals in accessing cheap credit and thus enhances the economic growth and general welfare in Romania. The creditor must be sure that he is protected against the bad faith or bad fortune of his debtor. He must be *informed* about existing security interests over his potential borrower's assets. He must be *certain* that, should the debtor default on the loan, he will be able to get his money back *ahead* of other creditors. He must become a *secured creditor*.

The Law on Security Interests in Personal Property, and the Administrative and Technical Regulations, are modeled in many aspects on US-UCC Article 9 and the various Canadian Personal Property Security Acts[8] (PPSAs). The Electronic Archive consists of a system for recording and publicizing security interests in personal property. A secured creditor

---

[6] Sometimes called the 'Electronic Archive of Secured Transactions', making reference to Uniform Commercial Code, Secured Transactions, Article 9, which inspired it.

[7] To assist in the setting up of the Administrative and Technical Regulations for the Electronic Archive of Security Interests in Personal Property, the World Bank launched an international selection process and the Center for Economic Analysis of Law (CEAL) from Washington DC, USA, including the experts Heywood Fleisig and Nuria de la Peña, who are also contributing to this work, was chosen.

[8] Personal Property Security Acts are based roughly on Article 9 of the Uniform Commercial Code.

will acquire a priority ranking over the collateral from the moment of registration (filing) of the security interest into the Archive.

Filing into the Archive grants to the secured creditor the right to satisfy the secured obligation with the collateral before any unsecured creditor (including the state), and before other secured creditor whose security interest or right in the collateral has a lower priority ranking. The Electronic Archive is only a system of notification of an obligation that may exist between the parties. Registration in the Archive does not confer validity to a security interest which would not be valid.

10.3 ARCHIVE ORGANIZATIONAL STRUCTURE: LICENSED OPERATORS AND AUTHORIZED AGENTS, OVERSEEING AUTHORITY AND BODY OF OPERATORS

The organizational structure of the Archive is to some extent atypical in the region. It was based on the idea that open competition would provide the best possible service for the Archive. As a result, the Law introduced the concept of 'operators', which would be licensed to operate the Archive but on a non-exclusive basis. All operators would however be overseen by an authority, the Ministry of Justice, and they would also be organized in the form of a body, a legal entity whose role is to ensure the proper functioning of the central database. The relationship between the four entities, operators, agents, Body of Operators and overseeing authority is illustrated by Figure 10.1. The discussion below will provide further details on each of these entities.

10.3.1 Licensed Operators and Authorized Agents

The Law provides that only *licensed operators* and their *authorized agents* can file information in the Archive. Operators are legal entities who have submitted an application to the overseeing authority of the Electronic Archive and demonstrated that they meet the requirements set out for this purpose. Each requirement has a maximum associated score that the applicant can acquire. Among the most important requirements are the territorial coverage of the applicant, its good name and reputation, and sufficient technical and financial resources to be able to perform its functions. Licensed operators can authorize other persons, authorized agents, to make registrations in the Archive.

All identification information regarding the address, telephone, fax and email address of the operators and their agents are made public on the official websites of the Archive. Typically, the authorized agents are in some way

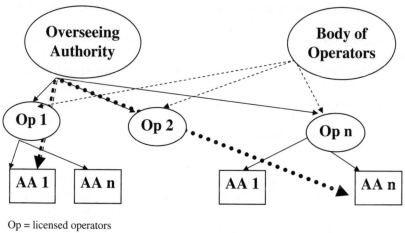

Op = licensed operators
AA = authorized agent

*Figure 10.1   Relationship between operators, agents, Body of Operators
             and overseeing authority*

related to the operator: for instance the Chamber of Notaries is a licensed
operator, which can authorize notaries who express an interest and comply
with the specific regulations to register security interests in the Archive.

At present, the licensed operators are:

- Chamber of Commerce and Industry of Romania;
- National Union of Notaries Public of Romania;
- Romanian Bar Association;
- Ministry of Public Finance (which acts as an operator exclusively to
  register its claims based on tax arrears);
- Banca Comerciala Romana (BCR) (which acts as an operator exclu-
  sively to register security interests where it acts as secured creditor);
- Transylvania Bank (which acts as an operator along the same model
  as BCR).

It is interesting to note how this open model has evolved over the years. It
has been interpreted in such a way that anybody can be licensed, provided
they fulfil certain conditions. Several private companies were initially
licensed in 2001 but their licences were revoked after a couple of years
because they failed to fulfil all requirements imposed by the overseeing
authority. Others gave up the activity because they concluded that the
actual returns were too low[9] or that offering registration services did not fit

with their image in the market. Conversely, whereas initially it was foreseen that banks would be the entities with the strongest interest in obtaining a licence, in reality, this interest did not materialize until later in the life of the Archive. Clearly the process was a learning curve for all parties, operators and overseeing authority, which took a few years.

Interestingly, although the nominal number of authorized agents has not changed much since 2001, the number of entries into the Archive increased appreciably (see Table 10.1). This seems to suggest that the number of agents does not bear a direct relation to the level of activity in the Archive.

10.3.2 Overseeing Authority

The overseeing authority is established within the Ministry of Justice. Its role is to supervise that the activity of the operators and authorized agents are compliant with the Law and the regulations.

The main functions of the overseeing authority are:

a. to license the operators and approve the authorization given by operators to agents;
b. to ensure that operators and their authorized agents file information in the Archive in compliance with the Law and regulations;
c. to administer and run the security copy of the computerized information management system and database of the Archive;
d. to issue administrative orders to further implement the regulations;
e. to inspect the operation of the Archive and control the activity of the operators and their agents;
f. to revoke licences of operators or authorizations of agents;
g. to approve the forms to be used for filings;
h. to work together with the Body of Operators to suggest and develop all necessary improvements and modifications of the Law and regulations.

10.3.3 Body of Operators

The Body of Operators of the Electronic Archive of Security Interests in Personal Property is a not-for-profit association with legal personality. The Body of Operators' role is to represent the operators vis-à-vis third parties and the overseeing authority. It administers and operates the computerized system of the Archive in accordance with the provisions of the Law and

---

9   All operators have to contribute to the costs of running the Archive, see below.

regulations, the administrative rules issued by the overseeing authority and the internal rules approved by the Body of Operators.

All operators are members of the Body of Operators and contribute to the costs of running the system, network, improving the software and hardware and others. Decisions are taken during the Body's General Assembly.

10.4   ARCHIVE'S PROCESSES: FILING OF FINANCING STATEMENTS

The Archive is a unique, centralized database. Filing and searching processes are described by article 2 of the Law.

10.4.1   Filing of Financial Statements

The legal acts that can be filed are not limited to 'pledges', as traditionally understood. They include:

a.   assignments of accounts receivables;
b.   conditional sales, as well as any other legal acts aimed at securing the fulfillment of an obligation with goods (as defined in article 6[10]);

---

[10]   Law on Security Interests in Personal Property, article 6:
  1. It is considered that all movables, tangible or intangible, are subject to the provisions of this title.
  2. It is also subject to the provisions of this title any tangible movable or movable which is an accessory to a real estate, but which can be removed or taken out of the real estate, except for the buildings and construction materials, even if the parties have named the respective contract a mortgage.
  3. By "buildings" is understood the erection of a structure, opening of a mine or starting a work carried out at the surface or underground. The phrase "construction materials" means those materials which are incorporated in a building and includes the goods affixed to a building in such a manner as they can be detached only by producing damage amounting to a greater value than that of the materials obtained as a result of the removal operation.
  4. This title also applies to the goods provided by articles 467–468 of the Civil Code.
  5. The following assets are subject to the provisions of this title:
    a. fungible and nonfungible stock of goods;
    b. the credit balances in deposit accounts, savings accounts or time deposits in banking or other financial institutions;
    c. deposit receipts, bills of lading and similar documents;
    d. shares and social parts in joint stock and limited liability companies;

c. all types of rental, including any leasing;
d. consignment contracts;
e. warrants and deposit receipts;
f. privilege claims, judgment liens, warehouse receipts and tax liens on property.

The *financing statement* refers to the information recorded by a licensed operator or an authorized agent in the Archive that accurately represents the content of the financing statement form as it was submitted by the applicant.

Each financing statement is given an *identification number*[11] that establishes the priority order. An initial financing statement is given a five-year validity from the moment it was filed in the Archive. The validity can be prolonged for another five years, if a continuation financing statement is filed before the expiration of the initial financing statement.

Any person who wants to file a financing statement must fill in the financing statement document form with the necessary information needed to clearly identify the secured creditor, debtor and collateral. The document form can be paper-based or electronic. If the document form is electronic,

---

e. the rights to exploit natural resources and to operate public services, under the law;
f. rights arising from patents, trademarks and other intellectual, industrial or commercial property rights;
g. accounts receivables, whether secured or unsecured;
h. negotiable instruments, including instruments secured by a mortgage;
i. all the personal property of the debtor which may include goods in circulation and future goods;
j. forest, agricultural crop, minerals and hydrocarbon to be extracted or which have been extracted;
k. insurance policies;
l. the right arising from rental or land lease of real property;
m. equipment, installations, agricultural machinery and the like;
n. corporate rights;
o. any right, whether or not exclusive, to deal with personal property or to provide services, that may be assigned by the grantee notwithstanding that the assignment is subject to restriction and notwithstanding that the assignment may require the consent of the grantor or any other person;
p. rented or leased personal property for a period longer than a year;
q. any such other goods.

[11] The identification number has the following structure: yyyy-fffffffffffff-LLL, were, yyyy is the year of filing, fffffffffffff is the numeric result of an algorithm that combines date, hour, minute and second of filing and LLL is a random combination of letters.

then it must be signed using an advanced electronic signature based on a qualified certificate of the signatory. Within 24 hours of filing a financing statement, a secured creditor must send a copy to the debtor.

It is possible to file an *intention* to file a security interest, for example when parties are negotiating a secured financing transaction but have not yet entered into a security agreement. Such filing remains effective for two months. To keep the priority ranking, the creditor must file a *transformation* financing statement before the two-month period lapses.[12]

10.4.2   Documents Needed to File a Financing Statement

Filing financing statements is an administrative function: licensed operators and authorized agents are not expected to ensure the accuracy or legal validity of the information.

Operators and agents must process a filing as presented by the applicant. Only the secured creditor or the debtor, and their representatives, are allowed to file in the Archive. Representatives must be empowered through a mandate authenticated by a public notary to file financing statements on behalf of either debtor or secured party.[13] *Only* the creditor or his representatives may file *any* financing statement. The debtor or his representatives may only request the filing of initial financing statement or a statement of extension of interest in collateral, not any other type of statement.

10.4.3   Searching

According to the regulations, all information in the Archive is public. The Body of Operators must provide access to the public in order to allow the search in the Archive. Any person may search, read or copy the information free of charge. The official websites of the Archive are www.co. romarhiva.ro and www.mj.romarhiva.ro.

There are several criteria to perform a search: identification number of the financing statement, name of the debtor or secured creditor, ID numbers of Romanian juridical or natural persons, elements to identify the collateral (as for instance if the collateral is a motor vehicle it can be identified by the model name, chassis number or engine number). It is also

---

[12]   In this case the duration of the acquired rank of priority covers five years plus the period of time (maximum two months) from the moment when the intention was filed.

[13]   If the representative is a solicitor he does not need the mandate authenticated by a public notary.

Table 10.1 Number of filings 2000–2006

2000	2001	2002	2003	2004	2005	2006	Total
95	65 227	171 170	189 653	282 381	358 996	536 067	1 603 589

Table 10.2 Number of filings per type of parties

Type of parties	Number of filings
Creditor: legal persons	1 236 568
banks	803 598 (65%)
the state	163 105 (13%)
others	269 865 (22%)
Creditor: physical persons	3246
Debtor: legal persons	927 428 (75%)
Debtor: physical persons	309 140 (25%)

possible to use Boolean functions between criteria in order to perform a search.

There are also some supplementary criteria to be used, in order to limit the number of possible search results: period of time when the filing was filed, active or non-active financing statement, not modified filings, etc. The reason why these supplementary criteria were introduced was to ease access to the information without unnecessary burdens to the system.

Certified copies of a filing can be acquired only from a licensed operator or authorized agent. Certified copies may be used in courts of law or during the enforcement procedure against debtors.

10.4.4 Statistics

Table 10.1 shows the evolution of filings into the Archive.[14]As can be seen, the Archive's activities have been consistently growing since its inception, which is mostly explained by the growth of credit from banks.

Table 10.2 shows that banks are the most active users of the Archive. Indeed, the National Bank of Romania (the country's central bank which supervises all credit institutions) requires them to file all lending activities, contracts of credit and other similar acts in the Archive.

---

[14]　In the first year when the Archive became operational, 2000, activity commenced on 15 December 2000, which explains why in 2000 there were only 95 filings.

10.5 CONCLUSIONS

The first and the most important conclusion is that after seven years since the Archive became operational it may be considered a real success. Although initially the Law and the Archive were regarded by many traditional Romanian legal theoreticians very skeptically, they have managed to impose themselves as trustworthy tools in the lending activities of credit institutions and in other commercial or civil obligations.

The Law on Security Interests in Personal Property aimed and managed to enhance the economy by easing the access to cheaper credit for a larger category of people and companies.

The state lost its status as 'privileged creditor' which it used to have before the Law was brought into force. All secured creditors are now equal, the priority ranking depending on the time of filing in the Archive.

The Law allows a great variety of assets to be used as collateral: it is possible to grant security not only for goods that the debtor owns at the present time, but also for goods the debtor may acquire in the future. For instance a secured party can create a secured interest in a future crop, allowing agricultural works to be done in time.

The Electronic Archive of Security Interests in Personal Property bypassed traditional legal obstacles and allowed the use of modern and inexpensive technology for broad public access and filing. The cost of filing in the Archive is relatively low compared to the advantages it brings. The existence of private operators creates a competitive market for the service of filing, which benefits the Romanian business environment.

The most impressive effect was in the field of banking activity. Banks developed a large variety of products aimed at both business and natural persons. Credit has become cheaper and cheaper with every year that has passed.

The system is very liberal, non-bureaucratic, with very few restrictions. The main key-word is 'self-responsibility'. The only area where improvement is still needed is that of security interest enforcement: although the Law contained some provisions regarding the enforcement of the security agreement, it is still difficult for secured creditors to recover quickly and simply the unpaid debt by realizing the collateral.

The Law also contains international provisions. The opposability and priority order of the security interest are governed by the law of the place where the asset was located at the date when the security interest was created. Thus, many foreign companies and foreign banks have developed a wide commercial activity having secured their investments with assets located in Romania. The most active are the European Bank of

Reconstruction and Development, several Austrian banks and companies and several Dutch companies.

The collateral reform that began in Romania at the end of the 1990s has proved worth the effort made by those who have been involved with it. Hopefully, the legal framework introduced by the Law on Legal Treatment of Security Interests in Personal Property will continue to be improved and developed to meet the needs and demands of a modern market economy.

11. Challenges in implementing secured transactions reform in Latin America

Nuria de la Peña[*]

The lack of an effective framework for secured transactions in Latin America substantially limits its economic growth, as has been well emphasized in the preceding chapters. Legal restrictions on the use of collateral, moreover, reinforce the inequality in the distribution of wealth. The laws and institutions that support the use of collateral work well only for owners of real estate who have clear title to their land. Wealthy landowners have better access to credit, enabling them to add more easily to their wealth. This defective system of collateral most hurts those who are already disadvantaged – indigenous people, women and the disabled – the groups most heavily represented among the landless and holders of untitled land.

A major problem is the lack of an effective framework for using movable property as collateral for loans. Only new motor vehicles and titled urban real estate are readily accepted as collateral. Yet new motor vehicles represent less than 0.5 percent of the capital stock. Micro, small and medium-size enterprises typically have 95 percent of their assets in movable property

* The arguments set out in this chapter were first presented at the International Conference on Collateral Reform and Access to Credit, London, August 2006, sponsored by the EBRD and the World Bank. The views expressed in this chapter are solely the author's and do not represent the views or opinions of CEAL or the governments, institutions or countries it represents.

The author thanks her associates Fernando Cantuarias, Heywood Fleisig, Alejandro Garro, Lance Girton, Peter Winship, John Spanogle and Roberto Muguillo, who have all so actively and enthusiastically participated in the CEAL programs on which this chapter draws. She thanks also CEAL's many local attorneys, who have so helpfully collaborated in uncovering the intricate problems of collateral. She is grateful to all those interviewed, who have so patiently given their time to explain their business practices and the many challenges they confront. Finally, she thanks the many chambers, associations and foundations in Latin America that have provided their invaluable support to secured transactions reform.

rather than real estate. Most small farmers have no urban real estate, but their equipment needs amount to about 80 percent of their investment.[1]

Those owning no real estate or lacking formal title to their land do have assets: their movable property and land use rights. Under advanced collateral systems, this property could serve as collateral, or they could purchase on credit equipment that could serve as collateral. Yet because of the defective legal system for using collateral, they cannot obtain such credit.

These problems restrict credit for all small- and medium-scale enterprises. However, in relative terms, they fall most heavily on the poor, the region's small farmers and business people, precisely those whom most development programs and free trade agreements aim to reach. Their inability to use economically important property as collateral arises entirely from the legal system: it has no other roots, economic or noneconomic.[2]

11.1 CASE FOR REFORM: LIMITED ACCESS TO CREDIT

Since 1991, staff of the Center for the Economic Analysis of Law have conducted hundreds of interviews with lenders, farmers and businesses in Latin America for reports under programs of the World Bank, the Inter-American Development Bank and the US Agency for International Development (USAID).[3] In these interviews banks were questioned about the process of securing loans, including the terms and the types of collateral they required and the reasons that other types of collateral were not accepted. They were also asked questions about whether they were able to collect loans in default, how long it took and how much it cost. Merchants were asked similar questions about how they sold on credit. Farmers and businesses were asked about how they financed their operations, from whom and under what terms they had borrowed, what kind of collateral was accepted and their understanding of why other types of collateral were rejected.

The information gathered was then cross-checked with legal research on secured transactions laws in the country. In each case the limited access to credit reported in the interviews matched a limitation under pledge, mortgage, registry or other law relating to collateral.

The interviews also revealed many potentially profitable investment opportunities that went unexploited because the legal problems in using

---

[1] World Bank, Investment Climate Survey, world-wide, 2006.
[2] de la Peña and Fleisig (2001).
[3] Some of these reports are available on the website of the Center for the Economic Analysis of Law, www.ceal.org.

collateral broke the chain of credit. An equipment dealer in Uruguay for example had many clients to whom he was willing to sell on credit. But the dealer could not make such loans because he could not use his inventory and accounts receivable as collateral to obtain the additional financing he needed from a bank. While he had US$1 million dollars in farm equipment, his ability to borrow was confined to his capital in real estate, a small shed worth about US$30 000. Similarly, a flower exporter in Colombia had profitable export contracts, but could not finance the industrial refrigerators and other fixtures needed to better compete.[4]

Some of these problems can be seen in the examples throughout this chapter, which refers mainly to Latin American countries with a Civil Code tradition (excluding Brazil, Chile, Costa Rica, Panama, Paraguay and Venezuela, where no comprehensive research has been undertaken in this area). The chapter focuses primarily on movable collateral. To expand access to credit to its full potential, a secured transactions reform should also improve real estate collateral and the underlying system of property rights (see Simpson and Dahan, Chapter 8, this volume).[5]

11.1.1 Costlier and Riskier Financing of Accounts Receivable

One way in which legal restrictions limit access to credit in Latin America is through the ineffective laws available for using portfolios of accounts receivable and other small loans as collateral. Under advanced legal frameworks for secured transactions, lenders that make many small loans, and sellers and dealers that often sell on credit to small borrowers and farmers, can use such portfolios as collateral for further financing.[6] This can be done whether the loans or accounts in the portfolio are unsecured or secured with real estate or movable assets. Thus this secured transaction provides a crucial link in the chain of credit that links larger lenders to smaller borrowers; such as from banks and capital markets to microlenders, sellers and dealers and thence to individual borrowers and farmers.

Refinancing accounts receivable is simple under an advanced framework of secured transactions like those provided in Romania and Peru in their recent reforms (Figure11.1).[7] Such a system permits the original creditor to borrow by offering as collateral a floating security interest against a portfolio of its accounts receivable. The modern system gives the new lender

---

4   Fleisig and de la Peña (1994); and de la Peña and Fleisig (2006).
5   See de la Peña (2004).
6   de la Peña, and Fleisig (1997b); and de la Peña et al. (1996).
7   See de la Peña and Fleisig (2004); and the Peruvian law on security interests in movable property, Ley de la Garantía Mobiliaria of February 2006.

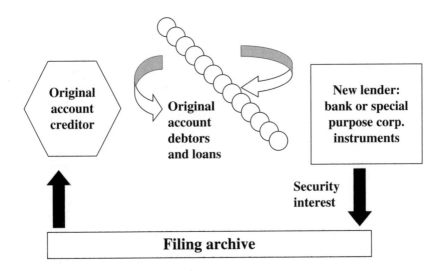

Figure 11.1   Accounts receivable financing under an advanced framework

clear priority in claims against the accounts receivable from the time the new lender files a notice of the security interest in a public archive or registry (without any requirement to notify the account debtors). This public filing gives the new lender priority relative to any assignees or pledgees and against the trustee in bankruptcy.

Moreover there is no need to transfer the accounts. They can stay with the original creditor and rotate, with the security interest 'floating' from the old ones that are paid off to new ones that automatically enter the pool. Unless there is a default, the account debtors continue their relationship with the original creditor. Because the original creditor is often better able to collect from them, the performance of the portfolio remains unaffected by the new financing.

In unreformed systems in Latin America the same transaction is both many times as expensive (in terms of fees) and many times as risky (Figure 11.2). To obtain financing against accounts receivable, the original creditor must transfer each account to the new lender. This system raises costs. Each assignment must identify a particular account or accounts, and in most Civil Code countries it involves paying the costs of a public notarial deed. Healthy businesses have a rotating portfolio of accounts receivable; old accounts are paid off as new accounts are generated. Under obsolete systems, as these old accounts are paid off, more assignments need to be made to transfer new accounts to the new lender. The accounts may rotate

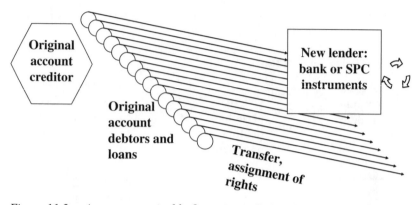

Figure 11.2   Accounts receivable financing in Latin American Civil Code countries

only afterwards, when the new lender issues shares, bonds or other instruments against its capital. Obsolete systems also increase risk. The new lender can establish priority only by giving notice of the assignment to each account debtor. Often, however, the new lender does not want to notify the account debtors because it may increase the risk of default. Such accounts are generated by debtors in transactions with local dealers with whom they have long-standing business relations that are costly to jeopardize. However, when the account is transferred to a new lender (perhaps a bank in the city) without such a relationship to the account debtor, the new lender may be less effective in collecting against them. The new lender could get around this by not notifying the account debtors of the transfer. However this merely changes the nature of the risk, since failure to inform the account debtors suspends any ranking of priority in the accounts.

Because of the riskiness of the transaction, efficient companies and lenders that expand their operations do not obtain additional financing using their portfolios of accounts receivable and small loans. One Colombian banker laughed when asked, saying accounts receivable were not collateral at all. In Colombia, for example, accounts receivable are often refinanced through an existing credit line secured with real estate. This financing does not expand as operators become more efficient and attain more accounts receivables. In Bolivia microfinance institutions often refinance their many small loans through an existing credit line guaranteed by the microfinance donors, no additional credit is given with the collateral of their portfolios of small loans. Many companies interviewed in Latin America were able to finance their operations only with their own savings.

When financing does not expand as operators become more efficient and acquire more assets, it limits their growth.

11.1.2 Higher Interest Rates

The limited access to credit in Latin America can also be seen in the interest rates that borrowers must pay, rates many times those in countries with advanced laws for secured transactions. The interest rates are higher even when country macroeconomic risk is taken into account.

In Bolivia, for example, the average interest rate charged on secured loans for new cars in 2005 was similar to that in the United States (Figure 11.3), with the small difference easily corresponding to the difference in macroeconomic risk between the two countries. For used cars, however, the average interest rate in Bolivia is considerably higher, far higher than in the United States. Why this difference? New car financing relies on the title transfer from manufacturer to buyer by the dealer and the state-certification and registration of that title. This supplements the secured transactions system. Used car loans lose the advantage of the chain of title back to the manufacturer and depend only on the state registration system of the pledge and the pledge regime for priority and enforcement, which are very weak. For loans secured by most other types of collateral, such as cattle, computers and equipment, there are no published data on loan terms or interests rates in Bolivia because there are no such loans.[8] Such loans are weaker than motor vehicle loans because they rely entirely on the legal framework for secured transactions, and have no support from the state-certified title and state registration system. Most lenders interviewed explained that they could not make such loans because the problems in the framework for secured transactions make these loans too risky.

11.1.3 Roadblock of Political Opposition

However powerful the case for reforming the secured transactions framework in Latin America, political opposition to such reform poses enormous challenges (see Fleisig, Chapter 3, this volume). In most countries reform of the framework for secured transactions has hit big roadblocks or made no progress at all.

Colombia and Nicaragua have active reform programs, but they face enormous political opposition from the legal community. After several efforts, programs in Argentina (a World Bank and Central Bank project)

---

[8] Fleisig (2006) p. 9.

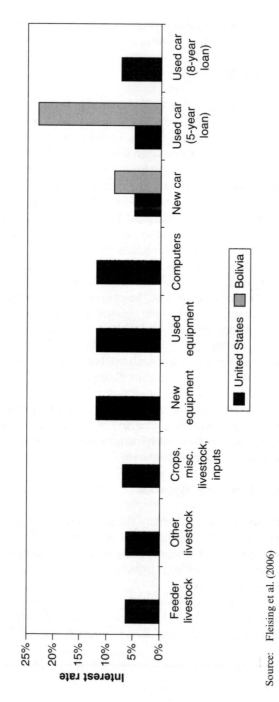

Source: Fleising et al. (2006)

Figure 11.3 Average interest rate for loans secured by different collateral, United States and Bolivia, 2005

and Bolivia (USAID's PREMIER) appear to have been suspended or canceled. El Salvador, where reform faces strong opposition from the registrar's office, has rejected several project proposals. Mexico passed a new law on secured transactions in 2000,[9] but this law left almost every key aspect of the framework for secured transactions unreformed. The new law expanded creation of security interests, but continued the old internally inconsistent system of priority of claims in collateral, the poorly run state registration system, and introduced a very limited reform for enforcing security interests. While Brazil, Chile, Costa Rica, Panama, Paraguay and Venezuela have not yet considered reform, though they show every evidence of having just as many problems in their secured transactions frameworks as the other Civil Code countries in Latin America, Peru is the only such country to have passed a comprehensive law on security interests in movable property in 2006.[10]

11.2   MAIN LEGAL RESTRICTIONS ON SECURED TRANSACTIONS

The legal roots of the economic problem lie in each of the four key stages of secured transactions: creation, priority, publicity (registries) and enforcement. To succeed, reform must address each of these stages. In all of them, however, reform is likely to encounter political opposition.

11.2.1   Creation

In Latin American Civil Code countries with unreformed systems of secured transactions, the law puts many restrictions on the creation of security interests. The law often not only restricts the types of property that can serve as collateral; it also may limit the types of agents that may enter into security agreements and the transactions that may be covered.

Parties that contract outside the law will find their security agreements unenforceable. A transaction outside the law might be used in a country for a while, but in times of economic distress it will soon be voided by the courts. Argentine jurisprudence, for example, provides many cases of pledges voided during the financial crises of the 1990s.[11]

---

[9]   Mexico, *Ley General de Títulos y Operaciones de Crédito*, 23 May 2000.
[10]   Peru, Ley de la Garantía Mobiliaria Law No. 28677, 1 March 2006.
[11]   de la Peña and Fleisig (1997a).

Laws of limited application

Some leasing, trust and warehouse laws permit only government-licensed lenders to function as secured lenders or trustees. These laws have had, in the long term, a very detrimental effect in Latin America. They not only prohibit secured transactions by other lenders; they also have created interest groups that now have a monopolistic niche in the credit market. These lenders often oppose reform in secured transactions because it would open their privileged position to all lenders. For example, interest groups of leasing companies and trustee companies in Argentina and Colombia and warehouse operators in El Salvador either do not support secured transactions reform or directly oppose it.[12]

Limits on floating security interests

Laws in Latin American Civil Code countries also often limit floating security interests and security interests in future property. Where pledge provisions require that collateral be specifically identified or that the debtor own the collateral before entering into a security agreement, they limit the financing of inventory and future crop.

In Nicaragua, for example, one Sandinista farmer interviewed said, 'I did not know at the beginning of the season how many hectares of coffee and how many of beans I was going to harvest, but the bank wanted a detailed list and description of each crop because so the *prenda* [pledge] requires in our Civil Code'.

Opposition to provisions allowing floating and future security interests often comes from legal conservatives, who believe that such provisions are contrary to the Civil Code.[13] Yet there is in fact no conflict with the Civil Code. In Nicaragua for example the provisions in the Civil Code on conditional obligations and those that set priority from the time of publicity address the legal issues posed by floating and future collateral (see also Mathernová, Chapter 9 and Ancel, Chapter 12, this volume, for further examples).

High notary fees

Another challenge to reform arises when the law requires that notaries be involved in the legal processes for creating security interests. Sometimes the law requires that a security agreement be validated by a notary or drafted

---

[12]   Views expressed to the author and her team during mission discussions on secured transactions reform.

[13]   See for example N. de la Peña, Memorandum to Claudia Aragón, Secretaría Técnica de la Presidencia, Nicaragua, re draft law discussion meeting with the Supreme Court, 26 November 2006.

as a public deed. And sometimes the Code of Civil Procedure allows the use of faster processes only with certification by a notary.

In some Latin American countries notaries' fees are high relative to the average income or to the value of the transaction. This is especially likely where a monopolistic regulatory framework allows notary associations to set the fees. When a reform proposes to remove notary requirements, therefore, the notaries put up powerful opposition.[14]

11.2.2 Priority

In most Latin American Civil Code countries the system for establishing priority among conflicting security interests and other claims in collateral remains fragmented, with different priority rules applying to different security devices. This inevitably leaves creditors uncertain about their priority ranking relative to other creditors.

The solution at first seems simple and straightforward: have one rule applying to all creditors, with the first to file a notice of a security interest in a public archive or registry being granted first priority. The reformed law would then need to be comprehensive, encompassing all security devices and possible claims in collateral. Also, it would contain some key public policy provisions to allow competition for additional financing, such as purchase money security interests, which should be given superpriority upon filing against the assets that such security interests finance.

Initially, most interest groups of lenders interviewed in Latin America fully agree with the first-to-file priority rule. As they look more closely at it, however, they oppose the public policy provisions that a 'first-priority rule' needs to foster competition (see below). A reform without these provisions will mean limited competition in the financial sector – a key reason for the limited access to credit for SMEs, small farmers, the poor and the landless in Latin America.

Resistance to competition from existing lending institutions

By most estimates private credit amounts to about 20–30 percent of GDP in Latin America, and banks account for as much as 90 percent of total private credit in most countries of the region. In countries with reformed systems of secured transactions, private credit amounts to as much as 220–300 percent of GDP, with banks accounting for about 40 percent of

---

14 See for example Association of Private Banks of Bolivia (Asociación de Bancos Privados de Bolivia) to Superintendence of Banks of Bolivia, Letter, 4 March 2005.

the total (see Fleisig Chapter 3, this volume).[15] In reformed legal frameworks, therefore, the 'bank business' is many times as large, though it occupies a smaller share of the total credit market.

Nevertheless, interest groups of lenders in Latin America, such as banks and microfinance institutions in Bolivia, sometimes oppose legal provisions that would allow more intermediary lenders to enter the credit market. These existing lenders rarely focus on the fact that allowing more lenders can increase overall credit. Instead, they focus on the 90 percent of the credit market that they now have and that they would have to share with other lenders. Protecting what they have becomes their objective, and they often do anything to oppose the reform.

In Bolivia in 2005, for example, banks[16] and microlenders[17] and local chambers of commerce[18] sent letters to Congress and the President opposing the reform. They raised many legal objections to reforming the country's pledge laws: common law versus civil law, incompatible systems, the possible security risks of an Internet registry, the constitutionality of creditor-administered enforcement and the like. After experts explained how all the legal issues could be resolved within the Bolivian legal system, the key issue that remained – the one that always remains – was a matter for political decision: whether to open competition in exchange for a much larger credit market.

How political opposition blocked beneficial reforms in Peru

Peru shows how effective political opposition can be in blocking beneficial provisions that would increase competition (see de la Peña 2001a). The Government of Peru did not have a secured transactions project that would provide them with international experts to develop their draft law. Instead, it commissioned a working party that worked on its own and modeled their law after the CEAL draft secured transactions law prepared for a project in El Salvador that was presented at the International Seminar on Secured Transactions in San Salvador in 2000. However, as the Peruvian working group adapted the model in preparing the final draft law, it removed precisely the provisions that would have opened competition. It is unclear why

---

[15] See for example de la Peña and Fleisig (2006).

[16] Letter, n.14 above.

[17] Association of Financial Entities Specialized in Microcredit of Bolivia (Asociación de Entidades Financieras Especializadas en Microfinanzas) to S. Smith PREMIER USAID project, Letter, 30 March 2005 (available upon request).

[18] Chamber of Industry, Commerce and Services of Santa Cruz (Cámara de Industria, Comercio y Servicios de Santa Cruz) to Bolivian Congress, Santa Cruz, Bolivia, Institutional Positions (Posiciones Institucionales), 22 April 2005 (available upon request).

they did this. Possibly, without supporting expert help, they did not understand the economic importance of these unfamiliar features; or, perhaps, they thought it was natural to defend the position of the dominant lenders; or, perhaps, they could not defend the public policy reasons when these provisions were attacked by dominant lenders.

- *Superpriority of purchase money security interests*: this feature promotes financing for new equipment by permitting dealers that sell equipment on credit to retain priority against such equipment over any other existing claims;
- *provisions that void restrictive covenants against creating security interests of subsequent priority in the same collateral*: loan contracts in Peru often include clauses requiring full payment of the first loan when a subsequent loan is secured with the same collateral. Provisions that void such clauses are needed to allow for the maximum divisibility of collateral and thus free otherwise frozen capital;
- *provisions establishing the priority of security interests in fixtures (movables attached to real estate) over mortgages in that real estate*: such provisions eliminate the requirement that the owner of real estate consent to the creation of a security interest in movables that will attach to the property, and void any clauses to that effect. Therefore, they often free borrowers from having to take a mortgage on their real estate in order to purchase industrial equipment through financing advanced by a dealer.

Excluding these provisions in the Peruvian reform will limit the economic impact of the reform in expanding access to credit beyond bank borrowers. Of course, priority rules are about balancing various interests. Yet such balancing must aim at increasing the social gain from expanding access to credit. These provisions eliminated from the Peruvian reform would have opened opportunities for lending by dealers and small creditors, thus creating a more competitive credit market in Peru. Banks also would have gained: when intermediaries such as dealers can lend at lower risk, they provide loans that banks can profitably refinance. Nobody expects a bank in Peru to lend directly to a poor farmer. But a reform of the secured transactions framework should expect that banks will refinance the loan portfolios of nonbank intermediaries, such as dealers of agricultural inputs and equipment. In turn, these intermediaries bring financing to small farmers by selling to them on credit.

Therefore, the opposition by Peruvian banks to these provisions seems shortsighted. They would also have expanded access to credit by nonbank lenders, but they would also have expanded many times the overall credit that banks could extend. Thus, those provisions that were eliminated would have increased the economic impact of the reform by expanding access to credit. It would have also fostered a more equal distribution of credit, because nonbank lenders can better reach most of the poor as well as small and medium-scale businesses.

Protection for consumer, labor and tax claims
Another key challenge in reform arises from the priority granted to consumer, labor and tax claims relative to security interests. Whether to afford protection to such claims is a public policy decision. Whatever protection a country decides to provide to such claims, however, a reform needs to emphasize transparency of the protected claims. That permits lenders the essential ability to assess in advance the equity value of collateral while still allowing the public policy choice of giving priority to the protected claims.

An effective law integrates protected claims into the overall framework of claims against property while minimizing exceptions to the priority system of contractual security interests in the same property based on order of filing. It does this in different ways: in some cases, by setting out predetermined amounts for protected claims and easily verifiable statements of taxes due, so that secured lenders will know the size of claims having automatic higher priority. In other cases, it requires public filings of all possible claims or interests in collateral, including tax, labor and civil liability claims in order for a prospective secured lender to take account of these claims when evaluating the collateral being offered.

11.2.3   Publicity

In a first-to-file priority system the law must designate where to file security interests, so that any potential lender can quickly determine whether the collateral offered by the borrower is subject to prior security interests or other claims. Ideally, for this purpose, that place would be a notice filing archive, based on the Internet. In a notice filing archive system, only a notice of the existence of a security interest is filed, offering important advantages in cost and accessibility (Figure 11.4).

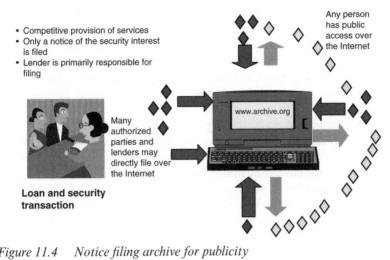

- Competitive provision of services
- Only a notice of the security interest is filed
- Lender is primarily responsible for filing

Any person has public access over the Internet

Many authorized parties and lenders may directly file over the Internet

www.archive.org

Loan and security transaction

Figure 11.4   Notice filing archive for publicity

All Latin American Civil Code countries that introduced a modern system use a first-to-file system to establish priority. However, their first-to-file systems fail to take advantage of the great simplification possible with a modern notice filing system. Instead, they inappropriately adopt many of the paper and manual filing features of the system for recording real estate (Figure 11.5). Such a registration system is many times more costly than a notice filing archive, for two main reasons.

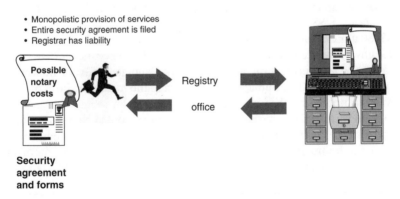

- Monopolistic provision of services
- Entire security agreement is filed
- Registrar has liability

Possible notary costs

Registry

office

Security agreement and forms

Note: Projects that introduce forms and computer systems at the registry offices do little to improve the publicity system if papers or paper forms still must be presented to the registry or scanned into the computer system. The ability to retrieve information is limited when access to the registry records continues to be permitted only through registry offices.

Figure 11.5   Registry for publicity

First, under the registration system in most Latin American Civil Code countries, the law requires the filing of the entire security agreement, not just a notice of its existence. As a result, the registry must store more information than is necessary, increasing its costs (for contrast see Lupulescu, Chapter 10, this volume). Computerizing a registry by itself does not help, because parties are still required to bring the paper security agreement or paper form to the registry.

Second, the law assigns the liability for recording correct information to the registry, not to the private lenders. This liability forces the registry to undertake costly legal functions to verify that the information in the security agreement conforms with the law before recording it. It also forces the registry to keep a paper or scanned copy of the security agreement for verification purposes.

Imposing these liabilities on the registry adds enormously to its operating costs. A registry system such as that in Colombia needs software, scanner equipment and substantial computer storage space. It needs many registry employees, including many lawyers, in several parts of the country to enter the data and verify information, along with the attendant payroll, office space and administrative expenses. Both initial and operating costs are very high.[19] Oddly, even though this responsibility is used to justify the higher costs of verification and record keeping, its economic value to users is unclear. No Latin American registry, to our knowledge, has ever taken financial responsibility for errors it committed in the registration process.

By contrast, notice filing systems, in which lenders are responsible for the information filed and often also make filings directly into the archive, operate at a much lower cost. A notice filing system with these characteristics, serving an entire country with a population of about 25 million would cost about US$50 000–100 000 to set up, with operating expenses of US$150 a month for rented Internet server space and staff costs for about three government employees for supervision. All other costs, for data entry, legal review and verification, are borne by the lenders as part of their work to process a loan. The public can freely access the archive at no cost from any computer with a Web browser.[20]

Access to a registry system is also often more limited than to a notice filing system. The requirement to file the entire security agreement results in too much information in the registry, raising issues of privacy for the parties involved and concerns about providing full public access. No such

---

[19] See de la Peña and Fleisig (2006).

[20] Romania for example has implemented a public Internet-based archive under a notice filing system (see de la Peña and Fleisig 2004). The model for this archive is being followed in the secured transactions reform program of the government of Nicaragua. It is available at www.ceal.org.

concerns exist with a notice filing archive, and lenders can easily search for prior claims in collateral.

Most registry systems in Latin America are run by the government. But even when they are run by the private sector, they do not permit competition in the services they provide. So there is effectively no incentive for providing good registry filing services. By contrast, in the most advanced notice filing systems, competition is introduced when the law authorizes lenders and other persons to file security interests directly in the archive. Competition is opened both for filing services and for searches of the archive through its Internet site (see Lupulescu, Chapter 10, this volume).

Finally, registry systems in Latin America present common 'registry problems', which can increase risks for lenders. There can be errors in receiving and archiving paper, and paper-based searches are likely to be less accurate than a computer search of a notice filing database. Moreover, they often establish priority by the date of filing rather than by the date and time (hour, minute and second), opening possibilities for conflicts in priority.

With all the drawbacks of registry systems, who would oppose switching to a competitive Internet archive and notice filing system? All those who gain from the inefficiencies of a registry system: the registry employees, the politicians who award them the jobs, the courts that depend on the registry fees, the lawyers preparing the complex filings.[21]

Meanwhile, these expensive publicity systems have their most detrimental impact on small loans and on the refinancing of large numbers of small loans, both secured and unsecured. This limits the success of a secured transactions reform in expanding access to credit to small and medium-size enterprises and the poor.

11.2.4   Enforcement

Enforcement of secured loan contracts in Latin American Civil Code countries remains a long, expensive and risky process, limiting the economic value of collateral.[22] Even Mexico and Peru, which have undertaken secured transactions reform, have yet to address enforcement problems. Mexico provides for a quick out-of-court sale, but the new law

---

[21]   See for example Chamber of Industry, Commerce and Services of Santa Cruz (Cámara de Industria, Comercio y Servicios de Santa Cruz) Bolivian Congress, Santa Cruz, Bolivia, Institutional Positions (Posiciones Institucionales), 22 April 2005 (available upon request) and Chamber of Industry, Commerce and Services of Santa Cruz to S. Smith PREMIER USAID project, Letter, 25 June 2005 (available upon request).

[22]   See de la Peña and Fleisig (2001).

left repossession unreformed. Peru provides for notary repossession rather than privately administered ('self-help') repossession.

The high costs of enforcement in Latin America stem from fees charged by lawyers, notaries, the courts and judicial officials as well as from the time required to complete repossession and sale. The long delays also increase risks for lenders. In rural areas lenders may face even higher costs and risks because of lack of availability of the enforcement mechanisms provided by law (for example lack of access to courts or notary services where the law requires court or notarial enforcement).

Legal and judicial interest groups are often strongly opposed to reforming enforcement systems. They particularly oppose extending enforcement rights to creditors and permitting creditor-administered repossession and sale of collateral. They often justify their opposition by arguing that out-of-court enforcement is unconstitutional in their country.[23] Legal research by many reform programs has shown that constitutional arguments do exist that favor creditor-administered repossession and sale of collateral over due process clauses in the constitution.[24] Yet legal and judicial groups often cling to their unconstitutional arguments in opposing the reform.

An enforcement system that is expensive may still support bank lending and large or medium-size loans. But it will limit lending by microlenders, dealers and other non-bank lenders, which can often reach farmers and poor people more effectively and efficiently.

11.3 STATUS OF THE REFORMS – AND HOW TO MOVE FORWARD

The gap between incomes in Latin America and the high income OECD countries is widening.[25] At the same time that Latin America falls behind in its development efforts, it barely makes progress in reducing poverty. Between 1990 and 2003, LAC reduced its incidence of extreme poverty by less than any other region except sub-Saharan Africa.[26] The limits on the use of col-

---

[23] See for example Letters, n.14 above and Memorandum, n.13 above.
[24] See for example de la Peña and Fleisig (2006), Annex I: Constitutional Law Issues by Marcel Tangarife.
[25] Income per capita in Latin America was 13.9% that of the high-income OECD countries in 2000 but only 10.9% of that income in 2005 (World Bank, 'Key development data and statistics', available at www.worldbank.org).
[26] The incidence of extreme poverty (population living on less than US$1 per day) fell 19% in Latin America between 1990 and 2003. It fell by more in all other regions except sub-Saharan Africa (+1%) and Eastern Europe and Central Asia (+280%). World Bank (2006) Table 2.3, p. 60 available at www.worldbank.org.

lateral, which have kept private credit at about 20–30 percent of GDP in most Latin American countries, remain a major constraint to economic growth.

Despite these high stakes, the approaches to reforming secured financing in Latin America remain unsuccessful. There have been limited reforms to the pledge and accounts receivable laws in Argentina, Uruguay and Honduras. The pledge, however, is such a restrictive security device in Latin America's Civil Codes, and it has been so restrictively applied by the courts for so many years, that it remains a very ineffective device for expanding secured lending.

Factoring laws to address accounts receivable financing have also had a limited impact, because the reforms have retained a system of transfer of the loan portfolios (see Figure 11.2 above). Laws for the securitization of mortgages have suffered the same legal problems as those for accounts receivable, as they include only a system of securitization with transfer. In addition, securitization laws in Latin America have not resolved the secured transactions problems in the underlying original mortgages. Therefore, these securitization reform programs have led to more financing mainly for those that already had mortgage credit, without expanding mortgage financing to the poor (see Simpson and Dahan, Chapter 8, this volume).

On the most advanced end of the spectrum, the reform in Mexico included some features of an advanced secured financing system. It did not include a comprehensive system of priority, however, nor did it resolve all priority conflicts among lenders. At the same time the reform retained the unworkable registration system. And its enforcement provisions left repossession untouched. These are key economic stages of secured transactions, and all remain unreformed in Mexico.[27]

Peru has a more advanced secured transactions law. Yet as noted, the provisions which would have allowed more competition from nonbank creditors were removed. Peru's filing system is still under construction, and meanwhile old models are in use. In addition, provisions for repossession of collateral introduced a notary requirement.

Why such spotty reforms? What have been the key obstacles?

11.3.1   Key Obstacles to Reform

Obstacles to this reform interact in a complex way, including elements of narrow self-interest,[28] ignorance of law,[29] ignorance of the economic

---

[27] For a discussion of the problems in Mexico before the reform, see de la Peña (1996).

[28] See for example Institutional Position, n. 21 above, para. 8–11.

[29] See for example Chamber of Commerce of Quito, Ecuador (Cámara de Comercio de Quito) to Superintendent of Banks of Ecuador, Letter (email), 18 February 2005 (available upon request).

consequences of law[30] and a broad diffused support that seldom leads to local action.

Donor agencies and international development institutions and governments in the country lack the technical expertise to effectively join the debate. Local private sector interest groups in the region often have a better understanding of the issues. But their support is diffused across many sectors, making it difficult to reach common agreement. Moreover, this support is not consistent and is often countered by the opposition of lawyers and other powerful interest groups. Sometimes this opposition stems from benefits from the state and private monopolistic frameworks provided under the existing laws and sometimes from ignorance (see similar problems raised in Dahan and Simpson, Chapter 5, and an example of successful reform in Mathernová, Chapter 9, this volume).

With some limited and important exceptions, the judicial powers in the region have most aggressively opposed the reform. The legal and judicial groups of the region rarely see the links between legislation and economic outcomes. Lawyers and justices often are not used to considering the overall transaction costs of expensive legal processes that have no clear public policy justification, or acknowledging the impact that small legal requirements can have on small and medium-size enterprises and the poor.[31]

The executive and Congress have been most supportive of reform in some countries. Yet the conflicting positions they hear from their constituencies leave them paralyzed to act. In Bolivia, for example, Congress gets no support for the reform from banks and the local chambers of commerce.[32] Bolivian banks and microlenders oppose the reform because it would bring other lenders into the credit market.[33] The chambers of commerce are reluctant to improve registration because it would mean sharing their monopoly in processing registrations of commercial pledges.[34] Ironically, the President of the Bolivian Supreme Court and some of its justices support a new law on secured transactions – an exception worth noting given the opposition of other courts in the region.

The Organization of American States' (OAS) model law on secured transactions and the USAID Commercial, Legal and Institutional Reform project represent promising regional efforts. So does the legislative guide on secured transactions developed by the United Nations Commission on International Trade Law (UNCITRAL). But models always need to

---

[30] Ibid.
[31] See for example Memorandum, n.13 above.
[32] Letter, n.14 above Institutional Position, n. 21 above and letter, n. 21 above.
[33] Letter, n.17 above, para. 7.
[34] Institutional Position, n. 21 above, para. 8–11.

develop general principles so that they can accommodate variations in each country. Moreover, they often need to sacrifice many best practices in favor of reaching common ground. As a result, regional models often have limited economic impact because they are unable to include the key legal features needed, particularly new provisions, revisions and derogations relating to publicity, enforcement and competition. The OAS model law on secured transactions, for example, recommends a troublesome registration system as represented in Figure 11.5.[35] So it may be better to rely on regional models in Latin America only in regard to their best features and for creating public awareness of the need for reform rather than for generating effective reform within a country.

International conventions (such as the UNCITRAL convention on receivables financing and the Convention on International Interests in Mobile Equipment (Cape Town, 2001) under the International Institute for the Unification of Private Law (UNIDROIT)) can lead to reform of local laws, if a country adopts them. But these conventions are too limited in application to achieve much economic impact in a country; some of these assets would represent less than 5 percent of the capital stock in the country.

Best international and regional alternatives would include model laws, principles and standards developed by institutions that rely mostly on expertise, rather than on the agreement of various jurisdictions, and that use economic analysis, such as the standards, indicators and benchmarks of the Legal Matrix of the Alliance for the Accountability of Property Rights[36] presented at the Summit of the Americas in 2005 and the EBRD Model Law on Secured Transactions.[37] Another route is to adopt international conventions that have a strong participation of leading business communities (for example the UNIDROIT convention), which may compensate for the lack of economic analysis of many instruments, and rely on them as models for domestic law with an expanded scope of application.

11.3.2 Project Design

In the coming years the key challenge in the reform of secured transactions is to design reform projects that draw on adequate expertise and pay adequate attention to political opposition. Past reform programs ignored political opposition. Some programs proposed rapid execution, drew on little technical expertise and included no resources for ensuring broad legal

---

[35] *Ley modelo interamericana sobre garantías mobiliarias*, arts. 35–46.
[36] Available at www.landnetamericas.org.
[37] Available at www.ebrd.com.

participation and promoting broad public awareness. While it may be possible to do the technical work in a short period, activities to address political opposition require much longer time frames and considerable expertise. It is unreasonable to expect the local legal community to reason its way independently through the principles of complex laws from the industrial countries that have included contributions from hundreds of lawyers over more than 50 years.

Of critical importance in project design is to draw on expert support in drafting legislation so that it addresses key economic details of reform. When the drafting process involves no input from economists, new legislation often leaves out many of these details. Moreover data on the potential economic gains from the reform are necessary to gain political support.

Incorporating economic indicators of success into reform programs can also be useful. Focusing on economic outcomes can provide flexibility in legal drafting. Whether civil or common law sources are used, the ultimate focus of reform programs should be on meeting certain economic targets in creation, priority, publicity and enforcement. By contrast, legal programs that present reform as consisting merely of having passed a secured transactions law may give a false impression of success. (see Fleisig, Chapter 3 and Dahan and Simpson, Chapter 5, this volume).

Government political action could focus on two fronts: on one front, setting up a government program on secured transactions reform that is comprehensive and that allows for the required time and expertise; and on a parallel front, governments and IFIs could link their credit lines to disburse for new instruments using the new legal devices.

Donors and international development institutions (such as USAID, the Millennium Challenge Corporation, the World Bank and its International Finance Corporation, and the Inter-American Development Bank and its International Investment Corporation and Multilateral Investment Fund) continue to play a key role in helping governments develop reform programs in secured transactions. These institutions could link the benefits of secured lending with their programs in advancing health, the environment, infrastructure, private sector development and banking or rural finance or in providing private project financing. For example they could address the problems in financing medical equipment, environment-friendly technology and future crops. Such sector programs could manage full reform activities or undertake diagnostics and produce indicators of the economic effects of restrictions on secured lending.

Latin America will simply not grow unless it improves its secured transactions frameworks so as to expand access to credit to permit exploiting high-return investment opportunities. Donors and international development institutions can help make the case for such reform through explaining and developing programs around links between secured financing and the economic problems in the region. Some of those links lead to specific benefits, such as in the way financing medical equipment can improve health. Others lead to broad economic gains, such as in the way secured lending can promote private sector development, help realize the benefits of free trade and lower risk for the financial sector by allowing diversified loan portfolios and opening financing by nonbank lenders – and in the way the ability to use movable property as collateral can expand access to credit for the poor and landless and produce a more equal distribution of wealth.

REFERENCES

de la Peña, N. (1996), 'México: identificación de los problemas de garantías para financiar bienes muebles en el sector agropecuario', *El Foro*, **9** (2), 2.

de la Peña, N. (2004), 'Legal issues for strengthening property rights in the blueprint of standards, indicators and benchmarks', July, Landnet Americas program, available at www.landnetamericas.org/Alliance/alliance.asp?documentID= 3866.

de la Peña, N. and H. Fleisig (1997a), 'Argentina: cómo las leyes para garantizar préstamos limitan el acceso a crédito', *La Ley* (Buenos Aires), **61** (47), 1–2.

de la Peña, N. and H. Fleisig (1997b), 'Peru: how problems in the framework for secured transactions limit access to credit', *NAFTA Law and Business Review of the Americas*, **3** (33), 40–6.

de la Peña, N. and H. Fleisig (2001), 'Marco legal e institucional de garantías reales mobiliarias en países de la región', paper presented at the regional workshop Desarrollando la Economía Rural de Puebla a Panamá, Inter-American Development Bank, Guatemala City, March, available at www.iadb.org/regions/re2/en2/Nuria.doc; also published in *Revista de Bancos y Empresas*, Editorial Depalma, Buenos Aires, **1** (3).

de la Peña, N. and H. Fleisig (2004), 'Romania: law on security interests in personal property and commentaries', *Review of Central and East European Law*, **29** (2), 133–217.

de la Peña, N. and H. Fleisig (2006), 'Colombia: expanding access to credit—case study on secured transactions', report prepared for DAI Inc. under USAID Office of Broad-Based Economic Growth in the Bureau for Latin America and the Caribbean and funded through the BASIS Rural and Agricultural Finance program, available on request at www.ceal.org.

de la Peña, N., H. Fleisig, A. Arias, R. Chatara and B. Valdez Iraheta (2001a), 'El Salvador: Draft Law on Security Interests in Movable Property (*Anteproyecto de ley de garantías reales mobiliarias*) with Commentaries', San Salvador: El Salvador Ministry of Economy, National Competitiveness Project.

de la Peña, N., H. Fleisig, A. Garro and R. Muguillo (2001b), 'Costo económico de los defectos en el marco legal Argentino para los créditos con garantía de bienes muebles', in *Poder Judicial, Desarrollo Económico y Competitividad En*

La Argentina, vol. II, Buenos Aires: Editorial Depalma for FORES and CONICET, p. 1.

de la Peña, N., L. Girton and H. Fleisig (1996), 'Financiamiento de cuentas de crédito', *Estudios de Derecho Commercial*, Colegio de Abogados del Departamento Judicial de San Isidro, Instituto de Derecho Commercial Económico y Empresarial, Argentina, **13** (45).

Fleisig, H. and N. de la Peña (1994), *How Legal Restrictions on Collateral Limit Access to Credit in Uruguay*, Washington, DC: Center for the Economic Analysis of Law.

Fleisig, H., M. Safavian and N. de la Peña (2006), *Reforming Collateral Laws to Expand Access to Finance*, Washington, DC: World Bank.

Association of Private Banks of Bolivia (Asociación de Bancos Privados de Bolivia) to Superintendence of Banks of Bolivia, Letter, 4 March 2005.

Association of Financial Entities Specialized in Microcredit of Bolivia (Asociación de Entidades Financieras Especializadas en Microfinanzas) to S. Smith PREMIER USAID project, Letter, 30 March 2005 (available upon request).

Chamber of Industry, Commerce and Services of Santa Cruz (Cámara de Industria, Comercio y Servicios de Santa Cruz) to Bolivian Congress, Santa Cruz, Bolivia, Institutional Positions (Posiciones Institucionales), 22 April 2005 (available upon request).

Chamber of Industry, Commerce and Services of Santa Cruz (Cámara de Industria, Comercio y Servicios de Santa Cruz) to S. Smith PREMIER USAID project, Letter, 25 June 2005 (available upon request).

Chamber of Commerce of Quito, Ecuador (Cámara de Comercio de Quito) to Superintendent of Banks of Ecuador, Letter (email), 18 February 2005 (available upon request.)

N. de la Peña, Memorandum to Claudia Aragón, Secretaría Técnica de la Presidencia, Nicaragua, re draft law discussion meeting with the Supreme Court, 26 November 2006.

World Bank (2005), *World Development Report 2006: Equity and Development*, New York: Oxford University Press.

World Bank (2006), Global Economic Propects 2007: Managing the Next Wave of Globalization, Washington DC: World Bank.

12. Recent reform in France: the renaissance of a civilian collateral regime?

Marie-Elodie Ancel

12.1 BACKGROUND

'Impossible is not French'. That is what Napoléon replied (or is reputed to have replied) to one of his generals who considered a certain military manoeuvre to be impossible. For a long time, reforming French secured transactions law seemed unthinkable. A major change has finally happened with the Ordinance of 23 March 2006, which has created a Book IV dedicated to security rights and guarantees in the Civil Code.[1]

The purpose of this chapter is to present this reform's main departing features from the former regime, as well as the processes which led to its adoption. Unsurprisingly, the reform was led (and misled in some aspects) by political forces which made the new regime far less rational and balanced than one would have liked. Yet this example of a civil law country reform may well provide some important lessons and inspirations to other countries, and also destroy some of the myths surrounding the so-called civil law tradition.[2]

12.1.1 Original Coherence

French law was based on very strong and, seemingly, inflexible foundations which were laid down two centuries ago when the French Civil Code (FCC) was drafted. At that time, just after the Revolution, France was eager to recover peace and stability. So strict principles were adopted to take into account the interests of all stakeholders, based on the understanding of those interests at that time:

---

[1] French Civil Code (FCC), art. 2284 et seq. Access to the FCC in French, English and Spanish is available at www.legifrance.gouv.fr.
[2] Du Marais (2006); Association Capitant (2006).

1. Of course, secured creditors had to be in a strong position, especially vis-à-vis third parties. That is why possession of the collateral by the creditor was required for the existence of the security interest (FCC, (ex) art. 2076).

2. Debtors had to be protected against abusive creditors and usurers: many spoliations had happened in these times of trouble. Again that is why possession was required, and not only for perfection but also for the constitution of security rights on movables (FCC, (ex) art. 2071); being required to surrender possession to create a security right, the debtor was thus supposed to realize the importance of the operation.

3. Obviously, possession could not be granted on future assets and security rights on a generic class of assets were complex to achieve. So a creditor could not obtain a security right over all the assets of the debtor. This impossibility was meant to keep some balance of power between creditors and debtors.

4. In addition, the secured debt had to be specifically quantified, which again was designed to protect debtors (FCC, (ex) art. 2074).

5. Foreclosure and private sales as methods of enforcement were prohibited, even if agreed between the parties (FCC, (ex) art. 2078); lawmakers feared that secured creditors would keep the charged assets and gain an undue windfall or sell them off, which would be detrimental in both cases to the debtor.

6. Third parties, and especially unsecured creditors, were also taken into account, for instance they had to be given a clear view of the situation: the debtor having lost possession of the collateral, unsecured creditors knew that they could not levy on this asset. And they also had to be protected against secured creditors' greed or, on the other hand, casualness. That is another reason why foreclosure and private sales were prohibited.

While these features may sound unthinkable and certainly in complete contradiction with the economic rationale of secured transactions as understood today, it is essential to stress that this legal framework was rooted in a particular sociological, political and economic environment – that of early nineteenth century France. Contrary to what is often stated, civil law tradition is not insensitive to what is going on in 'the real world' or strongly dogmatic. These rules related to a particular moment in France's economic and historical context. For this reason one should not consider that the aforementioned legal rules are intrinsic to civilian countries. In fact, these rules have been significantly amended or even completely changed, as will be seen.

Second, security law was principally dealt with by statutory law and not by judge-made law. In principle, this is a good thing. Everyone (debtor, secured and unsecured creditors) must be able to ascertain their respective position beforehand. It is often noted that 'statutory law is slow and costly to change' whereas judge-made law provides more flexibility[3] (although changes to case law may generate a lot of externalities), but in the field of secured transactions, ex ante certainty and clarity are of primary importance. When a country wants to improve its secured transactions regime, it usually does so through a legislated body of law. As a result, since 1804, French courts have played a modest role in updating these rules. The reason for this does not lie in a particular incapacity of civilian judges (or 'French legal origin' judges) to react to changing circumstances.[4] Tort law, contract law and the law on personal guarantees, for example, have been profoundly developed by case law, sometimes in a very creative manner. In the field of secured transactions law, however, this judicial shyness can be explained by the fact that, in the French perception of security law, many stakeholders are involved. Judges probably did not feel it legitimate to modify (at least directly) legal rules whose effects range beyond secured creditors and debtors.[5]

12.1.2 Growing Need for Change

French secured transactions law had yet to evolve to adapt to new economic needs. It did so from the middle of the twentieth century, mainly in two ways.

Numerous types of security rights, often limited to specific industries, were created by law but not included in the FCC. Each of these security rights has its own particular regime, which often profoundly deviated from the principles of the FCC. For example, since 1953, a specific law provided for non-possessory charges over motor vehicles. The creditor, who could only be the seller or the bank financing the purchase of the car, was deemed to be in possession of the car with an associated right of retention based on that fictitious possession. The charge was publicised in a special register held by administrative authorities.

---

[3]   Beck et al. (2002).
[4]   In the field of security law, the opposition between civil law and common law is far too rudimentary, see Sigman (2004).
[5]   For instance the French Cour de cassation decided that, except when expressly admitted by a specific text, fiduciary assignments of claims are not possible under the unreformed version of the FCC. The operation should be considered as a '*nantissement*', which is far less effective when the debtor is in insolvency proceedings (Cour de cassation, chambre commerciale, 19 December 2006). Whether such fiduciary assignments of claims are possible under Book IV of the FCC is controversial.

More recently, ownership right has been very much favoured as a form of security, especially from the early 1980s when retention of title (ownership) clauses were confirmed effective in the event of the debtor's insolvency. Fiduciary transfer of account receivables to banks was adopted in 1981 by the so-called 'Loi Dailly', and has been since widely used.[6] These laws demonstrated how inadequate the original collateral system had become. The fiduciary transfer of property has been particularly prized because it protects the owner-creditor even if the debtor is declared insolvent. And because in 1985 French insolvency law became more debtor-friendly than creditor-friendly (as it once was), ownership is often said to be the 'Queen of security rights'. Another sign of the creditors' dissatisfaction with security rights was the appetite creditors showed for personal guarantees. As a result, at the beginning of the twenty-first century, French secured transactions law has been deeply transformed compared with the original Napoleonic approach.

The FCC provisions had more or less lost any relevance as the possessory pledge does not suit modern economic life.[7] Yet specific regimes had been created to such an extent and in such a piecemeal manner that stakeholders were confronted with a puzzling patchwork of legislation, which in fact suited nobody. Secured creditors had difficulties getting information on their debtor's existing encumbrances: a debtor could be in possession of assets that he in fact did not own. Moreover, these secured creditors' rights were in real danger when the debtor went into insolvency proceedings, unless they had a right of retention or a fiduciary transfer of title over the assets. Debtors, notwithstanding the numerous specific statutes, had difficulties using some of their assets as collateral: stock-in-trade for example could not easily be charged. Third parties, in particular unsecured creditors, also complained of the lack of transparency: multiple specific registers had been created and existed side by side, making searching difficult; publicity of retention of title clauses and fiduciary transfers was not required, although it was required for some pledges and leasing contracts.[8]

12.1.3 Political Impulse and Political Traps

It was high time to reshape the French collateral regime.[9] In 2003, in the context of the bicentenary of the FCC, a review of potential reforms to

---

[6] Loi No. 1981-1, 2 January 1981, now codified (French Monetary and Financial Code, art. L.313-23 et seq.).

[7] Sigman (2004).

[8] Sigman (2005).

[9] Ancel and Evans (2005).

secured transactions law was initiated by the Ministry of Justice. A Consultative Report was released in the spring of 2005 prepared by a small group of academics and practitioners (including a judge, a lawyer and two bankers), led by Professor Grimaldi. The Grimaldi Report suggested inserting a new section in the FCC entirely dedicated to security rights and guarantees. This Report also suggested reconsidering seriously some of the traditional rules in French security law.[10]

These suggestions have been taken into account – but only partially. Indeed, having received the Grimaldi Report, the French government decided that the reform should intervene quickly and through an ordinance (a governmental order), to prevent inconsistencies which might arise during parliamentary discussions. The Parliament had to formally approve the use of an ordinance procedure on this matter and it did so by listing the scope of the reform for which authority was given to the government. Unfortunately the scope was very much reduced: among other things, fiduciary transfers were excluded and charges over financial instruments were to be left untouched; also, any substantive change regarding retention of title was prohibited. The result was the Ordinance adopted on 23 March 2006, which introduced in the French Civil Code a Book IV (FCC, arts 2284 to 2488) dedicated (a) to guarantees (FCC, arts 2287–1 to 2322) and (b) to security rights (FCC, arts 2323 to 2488), which failed to be as comprehensive as it could have been.[11]

In such a context, this chapter indicates two principal points: (1) Napoleonic countries can move towards a more efficient and credit-oriented secured transactions law, without getting rid of their civilian heritage – the Quebec Civil Code also furnishes strong evidence of the possibility of such a renaissance; (2) if the French reform does not go as far as it might have,[12] its shortcomings can mainly be ascribed to political factors rather than to civilian legal heritage. Napoleonic countries or French legal origin countries can see the French reform as an example of what can be done and of what should be avoided.

In order to address the question whether a civilian 'renaissance' or 're-birth' has happened in France, the French reform should be examined against the three key features of the Napoleonic approach regarding security rights, as mentioned above. In other words, is the new regime now once again connected with the sociological, political and economic environment? Are ex ante certainty and clarity now provided to all stakeholders? Have all the interests regained an acceptable balance?

---

10 The Grimaldi Report and the Grimaldi draft are accessible on the Internet.
11 Leavy (2006); Riffard (2007).
12 Leavy (2006); Riffard (2007).

12.2 CONNECTION WITH SOCIOLOGICAL, POLITICAL AND ECONOMIC ENVIRONMENT?

Obviously, compared to 1804, France is a completely different country. The economy is based on credit and usurers are mostly old memories; the need for security rights is greater than ever, especially for small and medium businesses; movables can be of considerable value; computerization is common. This change of circumstances explains the important substantive modifications, facilitating the creation, perfection and enforcement of secured transactions in French law.[13]

12.2.1 Creation of Security Rights

The most spectacular change is the extension of the scope of assets which can be charged. A charge may now be constituted on any present or future, tangible or intangible asset, or group of assets (FCC, arts 2333, 2355), provided they are described, in writing, in such a manner that they are made identifiable (FCC, arts 2336, 2356). If the charge regards intangible movables, it is called a '*nantissement*'. If the charge regards tangible movables, it is a '*gage*' (pledge).

This implies the admission of a non-possessory publicized *gage* over any tangible movable. This new *gage* can now be considered as the new principal legal instrument (FCC, art. 2333). The Grimaldi Report calls it an 'all-purpose' pledge (Grimaldi Report, p. 10), partly inspired by the US Uniform Commercial Code (UCC), Article 9 and by the Quebec '*hypothèque mobilière*', because it applies to all types of tangible assets. Indeed this new *gage* will certainly have a greater range than the possessory *gage*, which is not abandoned. It must be added that the regime of *nantissement* over intangible movables is aligned with the regime of this new non-possessory *gage*, except for *nantissement* on receivables, which is treated separately (FCC, art. 2355).

Dispossession by the debtor is no longer required for creating a pledge. Taking security over stock-in-trade is finally possible, as a general rule, under French law. When fungible goods are charged, the debtor can sell them if so agreed in the security document. The debtor will then have to

---

[13]   The mortgage regime was also deeply modified by the reform. For instance it is now possible to constitute a mortgage to secure future debts (*hypothèque pour sûreté de créance future*) or to use the same mortage to secure new debts (possibly due to new creditors) (*hypothèque rechargeable*). Reverse mortgage is also introduced into French law (*prêt viager hypothécaire*). However this part of the reform is outside the scope of this chapter.

replace the charged goods by goods identical in quantity and kind (FCC, art. 2342). Such an agreement between debtor and creditor should become the standard one in practice. In addition, because dispossession is no longer constitutive, several creditors may simultaneously hold security rights in the same asset or pool of assets.

Another key point is related to the scope of the debts which may be secured: future claims may now be secured by a security right on tangible and intangible movables (FCC, art. 2333; art. 2356 for charges over receivables; art. 2355 for charges over other intangible movables). Although used in practice and confirmed by case law, such practice nevertheless conflicted with the FCC's previous provisions, which required a 'fixed sum' (FCC, (ex) art. 2074). The FCC also states now very clearly that the secured debt extends to interest and costs (FCC, art. 2339). No restrictions are made regarding who the debtor or the creditor can be: the new *gage* and *nantissement* are available between all types of persons and organizations, for all sorts of debts.

12.2.2 Perfection of Security Rights

The French reform provides that registration is necessary to make the *gage* opposable against third parties (FCC, art. 2338). A Decree of 23 December 2006[14] describes the procedure: the creditor (or, one might imagine, the debtor acting on behalf of the creditor) files a rather detailed document, accompanied by the original security document, at the Registry of the Commercial Court in the jurisdiction in which the debtor is registered (as a company or as a professional) or domiciled. The data is fed into a nation-wide, freely accessible electronic database[15] permitting a search against the debtor's name and details.[16] One should denounce the nineteenth century flavour of this registration system.[17] Indeed, the Ministry of Justice has established a list of 17 types of assets which are likely to be used as collateral[18] and if one wants to know about all the *gages* constituted by a

---

[14] Décret No. 2006–1804, 23 December 2006, published in *Journal officiel de la République française*, 31 December 2006. The *Journal officiel de la République française* can be found on www.legifrance.gouv.fr.

[15] See www.infogreffe.fr:80/infogreffe/afficherGageSansDepossession.do.

[16] Compare for instance with the Romanian Archive system, which enables search according to various criteria (name of the creditor or debtor, serial number of the asset, identification number). See Diana Lupulescu, Chapter. 10.

[17] See Riffard (2007), who would have preferred an on-line notice filing by the secured creditor.

[18] See Arrêté dated 1 February 2007, published in *Journal officiel de la République française*, 10 February 2007: (1) animals; (2) clockworks and jewels; (3) music instruments; (4) equipments, furniture and products used for professional

debtor, one has to file 17 separate electronic requests. Moreover, the electronic national registry only informs about the existence of registered *gages*. Further details will have to be obtained at the local registry (at the inquirer's cost).

The registration system is also used to determine secured creditors' priority ranking (FCC, art. 2340) between registered *gages*. When possessory pledges were taken, the date of creation applies to determine the ranking order.

Another novelty regards perfection of a charge over receivables. Previously, the FCC required that perfection was dependent on a formal notification to the debtor of the charged claim or on his formal acceptance (FCC, (ex) art. 2075). This was really a burdensome and inefficient process. Since 1981, the Loi Dailly has provided that a charge on receivables that are due to legal persons or entrepreneurs in favour of a bank is effective against third parties as soon as this security agreement is executed. This rule has now been adopted for all charges over claims, granted to any creditor (FCC, art. 2361). Notice to the debtor of the charged claim is only required to make the charge opposable against him (FCC, arts 2362 and 2363).

12.2.3 Enforcement of Security Rights

Turning now to enforcement remedies, a change must be pointed out: foreclosure clauses are no longer generally prohibited unless the secured debt was a consumer credit (FCC, arts 2348, 2365). This means that the parties can agree that in case of default, the secured creditor would be allowed to keep the collateral in payment of the debt. However, the value of the collateral must be determined by an expert chosen by both parties or, if not, by a court, unless the asset is quoted on an organized market (FCC, art. 2348; such evaluation is not necessary for charges over receivables).

Overall, the French reform has gone a long way in trying to take into account the needs of the economic stakeholders and provide a more creditor-friendly climate.

---

purpose not listed in the other categories; (5) equipments other than electronic hardware used for non-professional purpose; (6) equipments related to sports; (7) electronic hardware and attachments; (8) house furniture; (9) intangibles other than shares; (10) currencies; (11) art objects, collector's items, antiquities; (12) shares; (13) publishing, press and other graphic industries products; (14) nonedible liquid products; (15) textile products; (16) food products; (17) others.

12.3   EX ANTE CERTAINTY AND CLARITY?

Has the reform, however, provided the certainty and clarity that stake-holders require? Creating a special part on secured transactions in the FCC has definitively sent a very positive signal that security law is a matter of concern in the French legal system and deserves a special place in the Civil Code. The main features of French secured transactions law is now clearly displayed for domestic and foreign market players. On the other hand, the new French security law still shows complexity.

12.3.1   A Reform, not a Revolution

One subject of astonishment, or even disappointment, is that the reform did not repeal the previously developed specific security devices and their separate regimes.[19] Possessory pledge is still available (FCC, art. 2337). Commercial *gage*, agricultural 'warrant' or pledge on an account for financial instruments are left unchanged. Retention of title is now included in Book IV but its regime, which was complemented by jurisprudence, was just slightly modified (FCC, art. 2367 et seq.). The *gage* over motor vehicles has even been given prominence by being inserted in the FCC and its use is now open to every type of creditor (FCC, art. 2351 et seq.).

As was stated previously, complexity was one of the main criticisms of French secured transactions law. So one may contend that complexity is now even worse because none of these previous devices has been repealed. Why? Two reasons can be put forward. The first one is that the legislator took a cautious approach. Some of these specific devices are useful and satisfactory for practitioners. For instance possessory pledge can still play a role because it remains confidential (which is a paradox because dispossession is traditionally explained as providing publicity) and because it provides the creditor with a right of retention. The French pledge on an account for financial instruments was also vigorously defended by French banks. The logic presumably was not to destroy the existing strengths. Other devices may be obsolete and would be expected to fall into disuse naturally: the market will make its choice; only the strongest will survive – at least, this way of reforming could be praised for its humility.

However, there is another (and probably a more realistic) reason behind this seemingly humble taste for diversity in the field of secured transactions. The Grimaldi Commission was not allowed to modify insolvency law, in particular by granting a strong position to all secured creditors in

---

[19]   Leavy (2006); Riffard (2007).

insolvency proceedings. The reason was that a separate working group, set up by a different department at the Ministry of Justice, had concurrently reviewed insolvency law and no serious attempt was made to co-ordinate the two projects.[20] The Commission thus took the view that it was important to at least keep the valuable protections which had already been granted to certain secured creditors in insolvency situations. Thus, retention of title now appears as a '*sûreté*' in the FCC (FCC, art. 2329) but it still gives an exclusive right on the asset to the creditor so he does not have to fear competing claims from other creditors. Possessory *gage* (or a *gage* relying on fictitious possession, like the *gage* on motor vehicles) still provides the creditor with a right of retention, which gives bargaining power in insolvency proceedings. This mismatch of concepts, old and new, has been the price to pay for a reform whose scope had been too strictly defined with no view on long-term benefits. Furthermore, the Ordinance, against the recommendation of the Grimaldi Report (p. 4), provides that insolvency law prevails over secured transactions provisions (FCC, art. 2287). As a consequence, many of the benefits of the new regime are lost to the secured creditors at the time when they need them most: foreclosure clauses become ineffective in insolvency (French Commercial Code, art. L.622-7) and, not having been granted a (fictitious) right of retention, the new non-possessory *gage* loses much of its interest because it does not have by law priority against unsecured creditors.[21]

12.3.2   Stock-in-trade Stuck between Parliament and Government

The Ordinance also contains a subject of bafflement: the creation of the so-called *gage des stocks* inserted in the Commercial Code (French Commercial Code, art. L.527-1 et seq.). This *gage* on stock-in-trade, which is available only to secure bank claims, is non-possessory and must be registered.[22] This new specific non-possessory *gage* is much less attractive to creditors than the all-purpose non-possessory *gage* included in the FCC. Creation formalities are heavy and foreclosure clauses are prohibited. Commentators are now discussing whether this special kind of *gage* is the only device available to bank creditors that take stock-in-trade as collateral. One should hope that it is not! How did this *gage* came to be instituted? The Grimaldi Report made no mention of it, very logically since the new

---

[20]   Leavy (2006).
[21]   But an on-going insolvency law reform project would precisely address this priority issue by granting the secured creditors such right of retention.
[22]   See Décret No. 2006-1803, 23 December 2006, published in *Journal officiel de la République française*, 31 December 2006.

non-possessory *gage* was precisely to make pledge over stock-in-trade easier. Its origin lies in bad co-ordination between the government and the Parliament during the negotiations on the Ordinance procedure. Creating an efficient security right over stock-in-trade was the top priority on the list established by Parliament, and because this to some extent relates to commercial matters, the Parliament decided that the new rules should be included in the Commercial Code. But it also decided that the government should provide in the FCC new means of extending the scope of the charged assets. The government followed these guidelines in the Ordinance rather rigidly, not realizing that doing so might create an ambiguity and make French security law even more confused than before.[23]

12.3.3 The '*Fiducie*' Taboo

As mentioned above, the Grimaldi Report wanted to address in the reform the fiduciary transfers which had been admitted on an ad hoc basis under French law. But the government decided to create a separate consultative group on '*fiducie*' so fiduciary transfers were removed from the Committee's scope of work. By a strange irony of fate, a Bill on the *fiducie* independently developed and submitted by Senator Marini took over the work of the consultative group. The *Fiducie* Act was adopted on 19 February 2007.[24] The availability of this device is limited *ratione personae* but it could be used to shelter security interests both from the constituent's general creditors and from the effects of insolvency proceedings of the *fiduciaire* (that is, more or less, the trustee). Apparently, a fiduciary transfer on movables does not need to be registered or publicized in any way and is not subject to any rules applicable to secured transactions, such as enforcement or priority. *Fiducie* is inserted in Book III of the FCC (FCC, arts. 2011–2031).[25] As a result, Book IV has somehow lost its comprehensiveness of the French secured transactions (FCC, art. 2329 for example makes no mention of *fiducie*), and the significance of the legal instruments it provides is cast into considerable doubt.[26]

Thus, as far as ex ante certainty and clarity are concerned, the French reform shows important and highly regrettable shortcomings, mostly due to political muddle and lack of a rigorous approach to reform. One can

---

[23] Riffard (2007).

[24] Act 2007-211, 19 February 2001, published in *Journal officiel de la République française*, 21 February 2007.

[25] Leavy (2007).

[26] The Fiducie Act gives in passing a legal basis to collateral agents acting in syndicated financings (FCC, art. 2328–1).

only hope that these shortcomings can be swiftly addressed to make French law simpler and more consistent.

12.4   BALANCE OF INTERESTS?

12.4.1   Debtors' Viewpoint

Some things never change: like the 1804 Civil Code's original secured transactions provisions, the 2006 Ordinance showed great concern for debtor protection. For instance, usually, the agreement of the debtor to the security document is required in writing (FCC, arts. 2336, 2356, 2368). This approach is particularly evident from the enforcement provisions. Judicially led enforcement remains the rule, as it is deemed to provide protection to debtors, and realization of the assets still has to be made through public auction based on a court order (FCC, art. 2346). This is regrettable because auctions may not always be the best and fastest way to generate a high value from the assets. The only exception to these rules is when parties have provided a foreclosure clause, by which the creditor can keep the collateral as payment of the secure debt.

12.4.2   Creditors' Viewpoint

It is difficult for a potential creditor to determine the existence of security interests on a debtor's assets because some security rights are publicized and others are not. The Grimaldi Report advocated publicizing retention of title clauses if the charged asset was over a certain amount. But this suggestion was not followed because the Parliament refused to give authority to the government to make any substantive change about retention of title. Moreover, preference rights, which are incredibly numerous in French law, are left unchanged because they too were excluded from the reform's scope.

Of course, complete transparency through registration is probably not realistic. Under the US Uniform Commercial Code, Article 9, for instance, some security interests will not be disclosed by a search of the public record because perfection will have been achieved by possession or control or automatically (although these are certainly exceptional situations).[27] But under French law the problem is that preferential rights, retention of title, fiduciary transfers and possessory *gage*, which all remain powerful security devices, are not required to be publicized.

---

[27]   Sigman (2005).

12.4.3   Third Parties' Viewpoint

In order to give maximum power to the new non-possessory publicized (registered) *gage*, the FCC provides that when registration is made, other persons claiming rights in the collateral are not protected by having acquired possession of the collateral in good faith (FCC, art. 2337, al. 3). Under the previous system, as in other legal systems, buyers of assets in the ordinary course of business could not be opposed pre-existing security interests. The French reform has thus produced a dramatic change impacting on third parties. But again one is baffled by the fact that it provided no exception to this rule, in situations where good faith acquirers should be protected by law. The situation is particularly bad because the search through the database is very tedious, as mentioned above, or even impossible when the inquirer does not know the precise name and other required details for identifying the chargor. We worry that undesirable effects may develop, which would discredit a laudable reform. At least, the hope is that sooner or later all registers will be merged into one user-friendly database.

So all in all, a more convincing balance of interests is still to be found.

12.5   CONCLUSION

'Impossible is not French', or is it?

We believe that all ingredients for a modern secured transactions system reform were present in France, but somehow failed to materialize, not because modernity was deemed against French legal traditions (although we do acknowledge that in some aspects, this played a role), but because of a confused political agenda and in some respects a rushed process (completely unnecessary). A renaissance of secured transactions regime is feasible for civil law countries. A non-possessory *gage* is compatible with civilian regimes. Spain for example created this device by legislation more than 50 years ago.[28] Registration is something a civil law country can deal with; it was first used in France for mortgages and then for specific types of security rights on movables.[29] Future debts can be secured, provided that they are determinable. More efficient enforcement remedies are possible, even though France's lawmakers still need to be convinced that market forces can be trusted. Coherent legislation is part of Napoléon's legacy. So every 'French legal origin' country should be convinced that 'Impossible is not

---

[28]   Sigman (2005).
[29]   Sigman (2004).

civilian'. That is the first major lesson the French reform teaches. But unfortunately, France has let down those that hoped for a clear leadership in this matter.

From a political point of view, the lesson is the following: reforming security law requires advanced legislative know-how, which French institutions seem to be lacking at the present time.[30] Those from civil law tradition would find much more inspiration from the 'Grimaldi papers' (the Report and draft law) than from the enacted Book IV of the French Civil Code. Furthermore, because secured transactions law is complex and intertwined with other aspects of the law, especially insolvency, no serious reform can be achieved without close co-ordination with these areas. That is the second most important lesson the French reform teaches us.

REFERENCES

Ancel, M.-E. and C. Evans (2005), 'Changing the colour of French security law', *Insol World*, **1**, 37.

Association Capitant (ed.) (2006), 'Réponse de l'Association Capitant aux rapports "Doing Business" de la Banque Mondiale', Société de legislation comparée, www.henri-capitant.org/rubrique.php 3?id_rubrique=24.

Beck, T., A. Demirgüç-Kunt and R. Levine (2002), 'Law and finance: why does legal origin matter', World Bank, Development Research Group Finance, Policy Research Working Group 2904, www.econ.brown.edu/fac/Ross_Levine/finance/ rlevine/Publication/2003_JCE_Legal%20Origin.pdf.

Du Marais, B. (ed.) (2006), 'Des indicateurs pour mesurer le droit? Les limites méthodologiques des rapports Doing Business', La Documentation française, www.ladocumentationfrancaise.fr/catalogue/9782110062444/index.shtml.

Grimaldi, M. (2005), 'Rapport du groupe de travail', 'Avant-projet de texte issu du groupe de travail', www.henricapitant.org/article.php 3?id_article=37.

Leavy, J. (2006), 'France's half-finished revolution', *International Financial Law Review*, **5**, 38–9.

Leavy, J. (2007), 'In France we trust', *International Financial Law Review*, **4**, 66–7.

Riffard, J.-F. (2007), 'The reform of the French secured transactions law: a revolution in half-tone', *Eurofenix*, **1**, 24–5, www.insol.org/emailer/march07_down-loads/Eurofenix.pdf.

Sigman, H.C. (2004), 'L'influence du modèle américain sur le projet de guide législatif de la CNUDCI: mythe ou réalité', *Banque et Droit*, **97** (5), 35–42 (in English), www.revue-banque.fr.

Sigman, H.C. (2005), 'The security interest in the United States: a unitary functional solution', in M.-E. Ancel (ed.), *Repenser le droit des sûretés mobilières*, Paris: LGDJ, Bibliothèque de l'Institut André Tunc, pp. 55–72.

---

[30] Leavy (2007).

Index